Praise for *Sel
The Art and*

MW00778255

"Dan Simon and Tara West shine a powerful light on *the* central principle that distinguishes mediation from nearly all other conflict intervention processes: party self-determination. With courage and clarity, they examine this abstract concept with practical examples and candid discussion that reveals the many real ways that mediators either support—or interfere with—party agency, choice, and the possibility of constructive interaction. In the end, the reader is left with a deeper and clearer appreciation for the importance of reflecting on their own (often subtle) practices to support parties as they work through their own conflicts. This is a must-read for all who seek to improve their mediation practice by better shining a light without casting their own shadow on the people who really matter in the mediation room."

—Kenneth H. Fox, founding director of Conflict Studies,
Hamline University; senior fellow, Dispute Resolution Institute,
Mitchell Hamline School of Law

"With the publication of *Self-Determination in Mediation: The Art and Science of Mirrors and Lights*, Dan Simon and Tara West have made a very significant contribution to mediation literature. Self-determination is a core value of the mediation process, and we finally have a comprehensive examination of this important subject. Simon and West apply their metaphor of mirrors and lights to a wide array of real-world scenarios to demonstrate how mediators can best support party self-determination. Everyone who believes in mediation's potential for resolving conflict will find an inspirational road map in this excellent book."

—James J. Alfini, dean and Professor Emeritus,
South Texas College of Law Houston

"Simon and West demonstrate that preserving party self-determination is what makes mediation a uniquely valuable conflict intervention process. They address the challenges that are involved in sustaining this core value and they provide a range of case studies that vividly illustrate how practitioners can align their core purpose with their intervention practices. An insightful and instructive volume for theorists and practitioners alike."

—Joseph P. Folger, cofounder and board president,
The Institute for the Study of Conflict Transformation;
coauthor of *The Promise of Mediation*

"Mediators, prospective parties, and their attorneys may sometimes wonder if it matters what label a mediator uses to describe their practice. In this book, Dan Simon and Tara West make it clear that it does matter. As committed transformative practitioners, Simon and West put self-determination at the center of their respective practices. The authors describe the specific interventions that allow them to honor party choice and provide detailed examples of the difference this makes to the people involved in the mediation process. They draw from their extensive experience to illustrate crucial moments in a wide range of cases and how and why, in each of them, they put decisions in the hands of participants. The authors' self-reflective approach to their own practices is evident as they describe occasional slips, acknowledging where they could have done better. Reading this book will help those in the conflict intervention field, and those who seek their services, appreciate that transformative practitioners bring unique value to the processes they guide."

—Judith Saul, fellow and board member,
Institute for the Study of Conflict Transformation

"Robert A. Baruch Bush and Joseph P. Folger's *The Promise of Mediation* dramatically sounded a bell that reverberated through and influenced the mediation field. Simon and West further that influence by shining a light on the research of self-determination as an important ethic for mediators and applying it to practice through experience. While 'mirrors and lights' may seem to evoke an evasive and performative 'smoke and mirrors' effect, Simon and West instead use skillful mirroring as a metaphorical prop for the role of the mediator to support party interaction and self-determination and to highlight party differences without diminishing their agency. It's a must-read for conflict practitioners and anyone in the business of supporting others."

—Kristine Paranica, JD, fellow of the Institute
for the Study of Conflict Transformation

"Since publication of Robert A. Baruch Bush and Joseph P. Folger's *The Promise of Mediation*, transformative theory has been much developed, but mostly in academic journals that are not available to practitioners. Here is a clearly written and accessible volume that expands on the important topic of self-determination in mediation and will be of interest to mediators, conflict coaches, and dialogue facilitators alike. The multiple case studies and examples make the volume highly engaging to read and ideal for teaching."

—Erik Cleven, Department of Politics, Saint Anselm College;
board vice president, Institute for the Study of Conflict Transformation

SELF-DETERMINATION IN MEDIATION

THE ART AND SCIENCE OF MIRRORS AND LIGHTS

DAN SIMON AND TARA WEST

ROWMAN & LITTLEFIELD
Lanham • Boulder • New York • London

Acquisitions Editor: Mark Kerr
Acquisitions Assistant: Sarah Rinehart
Sales and Marketing Inquiries: textbooks@rowman.com

Published in cooperation with the Association for Conflict Resolution.

Published by Rowman & Littlefield
An imprint of The Rowman & Littlefield Publishing Group, Inc.
4501 Forbes Boulevard, Suite 200, Lanham, Maryland 20706
www.rowman.com

86-90 Paul Street, London EC2A 4NE

British Library Cataloguing in Publication Information Available

Library of Congress Cataloging-in-Publication Data Available

ISBN 9781538153857 (cloth) | ISBN 9781538153864 (paperback) |
ISBN 9781538153871 (electronic)

♾™ The paper used in this publication meets the minimum requirements of American National Standard for Information Sciences—Permanence of Paper for Printed Library Materials, ANSI/NISO Z39.48-1992.

Contents

For our mothers

Acknowledgments

First we'd like to acknowledge whatever combination of forces brought the two of us together. During the three years we spent writing this book, we had many opportunities to support each other as coauthors and as friends. Given the challenges of 2020 and 2021, we especially appreciated having regular Zoom meetings where we could connect and commiserate with someone other than our cats. On the other hand, we also had many opportunities to experience the destabilizing impacts of conflict—for example, at the start of a writing session before Dan's morning coffee had taken effect and after Tara's third cup had very much kicked in. Whenever that happened, we found a way to regain a sense of agency and reconnect with each other. Our ability to weather these storms and continue to write with one voice surprises us. We are grateful to each other.

Next we'd like to thank the people who helped us find the path to getting this book published. Sharon Press introduced us to Michael Lang and Susan Terry, who were spearheading a joint venture between Association for Conflict Resolution and Rowman & Littlefield. Michael and Susan took our half-baked idea and turned it into something fully baked by encouraging us to home in on the concept of self-determination. They then coached us through writing a proposal, and then a better proposal, and then an even better proposal with the help of the full ACR/Rowman & Littlefield editorial board. Michael and Susan then added significant feedback and suggestions on drafts of our chapters that greatly benefited the book. Cheryl Jamison next joined the team as the managing editor for the project and added her own thoughtful feedback and support, which took the book to the next level.

Kathy Simon, Beth Rosenschein, and Shosh Dworsky each read one or more chapters and responded with insightful observations and helpful suggestions that improved the book. We are lucky Dan has two sisters and a cousin who are so literate.

Our most significant contributor, Al Dworsky (another cousin of Dan's), spent countless hours reading multiple drafts of each chapter and the book as a whole. Al's insights regarding both content and style were worth much more than the mug we gave him. In fact, there's no amount of feedback on Al's feedback that could sufficiently honor his contribution.

We would not even be talking about any of this had Baruch Bush and Joe Folger not developed and refined the transformative theory of conflict. Baruch and Joe's work, particularly on *The Promise of Mediation*, shaped our views of what supporting party self-determination could mean. They and their colleagues at the Institute for the Study of Conflict Transformation continue to advance the field of conflict intervention and to support mediators like us. And as if that weren't enough, Baruch also provided thoughtful feedback on the structure of our book, most importantly by reminding us that agency comes before connection.

Giuseppe Leone of the Virtual Mediation Lab organized the simulated mediation that appears in Chapters 1 through 5, and mediators Ben Davies and Lisa Jacobs portrayed the parties. Their contributions made that simulation worthy of all the attention we gave it. We would also like to thank Martina Cirbusová for contributing a dramatic story from her mediation practice for Chapter 7.

Real clients lived the anecdotes that made this book possible. Their efforts to gain a sense of control over themselves and to manage their differences gave us the material and the inspiration to understand and describe how it all works.

Finally, we couldn't have asked for more supportive and competent publishers than Rowman & Littlefield. While a number of people worked on our book behind the scenes (and painstakingly removed about 1800 unnecessary commas), we want to give a special thanks to Sarah Rinehart, Alden Perkins, and Mark Kerr. They gracefully managed to keep us in line and on time while also supporting our autonomy. We always knew we were in good hands with this team.

Reflective Practice and Deeply Held Values

elf-Determination in Mediation is the product of many years of reflective practice by two mediators with wide experience who are both deeply committed to the value of party self-determination as the heart and soul of the mediation process. While that value is almost universally trumpeted as the guiding principle of mediation, research has shown that it is quick to give way, in actual practice, to other values that are used to explain and justify intrusions on the parties' freedom to make decisions for themselves. Dan Simon and Tara West, the co-authors of this excellent book, make the case that it is rarely necessary or justifiable to limit party self-determination in mediation regardless of the situation, type of case, or parties involved.

The book's subtitle—*The Art and Science of Mirrors and Lights*—promises that this volume will be dedicated to concrete instruction on this subject, and the contents of the book make good on that promise. Simon and West provide what has often been requested by both mediators and publishers: a down-to-earth how-to guide to the practice of mediation as a party-centered process. The 2005 publication of Bush and Folger's *Promise of Mediation*, which included a case-study with commentary, offered concrete examples of how a mediator could support party decision making. However, that volume was equally or more concerned with establishing the overall framework of transformative mediation. In *Mirrors and Lights*, the entire volume is organized around multiple case-studies, recounted in detail, that show how a mediator can honor and support self-determination in actual practice from the beginning of a case to the end and at every point in between.

In his 23 years of practice, Dan Simon has mediated cases of all kinds, from family and divorce to employment and commercial cases—many including lawyers and other representatives. All these types of cases are presented in the book, and in each of them the focus is on how Simon found ways to support rather than supplant party decision making. At the same time, the authors take care to explain the why behind this practice—why it matters to the parties (and the mediator), and the beneficial results it produces. So each chapter, and each new case, not only illustrates the practice of supporting self-determination but also highlights the underlying value and benefits that make this practice worthwhile. In the course of showing all this, Simon and West also reference important new research findings that document the central claim that parties have both the capacity and the desire to make decisions for themselves not only about the final outcome of a case but about every step in the process.

Equally helpful in a concrete guide to practice, Simon and West are transparent about cases in which the mediator went off track in some way, substituting his judgment for the parties' and stepping in to supplant or shape their decisions. In short, Simon is not perfect, and the authors include his mistakes in order to show how he might have used his mirrors and lights to better effect—and in order to understand the kinds of pressures and temptations that lead even a committed practitioner to swerve from a focus on party self-determination.

The organization of the book also contributes to this end: It begins with a clear explanation of the essential value that lies behind supporting party decision making—that is, human autonomy and agency. It then shows in different chapters how this practice is also the best means of promoting sustainable resolution, addressing relationship concerns, and ensuring fairness. And of course, at each stage the authors present and explain concrete examples from actual cases.

Finally, *Self-Determination in Mediation* is an easy and very engaging read. The writing is consistently and admirably clear and powerful, the case examples interesting and challenging, and the underlying theme of self-determination always close to the surface. For mediators already using party-centered modes of practice, including transformative mediators, the book will provide new impetus and clarity to your work. For mediators using other modes of practice, the book will offer you an illuminating window into the ways that party self-determination can be supported in your own practice. For non-mediators, the book will interest you as an example of how reflective practice, based on deeply held values, can ground the work of any kind of professional practice.

And for all of us as fellow citizens, the book can contribute to strengthening our democracy by shining light on our inherent capacities for strength of self and understanding of one another—capacities that are being sorely tested today by social forces that would weaken and divide us. Simon and West's mirrors and lights, broadly deployed, can counteract those forces, preserving and increasing our strength and connection as fellow citizens.

I am gratified that through our association over the years I've been able to contribute something to the work of the authors of this book. And I'm immensely proud of what they've achieved in this volume.

Baruch Bush
Brooklyn, 2022

Introduction

We do not have to be told what self-determination means. We already know that it is just another word for freedom.

—Robert Williams, disability advocate

Mirrors and lights, when pointed in the right direction, improve our vision of ourselves and our surroundings. We (Dan and Tara) believe we can be most helpful as mediators when we illuminate our clients and their situation in this way. Mirrors allow the parties to see themselves without distortion. Lights help them see their situation and each other vividly. As they make decisions, we follow them with a flashlight, or even a spotlight, in whatever direction they choose to go. When we succeed, they have a clearer view of their power, their options, and the other's humanity.

Our idea of supporting party self-determination means assisting the parties in a process that they control. We reflect their conversation with the intention to help them make choices that are clearer, more conscious, and overall *better* from their own perspective. Self-determination means that we mediators minimize our role in guiding, leading, directing, or nudging. It means that we focus solely on supporting the parties as they figure out their own process and make their own choices, for their own reasons. It means that, in a sense, they have *more* self-determination than they would have had without our help.

Instead of literal mirrors and lights, we use words, facial expressions, and body language to reflect what the parties express as accurately and precisely as possible. Like a mirror, we help them take a good look at themselves. We also focus our attention on the interaction between the parties and where they stand in relation to each other. We tell them what we see, honoring what they say and how they say it, with as little modification as possible. We often repeat exactly what they communicate using their exact words. We help them confirm what they see and ask them where they want to focus next. Like lights, we allow them to see more clearly where they are, who the other person is, and where they can choose to step now.

Above we said, "Mirrors allow the parties to see themselves without distortion. Lights help them see their situation and each other vividly." This is the simplest way to put it, but of course it is not that simple. After all, it

1

is possible to see another person via *their* reflection in a mirror, and mirrors cannot reflect anything in the dark. So lights and mirrors work together and are present in almost everything we aspire to do. Throughout this book, we use the metaphors of mirrors and lights (as well as related words such as "reflect" and "illuminate") to describe our interventions and their likely effects. We choose whatever word seems most apt for that particular situation but urge you not to take these metaphors too literally. We are flesh and bone and not glass and photons, after all.

Enhancing each party's view takes nearly all of our attention. Holding up both a mirror and a light, and pointing each tool in the right direction, keeps us busy. Sometimes we find it challenging. Occasionally we want to share *our* perspective with the parties and tell them how *we* see things. We sometimes want them to see each other the way we see them and to treat each other with more kindness. We are tempted to think that if we bend the mirror a bit here, or put a rose-colored filter over the light there, we can help them see themselves and each other a bit differently. We forget that their own perspective is what matters and that our perspective is not entirely without distortion.

Our participation influences the parties. So we do everything we can do to resist our impulses to shape their perspective and instead focus that influence on supporting their self-determination. The choices we make about when and how to wield our mirrors and lights arise from our beliefs about people and what it means for them to have increased self-determination. Our assumptions about people in general, and about specific clients in particular, affect how we interpret what is happening in the mediation. Those interpretations also affect our choices about when and how to intervene. Our mirrors are inevitably distorted by our blind spots and misinterpretations; and where we focus our lights is never completely on target. Despite our best efforts, our biases distort our mirrors and color our lights.

Managing the urge to contribute our own perspective, or manipulate theirs, is a constant challenge. We want to feel helpful and be appreciated, and we are capable of doing more than holding up mirrors and pointing lights. We know things and we're witty. We (Tara and Dan) happen to be especially smart and hilarious. And it's hard to contain that. As David Letterman used to say, "There's no off position on the genius switch." So sticking to our simple job of paying attention to the parties is not that easy.

A leader is best when people barely know he exists, when his work is done, his aim fulfilled, they will say: we did it ourselves. —Lao Tzu

We are not alone in having these challenges. For many mediators, the desire to move the parties in one direction or another does not even feel like a challenge but instead feels consistent with the mediator's purpose. Many mediators have agendas beyond supporting party self-determination. Mediators talk about such goals as helping the parties reach an agreement or preventing the parties from reaching a bad agreement. For these mediators, self-determination, whatever it means, sometimes takes a backseat to these other goals. We believe self-determination belongs in the driver's seat.

In this book, we explore why self-determination is so important. We wrestle with why it is so hard to define, interpret, and apply to real-world situations. And we describe our efforts to support party self-determination in each moment and in every aspect of the process.

Maybe you have seen situations like the following and were unsure, as we were, about how to support party self-determination or even whether party self-determination should be your highest priority in that moment.

- Adam and Anna are mediating a parenting dispute. You believe Adam is threatening Anna with physical violence. You talk to Anna privately and she insists that she wants to continue mediating. Do you honor Anna's request and continue with the session? Or do you take some other action to protect her?
- Johnny lets his lawyer speak for him throughout the mediation. Even when you ask Johnny how he's doing, he silently looks to the lawyer, who quickly responds. Does Johnny have self-determination in this situation? If we attempt to change the interactions between Johnny and his lawyer, do we risk interfering with Johnny's (and the lawyer's) self-determination? Should we even be concerned about the lawyer's self-determination?
- Father and son have been in mediation for a year with no agreement in sight. The one thing that they agree on is that you (their mediator) are intelligent and fair. They ask you to arbitrate their dispute. How do you best support their self-determination at the moment they ask you to arbitrate?
- Bernice and Erik have been divorced for two years. A clause in their settlement agreement requires two hours of mediation upon the request of either party. Bernice frequently requests mediation, and Erik acquiesces. Bernice yells and calls Erik names throughout each session despite your attempts to help her communicate more effectively. Erik tells you that he agrees to mediate because he fears the legal consequences of saying no. What should you do?

There are at least two questions we mediators might ask ourselves when confronted with these sorts of dilemmas. One is "How can I best support party self-determination under these circumstances?" The other is "Are there other values to prioritize under these circumstances?"

A clearer understanding of what self-determination means will help mediators answer these questions. As we see it, self-determination exists along a continuum, present at all times to different degrees. It can also exist in different degrees vis-à-vis different people. For example, a party may exercise low levels of self-determination vis-à-vis their lawyer but high levels of self-determination vis-à-vis the mediator, who is supporting the party's decision to defer to their lawyer. Self-determination can also be viewed as a particular psychological state that affects *how* a person makes choices. A person can make choices, even the choice to defer to another, in a clear, conscious way, or they can make that choice in a state of turmoil and confusion.

As part of this exploration, we discuss the range of assumptions we can make about people in conflict and about human nature in general. Are people primarily self-interested? If so, why do they sometimes act in ways that appear harmful to themselves? To what extent do people naturally care about their connection and contribution to others? Why, in conflict, do they often seem to disregard each other so completely? Is it realistic to imagine that mediation can help people take better care of themselves and do right by each other? And is research available that we can turn to when attempting to answer these questions? We believe that by thinking more clearly about human capacities and limitations, which apply to both the parties and the mediator, we can view our role in a way that allows us to practice consistently with our intention to support, and even enhance, party self-determination.

The following beliefs inform our thinking about self-determination in mediation. We will share research that supports these beliefs.

- People at their core neither want to victimize others nor be victimized by others.
- People want to make their own decisions and solve their own problems.
- People are in the best position to know what decisions are right for them, and they are more likely to make good decisions when they feel supported.
- Autonomy, or the ability to make one's own choices, is important to people, and they often resist attempts to interfere with it.
- As mediators, we can only do so much—we are limited by our biases, the amount of information we have, and other practicalities (e.g., we cannot dictate the terms of an agreement, ensure that an agreement is signed, or enforce compliance with a signed agreement).
- There are exceptions to every rule (including this one).

We will also discuss a range of principles that guide our practices.

- **Party autonomy**—Above all, we value and choose to support each party's right to make their own decisions.
- **Mediator humility**—Recognizing the limits of our role and our awareness, we prioritize the parties' perspectives over our own.
- **Mediator self-awareness**—Instincts and impulses that seem to contradict our primary principles of party autonomy and mediator humility may

be telling us something important. They should be acknowledged and explored with awareness that they may arise from our biases.

- **Mediator autonomy**—We want to make our own decisions about our practices, taking into consideration our own needs as well as the needs of the parties.

Throughout this book, we return to these beliefs and principles, examining the evidence behind them and potential conflicts between them. We discuss how we can put our principles into practice as a general rule and in particularly challenging situations. We describe our efforts, in actual mediations, to maximize party decision making about every aspect of the process. We explain why we value that goal, above others, and we will tell stories of times we may have undermined our clients' self-determination despite our best intentions.

Although both of us have studied other approaches to mediation, the transformative approach, as articulated by Robert Baruch Bush and Joseph Folger in *The Promise of Mediation*,[1] has had the greatest impact on us. That model focuses on supporting party choice throughout the mediation process with the rationale that doing so maximizes the potential for parties to gain strength and clarity (empowerment) along with a greater appreciation of the other's humanity (recognition). We describe how that pattern has appeared in our own practices and has shaped our views of what it means to support self-determination. And we explore the ways this focus has affected our clients and us.

Many mediators, not only those who call themselves transformative, value party self-determination. Many mediators might say, "I support party self-determination by asking them at the start what their goals are. Then I help them pursue those goals." These mediators may remind the parties of their goals when the parties seem to be doing things that interfere with their goals. For example, if a party who said their goal is to settle their case holds rigidly to a position, the mediator might point out that their doing so is not consistent with their goal. We see party self-determination differently from that. We see it as something that happens in each moment. In the moment that a party insists on a certain outcome, we would remain completely supportive of that—we wouldn't even point out that it's inconsistent with what they said before—we would support them wherever they are in the moment regardless of whether it's consistent with earlier-stated goals. We also wouldn't have framed the mediation from the start as a process defined by their goals. We assume their goals are likely to change as a meaningful conversation progresses.

Depending on your orientation as a mediator, you may be surprised by our stories. You'll notice that the questions we ask ourselves during mediation are consistently some version of "How can I be most supportive of the parties' process at this moment?" We do not (or try not to) ask ourselves, "How can I get the parties to . . ." The difference between those two questions captures our understanding of our role in supporting party self-determination. In a way, that difference makes our job simple. And yet answering the question of how to be most supportive of the parties' process can be difficult.

Prioritizing party choice in each moment and in all aspects of the process honors and enhances party self-determination—both when viewed as the opportunity to make choices and when viewed as a psychological state akin to agency. Further, perhaps paradoxically, we believe that prioritizing party choice can yield the benefits that we have sometimes hoped we could achieve by more directly guiding the process. Opportunities for parties to make choices present themselves as parties decide what to say, how to say it, or whether to say anything at all. We believe that supporting the parties in each of these moment-by-moment decisions generally enhances the parties' willingness and ability to make clear and thoughtful long-term decisions. This approach also tends to lead to agreements that work for all parties. It can even lead to better relationships between the parties and better outcomes for affected others such as divorcing couples' children. In contrast, we conclude that our efforts to guide, persuade, or educate parties generally decrease the likelihood of these positive outcomes.

In the first half of the book, we describe our understanding of people's basic psychological needs and capacities in relation to self-determination and connection. We also discuss how the experience of conflict can interfere with each party's ability to meet their needs and exercise their capacities to do what they are normally willing and able to do. Additionally, we share stories, including the full transcript of a mediation Dan conducted, to demonstrate these principles in action. The first half of the book lays the groundwork for the second half where we explore the most common challenges mediators confront when they focus on supporting party choice in all aspects of the process.

In Chapter 1 we explore the relationships between the concepts of agency, autonomy, and self-determination. We ask why these concepts are valued and how they relate to human fulfillment. We observe that increased agency doesn't necessarily lead to an agreement or to harmony between the parties but still matters to the one whose agency is enhanced. We also observe, via a transcript of a mediation, how Dan starts a mediation with the goal of giving the parties every possible choice about the process.

In Chapter 2 we explore the parties' condition when they enter mediation. Powerlessness and alienation dominate their experience. The parties' interaction reinforces those feelings, resulting in the vicious circle of conflict. We share stories demonstrating that this emotional experience of conflict plays a more important role in the parties' decisions than does their desire for a particular tangible outcome. We demonstrate the importance of "following the heat" during a conflict as the mediator supports each party's choices even when the choices may temporarily escalate the conflict.

In Chapter 3 we share mediation stories that illustrate how supporting party self-determination through reflecting and summarizing the parties' different perspectives can lead to both increased agency and inspiring moments of connection. The parties in these stories make thoughtful, compassionate decisions that honor both their own and each other's humanity. We also share research findings illustrating people's deep-seated motivation to connect with others.

In Chapter 4 we share stories of parties arriving at solutions that the mediator could not have predicted when the mediator refrains from attempting to solve the problem for the parties. We see how parties gain clarity about their needs, limitations, options, and priorities through their own efforts. We also share research suggesting that not only are parties capable of solving their own problems, they *want* to solve their problems and they thrive when doing so. Finally, we share research suggesting that the more freedom people are given to make their own decisions, the better (e.g., more creative, durable, and considerate of the needs of all) those decisions tend to be.

In Chapter 5, we integrate material from the first four chapters and offer a more detailed description of the practices we believe effectively support party self-determination. We then share the reactions of Ben and Lisa, the real-life mediators who participated in the transcribed role play featured in the first four chapters of this book, as they share how it felt to have their conversation supported by Dan.

In Chapter 6 we address mediators' common impulse to try to move the parties toward an agreement or another good outcome. We illustrate the challenge of trying to remain supportive of the parties' choices while also feeling tempted to nudge the parties closer together. We show that in many of our cases, nudging the parties backfired. We demonstrate that such guidance, even when potentially helpful with an immediate problem, was likely unnecessary. Moreover, such guidance does not promote party self-determination, and the long-term consequences are unknowable.

In Chapter 7 we address the mediator's role when we are tempted to protect one party from another. These situations include apparent power imbalances, which could take many forms, and deliberate, forceful attempts at coercion. We share stories of these challenges, how we handled them, and what happened next. We discuss our options, given the limits of our role, and ways that we can support party self-determination even when withdrawing from the case.

Chapter 8 explores how we support party self-determination in the context of constraints that seem to limit party choice. Examples include confidentiality rules, disagreements between the parties about the process, expectations of program administrators, and our additional roles or obligations. Although these constraints limit our ability to fully support party decision making, we discuss ways that we can maximize party choice within these parameters.

Chapter 9 addresses how lawyers, union representatives, and other advocates can interfere with the parties' choices. We explore whether supporting the *advocates'* self-determination should be the mediator's concern or whether doing so comes at the expense of the parties.

Chapter 10 addresses the choices that mediators must make about how to practice their craft. Given the limits of what can be known about the short- and long-term effects of our interventions, our choices are often made based on our own values and priorities. While our experience and the research suggest that vigilant support of party choice leads to positive outcomes, we can never know, with certainty, what would have happened had we used a different approach. We explain why we nonetheless remain committed to supporting party self-determination above all else.

The appendix contains a reference list that includes all sources cited within the book in addition to other helpful resources (e.g., websites and videos).

The complexity and uncertainty of human conflict and the field of mediation mean we mediators must decide for ourselves how we want to help. We (Tara and Dan) believe that honoring party self-determination is not only valuable to the clients we serve, it is also of great value to us, the mediators. Making clear decisions about how we will practice our craft, based on respect and compassion for our clients, is a gift to ourselves as well as our clients. We hope this book helps illuminate your path. Thank you for taking this journey with us.

Note

1. Robert A. Baruch Bush and Joseph P. Folger, *The Promise of Mediation: The Transformative Approach to Conflict* (San Francisco: Jossey-Bass, 2005).

CHAPTER 1

Self-Determination Matters

There is a certain enthusiasm in liberty, that makes human nature rise above itself, in acts of bravery and heroism.

—Alexander Hamilton

Self-determination matters. Scholars, ethical codes, and many mediators identify it as the defining trait of mediation, and philosophers consider it central to human dignity. Yet in mediation, as in other areas of life, few agree on what self-determination looks like in practice and whether it should sometimes take a back seat to peace, safety, or another important value. Self-determination *could* mean something as simple as an absence of coercion or force, but we believe it means much more than that. As we see it, related concepts such as agency, autonomy, empowerment, and freedom, which mean much more than a simple lack of constraint, suggest why self-determination is so important and meaningful.

Among mediators who discuss the topic, everyone seems to agree that self-determination is the defining characteristic of mediation. According to the Model Standards of Conduct for Mediators, "self-determination is the act of coming to a voluntary, uncoerced decision in which each party makes free and informed choices as to process and outcome."[1] We can interpret this definition, and the terms within it, in a variety of ways. In fact, we suspect it was written that way by necessity. In a private conversation with one of the drafters of the revised model standards, she explained that the drafters represented a broad constituency. She said that though there was fundamental agreement on this high-level description, there probably would not have been if the drafters had gotten more precise. Therefore, any definition the committee could accept had to be vague enough to accommodate each drafter's view. The result was a definition that can be and is interpreted differently by different mediators.

*Obviously, a term or
construct that can mean
anything will eventually
mean nothing.*
—Wolf Wolfensberger

If the ambiguity within the definition of self-determination were not enough, there are standards and guidelines that seem to conflict with the principle of party self-determination. For example, the Model Standards of Practice for Family and Divorce Mediation direct the mediator to "assist the participants in determining how to promote the best interests of their children"[2] and to consider terminating the mediation when "the participants are about to enter into an agreement that the mediator reasonably believes to be unconscionable."[3] In these cases and others, the guidelines suggest that the mediator must evaluate the parties' decisions, compare them to the mediator's own sense of best practices or a conscionable agreement, and then exert influence on the parties that is consistent with those evaluations.

We'll return to the model standards in subsequent chapters. What is clear from this brief glance, though, is that such guidelines alone do not provide a definitive answer to the question of what self-determination should look like in mediation and why it matters. For a broader view on the subject, we'll turn to other definitions and applications of self-determination.

Mediators and scholars in other fields often use "agency" and "autonomy" interchangeably with "self-determination"—words that may best capture the spirit of the concept. For example, transformative mediators Robert Baruch Bush and Peter Miller equate self-determination with agency, which they define as "the self-aware and reflective assertion by an individual of the intentional choice to make decisions affecting their life circumstances."[4] This formulation is similar, but not identical, to the description of autonomy offered by psychologists Richard Ryan and Edward Deci. They identify autonomy as a state where "one's behaviors are self-endorsed, or congruent with one's authentic interests and values."[5]

Some fields hold self-determination to be a value in and of itself. For instance, social work, particularly in the area of eldercare,[6] values it highly. The National Association of Social Workers defines self-determination as the quality of a person who is "psychologically able to make decisions, has the power to do so, and is not prevented or directed otherwise."[7] Social workers put a premium, at least in theory, on people's abilities to make their own choices and to live their lives according to their own values. Even when a clinician sees their client's choice as unwise, or even harmful, serving their

*Freedom is not worth
having if it does not
connote freedom
to err. It passes my
comprehension how
human beings, be they
ever so experienced
and able, can delight in
depriving other human
beings of that precious
right.* —Mahatma Gandhi

client well often means supporting the client's autonomy. Of course there is a point where the professional draws a line, and not all social workers agree on where that line should be. Nonetheless, the field of social work values self-determination because the ability to make one's own choices and live according to one's own values is considered essential to human dignity.

Similarly, the fields of special education and other services for people with disabilities value self-determination.[8] Professionals in these fields seek to maximize clients' opportunities to make their own choices, and they are careful not to falsely assume clients lack the capacity to do so. As with social workers, not all educators view self-determination the same way or make the same decisions when attempting to support the people they serve, but the field recognizes and celebrates the self-determined life as a good in and of itself.

"Self-determination" is not a mere phrase; it is an imperative principle of action.
—Woodrow Wilson

Beyond the world of the individual client, self-determination also features prominently in political theory and international relations. In fact, self-determination is recognized as a fundamental right by virtue of which people can "freely pursue their economic, social and cultural development."[9] The term "self-determination" is enshrined in a number of charters and constitutions, and related words such as "liberty," "freedom," and "autonomy" appear in documents declaring individual rights. For example, the Declaration of Independence declares liberty to be an unalienable right of the individual.

In all of these fields and areas of life, self-determination is considered a primary principle and is held in high regard—largely because of the recognition that human dignity requires the ability to make meaningful choices. Self-determination is valued for another important reason: The highest quality decisions are the ones people make for themselves. People in positions of influence or authority have less information about the values and preferences of the people they serve than do the people themselves. Also, authority figures may prioritize their own interests over the interests of those they serve.

Power tends to corrupt, and absolute power corrupts absolutely.
—Lord Acton

Mediators can also be seen as authority figures with the same limitations as other authority figures. As we see it, putting as many decisions as possible in the hands of our mediation clients—the people most affected by those decisions—should lead to better decisions overall. Even a very wise, talented, and altruistic mediator has their own biases.

We view self-determination as both more and less than freedom from coercion or constraints. It is more than freedom as it requires a psychological state—one of intentionality, awareness, and congruence. It is also less than freedom as it does not require a lack of restrictions.[10] Decisions need not be *completely* free to be self-determined. Life is full of unavoidable limits, parameters, and consequences for our actions. The presence of *some* restrictions cannot negate our ability to experience self-determination; in fact, the quality of our decision making may be particularly important within certain constraints. It is when we are being pulled in different directions and the decisions we need to make are difficult that clarity and awareness are most needed. Our choices are particularly important, and our strength in making them especially inspiring, when something important is at stake. We find it meaningful to make clear, strong, *difficult* choices and inspiring to see others do so.[11]

Freedom is what we do with what is done to us. — Jean-Paul Sartre

Self-determination can mean much more than the ability to say yes or no. It can mean choosing one's own course clearly and consciously. It can be seen in the hero's journey in which the hero gives up the comfort of the familiar to embark on a risky adventure, rise to challenges, and return transformed. In these stories, the hero breaks from convention, asserts an unpopular opinion, or stands up to the more powerful mob.[12] The protagonist struggles to overcome obstacles by making strong, thoughtful choices and usually learns something important along the way. One who has been deeply hurt, or whose actions have hurt others, gains clarity about who they are and finds the strength to act on that insight. They make a conscious choice to put their own—or someone else's—needs first. The exact choice is less important than the feeling behind the choice. Strong, intentional decisions earn our admiration.

When we view self-determination this way, it is an important psychological need essential to the ability to thrive and flourish as a human being.[13] When this need is under threat, people try to restore it by resisting others' attempts to control them. Over 50 years of research on *psychological reactance* (the drive to regain freedom that has been lost or is under threat) demonstrates that efforts to control behavior often backfire.[14] When people feel pressured to change their attitudes or behaviors in one direction, their natural tendency is to resist that pressure and head even further in the other direction. As one family court judge put it in support of his position that divorce cases be removed from the court setting, "The normal response of a healthy adult when faced with coercion is to resist."[15]

Research demonstrates autonomy's importance to all forms of human flourishing including our ability to connect with others.[16] As we will discuss in Chapter 3, autonomy is essential to our ability to connect with others and act with compassion—doing something kind is more meaningful to both the doer and the receiver when it arises from the doer's initiative.[17] People with a strong sense of self-determination (or agency) are more likely to act consistently with their values, which almost always include standards about how they treat others.

Perhaps the biggest challenge for mediators in focusing on party self-determination is that we fear that doing so will diminish our role. Many professionals, including mediators, view their role as providing advice or guidance based on relevant knowledge. If the parties are making the choices about both process and content, we wonder what choices we, as mediators, get to make. If we mediators do not provide guidance or direction within the process, we may worry that we are unnecessary. What is our role if we fully support the self-determination of the parties? Although maximizing party choice means there are fewer choices of a certain kind for the mediator, there is still much for a mediator to do.

What we do is provide mirrors and lights. These interventions, which can have a great impact on party self-determination, require focus and skill. Keeping the mirrors and lights directed at the parties is difficult. It also requires us to let go of making a show of our expertise.

To illustrate the sorts of interventions that directly enhance party self-determination, what we are calling mirrors and lights, we turn to the transcript of a workplace mediation that Dan conducted. From the very start of the mediation, immediately after greeting the parties, Dan lets the parties know they can choose what happens first.

"Would it make sense for me to say a few words about how I see this conversation going at this point? Would that be okay?"

These were the questions Dan posed to the mediation participants, Ben and Lisa, at the beginning of a recorded role play of a workplace discrimination case, which we will use to illustrate our methods, along with the parties' reactions to them. From the very start, Dan wanted to communicate that Ben and Lisa were the decision-makers for every aspect of the process. If they had said there was no need for his introduction, he would have jumped straight to, "Okay, how would you like to start?"

We will share the full transcript (edited for clarity) of this simulated mediation throughout the next three chapters to demonstrate one method of supporting self-determination in mediation. You can also watch a video recording of the role play.[18] In the meantime, Ben responds to Dan's invitation.

Ben: Yeah, I think that would probably be helpful because I've never gone through mediation before, so, yeah, for my benefit at least, I think. Yeah.

Dan: Okay.

Lisa: For mine as well. I haven't done a mediation yet, so thank you.

Dan: Okay. Well, as I see it, it's really very simple. You two, I understand, have some differences, and my hope is to help you have the best possible conversation about those differences, or whatever it is that the two of you want to talk about. So I'm here to serve you in that. I'll do some things that I hope enhance the conversation, but by all means, keep me posted if anything I'm doing doesn't feel helpful.

{I no longer say "best possible conversation" because that could imply that I'm the judge of what a good conversation is. Now I like to say "whatever conversation you want to have" to make it clear that they get to decide what sort of conversation it is.}

So, you'll hear me do some things like reflect what I hear each of you say, just to help confirm that you've said what you meant to say, and that the other person got a chance to hear it. I may also summarize what I've heard you both say, so that you have a chance to kind of think about where you see things in relation to each other.

And this is your conversation. This process is voluntary as far as I'm concerned. And I really mean that, that we should only do it for as long as each of you feels like it's worth doing. We have up to an hour to do it today, but there is no obligation as far as I'm concerned that we use that whole hour. We really only should do this for whatever period of time both of you feel like it's helpful.

{Notice that I was not merely saying that, by definition, mediation was voluntary. I meant they could actually choose at any moment to end their participation, with no pressure or judgment from me.}

This is confidential as far as I'm concerned. I won't tell anybody anything that was said here. If it happens that you want me to take some notes about things that you've agreed to or about any other aspect of your conversation, which I would then deliver to you, I'm happy to do that. But I won't speak outside of here about what happened. My hope is that this helps you feel free to speak openly without fear that something will be used against you somehow.

{I no longer like to say that last sentence. It's not my business to hope that they feel free to speak openly—they may have good reason to feel guarded with each other so I don't want to try to nudge them toward openness. How open they are, like everything else possible, should be their choice.}

Any ideas that you have for what will make this conversation as helpful, meaningful, productive as possible, please keep me posted. For example, if it would make sense to talk privately with me at any point, we can do that. If it would help for you to take a break at any point, by all means. If you have any other ideas. . . . If there is somebody outside of the three of us that you would like to consult with at any point, as far as I'm concerned, those are also possibilities.

I hear that you haven't participated in mediation before, but in case you've heard about how mediation goes from others, I just want to clarify a difference that I may have from some other mediators. And that is that sometimes I've heard other mediators say that the mediator controls the process and the parties control the outcome. I don't see myself as controlling this process. I see this process as being up to the two of you, and my job is to support that.

I'm somebody for you to turn to for help as you have this conversation but not as the person who directs the conversation. Does that raise any questions or comments?

{The two paragraphs above may go without saying—the parties will experience soon enough what it means for them to control the process. On the other hand, since it's unusual to encounter a professional whose main goal is to support the clients as they make their own choices, I believe that the point is worth emphasizing.}

Ben: I'm just wondering about agenda, what issues we're going to be looking at. I mean, who would be the person to set that?

Dan: Well, as I see it, those are your choices. And so, for example, if you have some things that you would like to confirm that we're going to cover at this point, by all means, you're welcome as far as I'm concerned to kind of list those, as are you, Lisa. In fact, it might make sense, if that's okay with the two of you, kind of where to start, if you would like to say what you hope to cover today.

{Ben's question about agenda threw me a little. I don't love my last sen-
tence, which implied that I agreed that starting with an agenda was the right thing to do. It's certainly okay for one of them to do that, but I may have given the impression that *I* prefer that. I'm glad they didn't assume they had to start with an agenda and instead launched into Lisa simply sharing her perspective on the situation.}

Ben: Yeah, I mean, I think it probably makes sense if Lisa went first, because you know, this is really your case, Lisa. So I would be quite interested to hear from you first.

Lisa: Okay, that works for me.

Dan: That works for you too?

Lisa: Yeah, that works for me.

Dan: Okay, feel free.

Ben: Okay.

Lisa: Okay. Well, I'm really frustrated here and angry.

From the very start of this mediation, Dan aims to support the parties in making their own decisions as they deal with their conflict. The act of mak-ing decisions brings with it a sense of agency and competence, which allows them to feel clearer, calmer, and more willing to continue making decisions for themselves. Dan does not evaluate the quality of these decisions—the important thing is that the parties are making them, and the mediator draws attention to that fact. Dan acts consistently with his attitude that the parties, and not he, are the ones in the best position to make these decisions. As the parties walk down the path of their conversation, Dan's role is to point a flashlight at the forks along the way. When Ben asked about an agenda for the meeting, Dan pointed to the fork in the road by saying "Well, as I see it, those are your choices. And so, for example, if you have some things that you would like to confirm that we're going to cover at this point, by all means, you're welcome as far as I'm concerned to kind of list those, as are you, Lisa."

Because Dan has already put decisions in Ben and Lisa's hands, they have started making choices. Would they like to hear Dan describe the process?

Are they going to set an agenda? Who will speak first? Although these decisions may not seem significant, they give the parties the experience of making choices within the process. The parties become aware that they have the opportunity, as well as the responsibility, to steer their own course.

The goal of this approach is to support parties in a way that maximizes their ability to make clear decisions despite the complexities of their situation. We hold up a mirror to the parties, putting their words back into the room so that they can better hear themselves and each other. We reflect, as accurately as possible, both the words and emotions that the parties convey. We do so to honor their choices about what and how they communicate. We also reflect the parties to help them see that however disempowered they feel, they are at least heard by the mediator. The reflections also give parties the opportunity to respond by refining or revising their message, increasing their sense of agency in the process.

We focus lights on the parties and their situation as well. We summarize portions of the conversation, helping them see more clearly the topics they covered and the perspectives they have shared on those topics. We additionally point out opportunities to make choices by checking in with them about what they would like to do next.

These practices slow down the conversation and provide the parties with greater opportunity to make choices. Those choices often lead to increased clarity, confidence, and an openness to hearing the other's perspective even if they disagree. But even slowing down the conversation only happens if the parties are open to it. We defer to the parties' preferences if they choose to quickly talk back and forth, over each other, or over us. While we sometimes interrupt the parties with a reflection or to offer a summary, if they continue talking or decline our offer to summarize, we defer to them. In that case, we step back and remain available to offer support if they choose to take advantage of it. Since we see the parties' challenge as being, at its core, their diminished sense of agency, our goal is to provide a process they control and not one we impose on them.

We do not evaluate whether the conversation is going well. The question instead is whether we are doing everything we can to give them choices. For example, if parties are talking over each other and appearing more and more frustrated, we might shine a light on that situation with something like "It looks like you're both getting frustrated with this conversation and you're both talking at the same time. If you're okay with how it's going, that's fine, but I'm just checking if you want to try something else." Our intention behind that check-in would not be to get them to change what they are doing but simply to remind them that they have choices. We are aware that the parties could feel criticized by us so we are careful to maintain the attitude that what they have been doing is genuinely acceptable to us.

Now back to Ben and Lisa.

Lisa: Okay. Well, I'm really frustrated here and angry. I've put my heart and soul into this job for eight years, and Ben, my boss, I thought I could really trust him. I've worked the hardest I could, or I can. I took all of my boss's advice on what to do to be a good worker, to open the possibility that I could receive a promotion at our company. The position that John recently accepted is for foreMAN. I didn't realize that you had to be a man in order to get that job.

The workforce at our company has more than 60% women in it, a lot of them my friends. We all work really hard. I've seen the figures and I'm the hardest-working person on our team, male or female. And do I get offered the job? Or even discussed the possibility of the job? No. It goes to John.

That made me so angry that all I can think of is the reason why I wasn't offered the position is because I'm a woman. And if you're in the United States, you're not supposed to discriminate against women, or people of other ethnic backgrounds. So that's all I can see here. And I'm just so flustered I don't know what to do.

I thought I could trust my boss. I thought I worked for a good company, and I, you know . . . All my hard work for the past eight years has been . . . I'm just not sure what to do. I'm very frustrated.

Dan: So, you are very frustrated, very angry. You're flustered. You don't know what to do. You feel that you have been working hard for eight years. You trusted your boss, Ben. You sought advice from Ben for how to do your job as well as possible. You feel like you've done everything you can to do a good job. The numbers show that you've been more productive than others on your team.

When John received this promotion, the only explanation you can come up with is that it's because he's a man. You said there are 60% women in the workforce. You said that you didn't know the word "fore-man" necessarily meant it has to be a man, but that's how you feel at this point. That the only explanation for John getting the job is that he's a man, and you aren't supposed to discriminate in the United States based on gender.

{My decision to reflect at that moment arose from a few factors. I jumped in immediately at her words "I'm just not sure what to do. I'm very frustrated." Those are very clear statements of diminished agency. Reflecting at that moment was an attempt to provide support right where she needed it. It was a way for her to experience that, despite her uncertainty and frustration, she *did* have the capacity to articulate that she felt that way. And she *was succeeding* at being heard. Her comment shortly before that, "I thought I could trust my boss," gave me an additional rationale to reflect. That expression of alienation from Ben was exactly the sort of thing that this conversation might have been able to help with. I wanted to shine a light on that aspect of Lisa's experience so that both she and Ben could contemplate it further. Another reason for reflecting then was that neither Ben nor Lisa seemed to have something else they wanted to say at that moment. If Lisa had continued to talk or if Ben had jumped in, I would have deferred to them. My intention was to help them see the conversation more clearly. I focused my lights on the choices Lisa was making and I held up a mirror so both she and Ben could take another look. My mirrors and lights helped them to see what Lisa was doing, increasing their opportunities to proceed consciously.}

Lisa: Yes, that sounds like what I mean to say. Yes, thank you.

{This comment from Lisa suggested that my reflection matched what she thought she'd said. I was hoping that this small bit of success that Lisa had had, to speak and be heard as she intended, reinforced her awareness of her competence, bolstering her sense that she could handle the situation she was in.}

Notice that even though Lisa is in the midst of feeling confused, powerless, and victimized, Dan remains fully supportive of her choices. He reflects, without reframing, her expressions of confusion, upset, and frustration as well as her expressions of distrust, anger, and judgment toward Ben. Dan shows no sign of trying to redirect the conversation or focus it on any particular aspect of the story. Next he continues to place all decisions about the process in the hands of the parties. In other words, Dan continues to allow space for Ben and Lisa to exercise their autonomy and increase their agency.

Dan: Your guys' choice—if you would like to speak at this point, Ben. Or if you have more to say, Lisa.

{There was a pause before I said this line, which suggested to me that Ben and Lisa thought I would let them know whether it was Ben's turn to speak or whether I had follow-up questions for Lisa. I remained clear that they got to decide what happened next.}

Lisa: Oh, I would like to hear what Ben has to say.

{Leaving to them this choice about who would speak gave Lisa the chance to say she wanted to hear what Ben had to say, and it gave Ben the chance to respond. Despite their differences, they were actively, autonomously collaborating with each other in having a conversation now.}

Ben: Sure. Okay. Well, essentially it comes down to this. This is an old company, and we are now a very large company. When we became a large company, we were taken over by another multinational, and you know, that's part of the reason we're in mediation today. It's because that's part of the new HR policy. They introduced a load of schemes where we take our commitment to equality very seriously.

The company did use to . . . It had a bit of a reputation, back in the '60s, for being very . . . You know, everybody knew everybody, and it was male-dominated back then. But Lisa just said, you know, 60% of the employees are women. That's quite a substantial number. Men are almost in the minority so I think it's nonsensical to call a company like this discriminatory.

The simple fact is, I've been friends with Lisa for a long time, okay, so I like Lisa, and she is a very good worker. That certainly isn't in question. But for the kind of job that John's been given, we've got to look at more than just simple productivity. We've got to look at leadership skills, and in particular, management ability. Now while Lisa has exhibited incredible productivity as a base worker, she hasn't taken the initiative to show management and leadership qualities. And this is something John has done.

He's actually sacrificed—it is my opinion—that he has sacrificed his own output, potentially risking his job, to develop his leadership skills and management skills, you know, helping out other members of the team. That's part of the reason he's been given this job, and I don't see Lisa's grounds for her allegation. They do seem to be most unfounded to me.

{I was aware that Lisa might have been taking Ben's comments any number of ways. Maybe she was finding what he was saying to be responsive to her, relevant, and persuasive. Or maybe she was finding it disingenuous and manipulative. I knew I wanted him to have the chance to speak in his own words if he wanted to; and I knew I wanted Lisa to have the chance to respond as she wished. I knew it wasn't my place to evaluate Ben's words other than to watch for opportunities to support him or Lisa. My main contributions during this monologue by Ben were to continue to pay attention to both him and Lisa and not to interfere with the choices they made.}

In this chapter we have introduced the idea that the mediator is someone who illuminates the parties and their situation but who does not push, direct, or even nudge the parties. We have described the importance of agency and autonomy in general and how they can be supported in mediation. Although promoting agency is a worthwhile goal in general, it is especially important for people in conflict. As we will discuss in Chapter 2, conflict tends to bring with it a *diminished* sense of agency, which leads to a vicious circle.

Notes

1. American Arbitration Association, American Bar Association, and Association for Conflict Resolution, "Model Standards of Conduct for Mediators" (2005), Standard 1.A.

2. Symposium on Standards of Practice for Family and Divorce Mediation Convened by the Association of Family and Conciliation Courts, "Model Standards of Practice for Family and Divorce Mediation" (2000), Standard VII.

3. Symposium on Standards of Practice, Standard XI.A.4.

4. Robert A. Baruch Bush and Peter F. Miller, "Hiding in Plain Sight: Mediation, Client-Centered Practice, and the Value of Human Agency," *Ohio State Journal on Dispute Resolution* 35 (2020): 597.

5. Richard M. Ryan and Edward L. Deci, *Self-Determination Theory: Basic Psychology Needs in Motivation, Development and Wellness* (New York: Guilford Press, 2017), 10.

6. National Association of Social Workers, "NASW Standards for Social Work Practice With Family Caregivers of Older Adults" (2010), Standard I, https://www.socialworkers.org/LinkClick.aspx?fileticket=aUwQL98exRM%3d&portalid=0.

7. Paul Spicker, "Social Work and Self-Determination," *British Journal of Social Work* 20, no. 3 (June 1990): 222.

8. Michael Wehmeyer, "Beyond Self-Determination: Causal Agency Theory," *Journal of Developmental and Physical Disabilities* 16 (December 2004): 338.

9. United Nations General Assembly, Resolution 1514 (1960).

10. Bush and Miller, "Hiding in Plain Sight," 21.

11. See Bush and Miller, "Hiding in Plain Sight," 37.

12. See Bush and Miller, "Hiding in Plain Sight," for demonstrations of agency in popular culture.

13. Ryan and Deci, *Self-Determination Theory*; Bush and Miller, "Hiding in Plain Sight," 5–6, 21–22.

14. Stephen A. Raines, "The Nature of Psychological Reactance Revisited: A Meta-Analytic Review," *Human Communication Research* 39, no. 1 (January 2013): 47.

15. Bruce Peterson, "Time, Perhaps, to Get Courts Out of Divorce," *Minneapolis Star Tribune*, July 12, 2012.

16. Ryan and Deci, *Self-Determination Theory*, 247, 250.

17. Netta Weinstein and Richard M. Ryan, "When Helping Helps: Autonomous Motivation for Prosocial Behavior and Its Influence on Well-Being for the Helper and Recipient," *Journal of Personality and Social Psychology* 98, no. 2 (February 2010): 239.

18. Dan Simon Mediation, "Transformative Mediation in Action: Workplace Discrimination Case Example," https://www.youtube.com/watch?v=Cq0upTnMbVc. The video recording also includes a discussion before and after the mediation among the mediators on the call (the parties were played by self-described facilitative mediators). Following the mediation, the role players share how they experienced the mediation as participants to the process.

CHAPTER 2

A Crisis in Interaction

Deterioration in human interaction is what [people] find most affecting, significant—and disturbing—about the experience of conflict.

—Robert Baruch Bush and Joseph Folger

Mediation clients are in a predicament. In addition to having a practical problem to solve, they are experiencing a *crisis in interaction*—a breakdown in the way they are relating to each other. That crisis affects the parties' thoughts, feelings, and behaviors in relation to themselves, each other, and the situation. This is the main, if not only, reason the parties are unable to solve the problem on their own. We believe that supporting the parties in ways that are likely to help them transform the interactional crisis is the most important assistance mediators can offer.

Bush and Folger describe the interactional crisis in *The Promise of Mediation*. According to their transformative theory of conflict, the crisis includes parties experiencing both *weakness* and *self-absorption* in relation to each other and to the conflict. That is, each party experiences, on the one hand, a sense of their own vulnerability, limitations, and lack of control (weakness); and on the other hand, a diminished sense of empathy, compassion, and openness to the other party (self-absorption). That self-absorption appears through parties viewing each other in a negative and suspicious light—seeing each other more as problems than as fellow humans. These experiences can reinforce each other: The more a person feels scared, confused, or powerless, the more they see and treat the other person in the conflict as an enemy. And the more a person is treated as an enemy, the more scared and confused *they* become, leading them to now see and treat the *other* person in the conflict as an enemy. This creates what Bush and Folger have termed the "vicious circle of conflict."[1] In the most extreme examples, the vicious circle leads to endless

litigation, or even violence. Some divorcing couples litigate for years, experience trauma throughout the process, and stay bitter toward each other for
the rest of their lives. Throughout the world there are border disputes and
conflicts between ethnic groups that go back generations and occasionally
still erupt in violence. In the cases we mediate, the vicious circle might not
seem this intense, but the pattern is similar.

As we discussed in Chapter 1, autonomy, or agency, is a basic psychological need. People want to be able to make their own clear, strong choices and
to feel like they are taking good care of themselves. As discussed above, weakness (or a lack of agency) is a common experience in conflict. The antidote
to this predicament, then, is a process that supports party self-determination
and helps each party regain their sense of agency. As mediators, we hold up
mirrors and lights that reflect and illuminate the parties' choices, allowing
them to see themselves and each other more clearly. That clarity increases
their sense of agency and strength (*empowerment*)[2] and contributes to their
growing ability to empathize with each other (*recognition*). This empowerment and recognition allow parties to escape the vicious circle, creating a
self-perpetuating *virtuous circle*.[3]

To view this predicament in action along with the mediator's interventions aimed at supporting party self-determination, let's rejoin Ben and Lisa.
If you recall, Ben had just shared his perspective, ending with "I don't see
Lisa's grounds for her allegation. They do seem to be most unfounded to
me."

{When Ben called Lisa's allegations "unfounded," he seemed to be experiencing the self-absorption aspect of interactional crisis. He was focusing on
what he saw as the invalidity of Lisa's perspective. That sort of focus is natural and common in conflict. If he were in another frame of mind, he might
have noticed that her allegations were plausible, or at least understandable.
He might have empathized with her disappointment even while he saw the
situation differently from her. He also might have anticipated Lisa's angry
reaction to his statement. Instead, Ben focused on his own perspective,
which was that discrimination did not occur. Ben's focus there kept them
both stuck in the vicious circle.}

Lisa: What do you mean, "most unfounded"? Most unfounded?! I put all my
trust in you, Ben, for the last eight years. You said, "Work hard. I will
help you get ahead." And now, now you're saying . . .
Dan: "Unfounded"—you don't understand how Ben can say that, after this.
After eight years of you trusting him, and him telling you he was going
to help you.

{I reflected Lisa at this moment because her reaction was so heated.
(A common saying among transformative mediators is "Follow the heat.")
Because this comment was so charged and because she was expressing
offense at what Ben had said, I believed it was central to the interactional

crisis that I was trying to help with. By holding up a mirror to Lisa at this moment, I gave her the chance to take another look at herself and her reaction, and to choose how to handle this challenge. This reflection oriented Lisa toward the decision she had just made about what to say and to her opportunity to make her next decision. It gave her another chance to increase her agency and to do so in a moment when she was confronting Ben. To make a choice in that moment held the promise of increased agency for her and, perhaps, a shift toward understanding Ben. The reflection also shone a light on Lisa, giving Ben a chance to absorb the reality of her anger and to contemplate how to respond. I had not reflected Ben throughout his longer monologue simply because there had not been an opportunity to do so without interrupting him. I do not try to reflect parties equally—I try to respond when there is something I can do to help at a difficult moment.}

Lisa: Yes, yes.

{At this moment, when Ben was dismissing Lisa's perspective, I was glad she knew that her reaction was being heard. Lisa chose what to say and she succeeded at being heard; she had power.}

Ben: Sure, I mean . . .
Lisa: And how could I know that John sacrificed . . . You know, that's easy for you to say that he was less productive in order for him to build his leadership skills, in order for him to open up the opportunity for him to be offered the foreman position. That was never discussed with me.
Dan: It was never discussed with you that John had done that? That he had taken initiative?

{This reflection was off. She meant she was never told that doing the things John had done would've helped *her* career. I had chosen to speak up, because Lisa appeared to be struggling around articulating this thought. It would have been more effective if I had reflected her meaning accurately. I think Lisa sensed that I was *trying* to be accurate so I didn't do much harm, and she simply continued trying to explain her point.}

Lisa: [speaking to me] You know, Ben told me if I work hard and I follow his advice, that there would be further opportunities with me in the company. So I trusted him. I listened to him. I did all that was told and expected of me. And you know, I would have hoped that I would have been informed about the position opening so I could have applied for it.
Dan: You followed Ben's advice.
Lisa: I did.
Dan: You trusted him.
Lisa: Yes.
Dan: You understood that he was going to help you make progress in the company, and you would have expected that he would have told you about this opening.

{I chose to reflect these comments because they were about how Ben had let her down. She appeared to be thinking of Ben mostly as the person who had betrayed her. The intensity around this part of her situation suggested that it would be helpful for me to reflect what she was saying both so she could continue to make choices about what to do about it and so Ben could hear clearly how Lisa was seeing things. These reflections seemed to give Lisa a boost that helped her to continue to articulate her perspective vividly.}

Lisa: Yes, yes. Ben says that, yes, the company does have a larger percentage of women working there than men. But how many of the managerial or supervisory positions have been offered to women? Well, the one right in front of me, you know, this one job opportunity that could have been presented to me, wasn't. So, I don't have a whole lot of information, other than that the women in our company are in the lower-level positions, and that doesn't seem like that's very good to me, or to the other women in our company.

Ben: Well, all I can say to that is one, your single case does not reflect what goes on in the rest of the company. This is one isolated case. We're not talking . . . This case isn't reflective and isn't representative of what goes on in the entire company, okay. I just think it's important to understand that.

{This would've been a fine place for me to reflect Ben, since it was, in effect, "You're wrong, Lisa," but since Lisa responded very quickly, my reflection would have interfered with her choice to speak at that moment so I thought it was better for me to stay out of the way. As always, the most important consideration was what choices the parties were making, and now Lisa was choosing to speak. Staying focused on the parties' choices promotes their agency and supports them in finding their own way out of their crisis.}

Lisa: Well, we can see, you know. I mean, if I pursue this further, and take legal action, I could go to the press. I could really make a big stink out of this and expose the company. Then you'll have to really prove that you're not discriminating against women.

Dan: You're saying, "We'll see about that. We'll expose . . ."

Lisa: I'm so frustrated that that makes me . . . I just feel like I could pull that lever at any time right now, because I am so angry.

Dan: You're so angry you could go to the press. You could make a big stink about it.

Lisa: I could, yes, yes. And you know, right now I'm just not getting a whole lot of . . . I don't feel like I'm being listened to, and that I'm being supported, and so it just feels like the rug has been just pulled right out from under me.

{Lisa's continued intensity and expressions of frustration inspired me to continue to reflect her comments. Her mention of legal action gave me a little twinge of wanting to prevent her from going in that direction. I used that twinge to remind myself that my job was to provide support for her, right where she was. Her mention of taking legal action meant, if anything, that she was in distress and wasn't sure what to do so I remained focused on listening to her and reflecting her accurately. I also assumed it was important for Ben to have the chance to experience the reality of how strongly Lisa felt so he could decide how to respond. It's especially important in these moments of intensity that the parties receive additional light on their situation. The interactional crisis can seem murky and confusing. Holding a mirror to Lisa, and shining a light on her frustration, gave both parties added opportunities to make clear choices. This is the essence of self-determination.}

Ben: Okay, Lisa. Look, the whole thing with John, he's . . . It is important to work hard. But the thing is, he's taken the initiative. You're saying that you're upset that opportunities weren't put in front of you, okay. Now, I don't mean to be patronizing about this, but John really went out there. He put in a lot of hours after work. He spent a lot of time networking and doing all these things off of his own back. He showed a lot of initiative.

Lisa: Networking? Network with who? With the big bosses? Your big bosses? All the guys? What? Did you go smoke some cigars and drink some brandy after work?

Ben: Well, not cigars and brandy.

Lisa: I was never invited. I didn't know about any of these networking opportunities.

Ben: Because he made them.

Lisa: I can check with my other female colleagues. I don't think they knew about any of this. It just seems like this old boy thing.

Ben: He made those opportunities. He went out there and he approached people off of his own back. Okay. He networked with everybody, not just the bosses, but also his coworkers. I believe he has had a few conversations with you. I think you know him. Don't you?

Lisa: Yeah. He and I work well together. I don't know what he did or said to you, but I don't hold anything against him. It's you that I'm upset at because I put my trust and my faith in you, and you let me down. So you know, I respect John for what he does. But you know, I've got the figure here that I am more productive than he is, so I should have at least been presented the opportunity to apply for that foreman position. And I wasn't.

{The back and forth between Ben and Lisa, though conflictual, seemed to be meeting both of their needs. As far as I could tell, they were both making clear choices about what they wanted to say, so I stayed out of the way.}

Ben: I mean, that's true. I'm not going to question your productivity. Okay? That's absolutely true and I stand by that. I always will. Okay? I just want to make you aware of that right now.

Dan [after a brief pause]: You do acknowledge that Lisa has been very productive.

Ben: Absolutely. One of the best.

Lisa: Yeah.

Dan: One of the best.

{I chose to reflect here because Ben's statement about Lisa being "one of the best" seemed central to their interaction. Any time one party shares their view of the other party, positive or negative, I assume it matters. The vicious circle tends to include negative thoughts and feelings about the other party, while the virtuous circle is characterized by more positive sentiments, so when a party expresses either negativity or positivity toward the other party, it is relevant to where they are in the interactional crisis. Holding up a mirror to those aspects of the interaction helps parties see where they are, giving them opportunities to make clear choices about where they want to go from there.}

Dan: I wonder if it would make sense for me to . . . You've covered a few different aspects of this situation. Can I just kind of summarize what I've heard? In case that helps clarify where you want to focus at this point? Would that be all right?

{The slowed pace of their comments at this moment suggested to me that I wouldn't be interfering with choices they were making if I offered to summarize. I also was aware that they had discussed a variety of aspects of the situation. I hoped that by organizing what they had talked about into the different topics they had covered, and by repeating what they had each said about each topic, I could give them the opportunity to make a clear choice about whether they wanted to revisit any of those topics or raise a new one. Because I believe supporting self-determination means supporting each party's choice in each moment, I only wanted to do so if they didn't prefer that something else happen at this moment, so I genuinely asked their permission.}

Ben: Yeah.

Lisa: Sure.

Ben: Yeah, absolutely.

Dan: Okay. So, you talked about the overarching question of the company's discriminatory policy, or not. And Ben, you've stated that you do not feel the company has been discriminatory, and in particular, recently policies have been put in place where equality is an important priority of the company. And you say that that's evidenced by the fact that 60% of the workforce are women, and that goes to show that the company is not discriminatory in general.

Lisa, you're saying that, well, yes, 60% of the company workforce are women, and yet in terms of management positions, your sense is that in fact women are under-represented. And certainly in this partic- ular instance of John being selected over you, that feels to you like an instance of discrimination.

Lisa: Yes.

Dan: Another thing you both talked about is basically Lisa's performance up 'til this point, and you both agreed that Lisa has been very productive. Ben, I think you said "the best," in terms of productivity. Or "one of the best."

Ben: Yeah. I did.

Dan: And I guess there's no disagreement about that. You've also talked about how it came to be that John, instead of Lisa, was given this promotion. And Lisa, you're saying that, given your productivity, it really doesn't make sense other than that John's a man. And to the extent that John may have done some networking, you see that as an old boys thing. They're out, you know, whatever, drinking scotch and smoking cigars, and you were never invited to that sort of thing, so you didn't have the opportunity to do that.

Ben, you're saying that the way that John earned this position was that he took a lot of initiative, worked a lot past his paid hours, past the workday, did a lot of networking. That he took his own initiative, you're saying that he made those opportunities happen. And you also say that, from your standpoint, productivity is not really the criterion that determines who should have this job, but it's management skills. And your sense is that John was the person with those types of skills.

And one more thing that you discussed was your relationship with each other. And Lisa, you said that you had trusted Ben to basically be a mentor to you in the company, and you had sought his advice on how to advance in the company. And you felt like you had a relationship where you could trust that he would advocate for you and would at least let you know about this opportunity coming up. And you feel incredibly frustrated that he has not lived up to that relationship. And Ben, you also acknowledged that the two of you have been friends.

{I intended to provide an accurate and thorough summary of what they had discussed, including areas where they disagreed, along with any strong negative emotions and accusations they had aimed at each other. By juxtaposing their differing perspectives on each topic they had discussed, I gave them the chance to see where they stood in relation to each other. As always, my intention was to illuminate, without coloring, their conversation. My summary seemed to lead Ben to further address one of the topics I had mentioned, as we will see when we continue their story in the next chapter.}

Ben's and Lisa's conversation is typical of people in the vicious circle of conflict. Each person feels in some way diminished by the other. Lisa feels disregarded and betrayed by Ben. Ben feels misunderstood and maligned by Lisa. Both are confused by the other's behavior, and their own positive self-concept (as a person who deserves consideration and trust) is under threat. In this state, they both find it challenging to empathize with each other. The lack of empathy from the other perpetuates the vicious circle.

Dan seeks to remedy this situation with his mirrors and lights. If he can help Ben and Lisa see themselves, each other, and the situation more clearly, they may be able to act on their preference for a stronger sense of self as well as their preference to be positively connected to each other. In addition to shining a light on their conversation as it plays out, he shines a light on their opportunities to continue to have agency in the conversation. He does so explicitly, for example, by asking for their permission to summarize. He does so implicitly by accepting all of the choices they make throughout the conversation, including what to say and how to say it.

Ben and Lisa provide one example of parties caught in the vicious circle. In later chapters we will see what the process looks like, in detail, as they move through it. Meanwhile, the following stories illustrate other forms that the vicious circle can take in different contexts. In this next case, Dan mediates a conflict between former business partners and attempts to support their self-determination as they struggle with the vicious circle, which evolves into a virtuous circle.

NO NON-COMPETE

"Mediation will just be a waste of time, but the judge wants us to do it. We'll probably just be going through the motions. These guys are too far apart. And they can't stand each other. You'll probably have to keep us in separate rooms."

I listened to this comment from the defense lawyer but didn't let it dissuade me from my position that my job was to help all of them have a conversation. Lawyers often say these sorts of things when they schedule mediation. For one thing, if they already thought a settlement was likely and that both sides could easily talk to each other, they would have had a conversation without me. Additionally, it's not surprising that the early stages of the litigation process would have only intensified their pessimism, distrust, and sense of powerlessness. Mediation conducted in the shadow of litigation rarely starts with anyone saying, "This should be easy."

I'm also aware that people may say these sorts of things because they believe it provides a strategic advantage. They want the mediator to know that they intend to stick to their position or at least continue to argue strongly about the rightness of their cause or the strength of their case. Often both sides genuinely believe that they are right and the other side is wrong. And they want the mediator to know that the other side is the one who's going to have to cave in. They may also believe that suggesting how strongly they feel about their case makes the mediator more likely to believe that their side actually *is* right. Often implied in those comments is the idea "We are not going to budge because we are right; they are not going to budge because they are stubborn, crazy, bitter, or dishonest." The belief that "we are right" and "the other is wrong" is also a common symptom of the vicious circle.

After confirming that both sides agreed to work with me, I had separate phone conversations with each side. I learned that the defendants (Bruce and Tony, co-owners of New Company) were former employees of the plaintiff (John, owner of Old Company). New Company was now competing with Old Company and was serving a significant number of Old Company's former customers. John was suing Bruce and Tony for $2 million. When I first talked to John and his lawyer, they told me they believed that New Company had no way of paying that amount and that John's real hope was to drive them out of business. The business involved selling software to beauty salons and then providing consulting about and service of that software.

In my phone conversation with Bruce, Tony, and their lawyer, I learned that they felt especially strongly about wanting to avoid seeing the other side. They found John's lawsuit offensive and unjustified. Bruce and Tony's lawyer said, "Neither Bruce nor Tony signed a non-compete. John really doesn't have a case. He's just trying to bully them out of business." And Bruce added, "Yeah, and I'd really rather not give him the false impression that we think his claims are in any way legitimate. I'd kind of hate to have to sit across the table from him as if he's entitled to a rational discussion about this. I basically don't want to give him the satisfaction." I explained to both parties (on the phone and in person) that I saw my role as being to help them have a conversation. If they preferred to communicate from separate rooms, that was their choice, but it raised the question of how they intended to get messages across.

I see my role as helping parties with their crisis in interaction. Consequently, I generally won't carry messages when parties are in separate rooms. When I meet with the sides separately, my goal is to help them get clearer on their points of view, what they want out of the situation, and what they want to say to the other side. I am not there to gather information for passing messages between them. Carrying messages would do little to shift their interaction.

Meaningful shifts in interaction require the parties to make choices about the interaction. My carrying messages would entail me, and not the parties, making the choices. When I carry a message, it is impossible for me to match the speaker's tone or to answer follow-up questions the same way the speaker would. Inevitably and unintentionally, I alter the meaning of the message, thereby diminishing the parties' control over how they interact. Worse, I often can't help but *want* to alter the message because of some belief I form about what will be helpful. That alteration would certainly mean that I was making a decision for a party, replacing the party's judgment with my own, and eliminating any opportunity for the parties to increase their agency around the interaction.

In my practice, I inform both sides that we could set up a phone call or video conference between rooms and that either party could send their lawyer to talk to the other side. The one exception to my policy is that I will facilitate negotiation between different rooms about what it will take for them to meet in the same room.

In this non-compete mediation, we staggered the parties' arrival times so that there would be no face-to-face contact, and I showed them to separate conference rooms. In addition to his lawyer, John had brought his CFO. Although I never learned their reasons, Bruce and Tony were adamant they did not want to see the CFO. After 30 minutes of negotiation, through me, about how they would hold the session, Bruce, Tony, and their lawyer agreed to meet directly with John and his lawyer as long as the CFO was not present.

When we all met in the same room, I reminded everyone, "This is an opportunity to have whatever conversation you want to have. You've all already signed the agreement to mediate, which reminded you about my commitment to confidentiality and about how these conversations are generally inadmissible in any future proceeding. Any questions or comments about the process?"

Everyone shrugged or shook their heads. I said, "So how would you like to start?"

As discussed in Chapter 1, I make it clear from the start of the session that the participants are in control of what happens in the mediation. Once I've given my brief orientation, I turn the process over to the parties. Saying "Where would you like to start?" allows anyone in the room to speak about anything they wish, including procedural questions or requests, going straight to offers and demands, or starting the way this group did.

Bruce's lawyer said, "It's traditional for plaintiffs to speak first—would you guys like to start (looking at John's lawyer)?"

John's lawyer said, "John, would you like to share what brings us here?"

While it is indeed traditional for plaintiffs to speak first, I didn't know whether this group would choose to do it that way. Here the defendants' lawyer had the chance to act graciously and invite the other side to speak first. That opportunity would have been lost if I had said, "Shall we hear from the plaintiff's side first?" Turning the process over to the participants also gave John's lawyer the chance to ask John if he would like to speak, and John had the opportunity to make that choice.

John said, "Absolutely . . . I started this business 25 years ago. And Bruce, you came along about 10 years in. I took a chance on hiring you—you had no experience. But I taught you what you needed to know and you got the hang of it, and you wound up being great for the business, and I paid you for that. The customers liked you and things generally went well. And I considered you a friend. There was even a point where we talked about you taking an ownership interest."

Bruce broke in at this point, "Yeah, what ever happened to that?"

"The crash of 2008 happened," said John. "I could barely pay your salary for a couple years, much less think about cutting you in on the tiny profits . . . So anyway, when you told me you were taking a job at 3M, as you know, I was sorry to see you go, but I understood. A corporation like that can pay better than I can. I figured I'd have to replace you, but that's life. So obviously, when I learned you were going into competition with me, I was pissed, and I regretted not having you sign a non-compete. And then when all those customers went with you, I talked to Bill here (indicating his lawyer) and I realized we've got some good claims and I've got serious damages. Last year was my worst one in 20 years. I had to offer all of my customers a free year of service so they didn't switch to you. I took a salary of zero and I had to lend the company $40,000. And by the way, when Tony over here went to work for you, that was the icing on the cake."

Tony looked down and shifted in his seat.

At this point, I reflected what John had just shared, in detail. I held a mirror to John's story so he and the others present could take another look. My intention was to honor the choices John had made so I did my best to accurately reflect all that he had said, including the positive and negative aspects. For instance, I reflected his acknowledgment that Bruce was great for business along with his complaint of serious damages. After this reflection, I did nothing to indicate what I thought should happen at that point. I wanted to leave space for the participants to decide what was next.

Bill (John's lawyer) spoke up and said, "Yes, so we calculate the damages on John's tortious-interference-with-contract claim at around $2 million."

Bruce said, "Okay, may I speak now?"

I shrugged and nodded, looking first at Bruce, and then at the others, to indicate that it was fine with me but that the choice belonged to everyone but me.

Everyone else nodded, and then Bruce told his story. "You did take a chance on me over 15 years ago and I appreciate that. And I did become very competent at selling the software, and customizing it, and solving all of the customers' problems that came up. And then I realized that you had no intention of making me a partner. So I started to consider other opportunities. I seriously considered that job at 3M but I decided I wanted to go into business myself and do what I already knew how to do. I figured you wouldn't be happy about that, so I let you continue to believe I was going to work at 3M.

"But I did not solicit your customers—several of them called me. I told them I left and that they should continue to work with you but many of them insisted on continuing to work with me. What was I supposed to do?" Bruce continued, "It's similar to when a doctor switches practices—patients who like that doctor often go where the doctor goes. They have no loyalty to his previous employer—they want to stay with the doctor himself. And they should have the right to. I had no intention of hurting your business, John. I figured you'd be fine and might even benefit from my work since I'm promoting SalonSoft as well. I understand why you're angry, but don't think you have any legal grounds for the lawsuit—there was no non-compete."

I now held up a mirror to Bruce by repeating the story he had shared, in as much detail as possible. I was giving him a chance to hear his own words and giving everyone else a chance to hear them a second time. I noticed that, as I often see in conflict, both parties view themselves as victims of the other. John's story described how Bruce had betrayed him and damaged his business. Bruce's story involved John mistreating him by holding out the promise of partnership and then refusing to follow through. When the vicious circle is at its worst, both parties accuse the other of victimizing them and then feel victimized by such accusations, leading to more accusations, and so on. As we have discussed, people prefer not to feel like victims, and they also prefer not to victimize each other. We can help them find their way out of the vicious circle by reflecting where they are and by shining a light on their opportunities to decide what is next. Mirrors and lights clarify and illuminate where they are and enhance their awareness of their ability to make choices. This is how mediation can provide parties with more self-determination than they were experiencing when they arrived.

John, who had been listening closely while Bruce told his story, responded, but this time he spoke directly to Bruce.

"But how could you do that to me, after everything I did for you?"

I sensed a shift at this point, John had gained the courage to address Bruce head on. His question expressed the core of his feelings about the situation. This was the sort of increased agency that Bush and Folger call an "empowerment shift," and it feels like a privilege to be present for these moments.

Bruce leaned forward in his seat and turned toward John. "You treated me just fine. I also made you a good amount of money. The real problem was that you never followed through on making me a partner. Whatever happened to that?"

"2008 happened," said John. "I started losing money. You wouldn't have wanted to become a partner then!"

"Yeah, but by 2012, things were booming again, and still no mention of partnership."

"I didn't know partnership was such a big deal to you."

"I don't believe that."

At this point, I felt encouraged. They were claiming their agency. They were confronting each other directly and plainly, addressing the heart of their differences. The details of their litigation seemed less important and they both spoke with passion and purpose. Also, though they were disagreeing, they were talking to each other in a way that felt deeper and more real. As they each claimed their agency, the vicious circle of conflict started to unwind. Bruce and John were looking at each other and taking each other into consideration. They were talking in a way that revealed that they cared what each other thought. They weren't out of the woods yet, of course, but it's hard for people who are having such a real conversation, and who are so in touch with their power and competence, to want to return to litigation mode. Tony had remained silent. It seemed that he understood that this lawsuit was based on the dynamics between John and Bruce.

John continued, "Well, regardless—your leaving and taking those customers nearly wrecked my business completely. And it was particularly poor timing because it drove down the value of the business when I was getting ready to sell it and retire."

I'm not sure if everyone in the room immediately saw the potential solution. I, myself, didn't know whether it would be feasible for Bruce and his company to buy John's business from him. I suspect each side hesitated to suggest it because they didn't want to appear overly eager.

After a pause, Bruce's lawyer said, "Would you be open, as part of a potential settlement, to talk about a buyout?" And John, who looked relieved, said, "Sure." Within an hour, the basic terms of the purchase of Old Company by New Company were worked out. The deal would require John to be paid in installments, over the next five years, from the profits of New Company. By the end, the mood in the room was jovial, and John and Bruce parted with a handshake that escalated to a hug.

The story of Bruce and John illustrates how powerful mirrors and lights can be and how their power both enhances and relies upon party self-determination. Dan did everything he could to illuminate where the parties were. That illumination allowed the parties, as well as their lawyers, to find their way from assuming that mediation would be a waste of time all the way to a satisfying solution and a hug. Dan did not lead the parties in any direction but only illuminated their situation in each moment and their opportunity to make choices.

While it's obvious that Bruce and John's story is partly about their relationship, sometimes the centrality of the relationship is even more obvious from the start of the mediation, with problem solving taking a back seat or, in the next case, a couch.

YOU CAN HAVE THE COUCH

A lawyer called, asking if I was available to mediate a property dispute. He asked how I'd deal with the fact that he would be present but the other party was unrepresented. I told him that it's the parties' choice whether they want one lawyer, two lawyers, or no lawyers present. I also mentioned that the parties are welcome to bring others (friends, family members, etc.) if they like.

I knew the lawyer's reason for asking me this was that some mediators have strong views about mediating when one party is represented and the other is not. As I see it, the parties are in a better position than I am to know what choices they need to make about that. Also I assume that most mediation parties are experiencing at least some aspect of the vicious circle of conflict and are therefore feeling disempowered. I like to give them every possible opportunity to make choices about the process. They can choose to bring a lawyer, a friend, or no one at all even while they may feel they otherwise have very little control of the situation.

Several weeks later, Phil arrived at my office with his lawyer, Bill, and Steve arrived with three family members, who were out of earshot. The four of us (Phil, Bill, Steve, and me) were standing in my waiting room as we discussed who should participate in the mediation.

Steve: My family is going to wait outside. They should NOT be involved. They HATE Phil right now.

Phil: Fine, but I'm paying my lawyer to be here. You're the one who sued me. He's here to protect my rights.

Steve: Well that puts me at a disadvantage.

Bill: It's my duty to represent Phil. I intend to participate.

I chimed in with "We could also start the conversation either with or without Bill present, see how that goes, and then switch at any time if anyone wants to."

I intended to let them know that they had options, now and throughout the process, and that I wasn't attached to any particular approach. It would have been even more consistent with my intention if I had instead reflected back their disagreement and then said, "It's your choice what we do here." Had I done that, they likely would have suggested something else that would have worked, with the added possible benefit of greater awareness of their ability to figure out for themselves how to work with each other.

Steve said, "In that case, fine, we can start with Bill here, and see how it goes."

It's possible that Steve's choice to bring three family members to the session increased his sense of control over the situation. I don't know when he made the decision that they would wait outside—he may not have known that was all he needed until he was standing in the waiting room. I imagine that simply having the opportunity to make that choice was enough to help him experience agency. Maybe that increased agency gave him the clarity and strength to suggest that they wait outside. Perhaps knowing that he could make another decision later further increased his sense of agency or enabled him to freely make a gesture toward Phil by agreeing to start the mediation with Phil's lawyer in the room.

I quickly gathered that Steve and Phil had lived together as life partners and that the dispute was very much like a divorce, with some disagreements about personal property. Bill pulled out the complaint that Steve (back when he had a lawyer) had served on Phil. Bill then asked Steve to provide a list of the property in question. Steve pulled out copies of the list for everyone present. Bill suggested that we address each item on the list and see if Steve and Phil agreed on any of the items so that he could check those off. All agreed that that would be fine, and Bill started reading the list.

Bill: Couch in the basement.

Phil: You told me I could have that one.

Steve: No, I didn't.

Phil: Yes, you did, you said I could have all the stuff we got from Terry and Dave, because they were my friends.

Steve: I knew Terry 20 years ago!

Phil: I know that, but when you moved out you said . . .

Bill interrupted and said, "Okay, let's skip that one. It's still in dispute." I did my best to reflect everything the parties said with my usual intention to give them an opportunity to contemplate what they have said and decide what to do next. I also reflected Bill's comment: "And you'd prefer to keep working down the list, and see which items are in dispute and which aren't." Bill said, "Yes, a lawsuit has been filed and we're here because the court has ordered us to go to mediation to resolve the property issues." I reflected that comment as well. I assume that the lawyers as well as the parties can benefit from having a mirror held up to them. I also wanted the parties to have another opportunity to decide how to respond to what Bill had said. Bill then listed another item.

Steve: That's mine. I definitely bought that.

Phil: Yes you did. You bought it AS A GIFT TO ME!

Steve: Yes, back when I thought you were going to be faithful to me.

The conversation continued, with heated exchanges between Phil and Steve, and with Bill saying such things as "Okay, that item is in dispute. Next item."

At one point Phil said, "You sued me! How could you do that?"

Steve: It was your idea! You told me to get a lawyer!

Phil: Yeah, but I just meant I didn't like how you were demanding all the furniture. I didn't really mean get a lawyer and SUE me!

Steve: Well, what was I supposed to think you meant when you said the words "GET A LAWYER!"

Phil: Well, where is your lawyer anyway?

Steve: I couldn't afford to pay him anymore.

Phil: So now I have to pay a lawyer because YOU SUED ME!

Steve: This was all your idea.

Phil: No it wasn't! You're the one who left!

Steve: Because YOU told me to!!

Phil: Oh my God!!! I just want this to be over!!!

Steve: You know, I don't really give a shit about any of this property!!

Phil: Neither do I.

After all of this, I summarized the conversation, including the questions about what each person meant in their farewell argument and including Bill's persistent attempts (interposed but not quoted in the above exchange) to bring the focus back to the list. Unfortunately, I let my biases influence my summary. I believed Bill's focus on the list was preventing the parties from having a more meaningful conversation, and my summary included saying to Bill, "You're saying that if we can get through this list, you'll be willing to back off and let these guys talk about what this is really about."

I winced after I said this because I had deviated from my commitment to reflect genuinely, without editorializing. One risk of my having done so was that Bill might have felt defensive and become more insistent that the parties stay focused on the list. Another risk was that everyone in the room would have realized I had an opinion about what should be happening and then might have succumbed to this pressure. I was pleased that next Bill said, "Yes, if we get through this list, I'll even step out of the room, and then these guys can talk about whatever they want." It was not my place to be pleased about that—when I'm in the right frame of mind I understand that the participants' choices are far more important than my preferences about their choices.

By forming an opinion about what the parties should be discussing, I deviated from my commitment to fully support party self-determination. I implied that Bill should get through the list quickly so that the parties could discuss what I believed they wanted to discuss. Had I been acting more in line with my intention to support all of the participants, without an agenda, I would have noticed that I had formed an opinion and then intentionally let that go. As we discuss in Chapter 9, we view, and treat, all participants, including lawyers, as parties to the conversation.

And that's how it went. Phil and Steve let Bill check items off his list. Bill left. Phil and Steve then discussed their feelings about each other and the ending of the relationship. Their conversation confirmed that neither of them was really attached to any of the property but that they both wanted to wrap up their relationship differently than they had the first time. They wept and hugged each other. Steve agreed to dismiss his lawsuit, and they both agreed to meet at Phil's house and sort out the property—forgetting about the list altogether.

As with the case of Bruce and John, the case of Phil and Steve demonstrates that "it's often not about what it's about." In other words, while the lawsuit that led to the mediation was a property dispute, the core of the conflict was interactional crisis. It was about how Phil and Steve were relating to each other. Before the mediation they were not sure they had the capacity to have a conversation with each other. During the mediation they discovered that, with the help of mirrors and lights to give them a clearer view, they could talk to each other. In that setting, they were able to regain their awareness of their own power and the other's humanity.

Although Phil and Steve provide an example of conflict between people who have been intimately connected, conflict between strangers can play out similarly. The participants in the following mediation had never met before and had no reason to believe they would meet after the mediation. Nonetheless, Dan conducted the mediation under the assumption that supporting each party's choices would help them reverse the vicious circle of conflict.

CHECK ENGINE

Paula and Peter arrived at the mediation ready to tell the story that led to their $15,000 lawsuit against Acme Auto Manufacturers. Dave, one of Acme's lawyers, appeared on the company's behalf.

I explained that this meeting was an opportunity for the participants to have whatever conversation they wanted and then asked them how they'd like to start. Paula started by saying that she had owned her certified used Acme for less than two months when something went wrong. She had been driving on the freeway when she saw the Check Engine light come on, and she immediately called Peter. While they were talking and within two minutes of when the light came on, the car lost power. Paula pulled to the side of the freeway and called AAA. The car was towed to the dealership, where an assessment was made. Paula and Peter learned that the engine had seized up completely and the vehicle was a total loss. According to the mechanic at the dealership, the water pump had failed, which led to the engine severely overheating. Paula and Peter next learned that their warranty from Acme did not cover this sort of damage. The warranty did cover the failed water pump, but according to Acme, Paula was responsible for the damage to the engine. Acme said that Paula would have had enough time to see the Check Engine light and elevated temperature gauge and to turn off the engine before it seized up. Paula and Peter were shocked by Acme's initial response. They had a variety of frustrating interactions with Acme customer service over the next several weeks, including calls not being returned and long delays before being able to talk to someone with any real authority. From the Acme dealer's mechanic, Paula and Peter learned that the cost of repairing the engine would be $9,000. Rather than having it repaired, they chose to sell the car as is for $3,000. Next they filed a lawsuit for $15,000 against Acme.

At the mediation, Paula described buying the car. She said she had initially offered to pay $14,000 but the salesman said that for an additional $1,000 the car would be certified. She chose to pay the extra $1,000. She was especially shocked that the extra $1,000 failed to include a warranty that would cover this sort of damage. Dave explained that *all* of the used cars that Acme sells are certified. He suggested that Paula had misunderstood the salesman. The salesman had probably meant that although he needed to receive $15,000 for the car, she might appreciate that the car would be certified. Dave added that even if the salesman had misrepresented that fact about certification, Acme corporation was not responsible; the dealership, if anyone, was responsible.

Peter and Paula expressed extreme frustration with how they'd been treated by Acme. They could not believe that Acme felt it was a good business practice to treat customers this way. Paula was absolutely sure that the temperature gauge had also failed. She would have noticed if it was showing that the car was overheating. Her experience was that the Check Engine light came on (a light that often signals non-critical problems), and two minutes later the engine was ruined. It was inconceivable to her and Peter that only two months after their purchase of this certified car, Acme would not honor their warranty. When Dave suggested that it was possible that Paula had somehow missed the elevated temperature gauge, Paula blew up, yelling, "How can you possibly know that?! Were you there?! I can't believe this!"

I reflected back to Paula, "You're wondering how he could possibly know that! He wasn't there. This is unbelievable." I tried to capture the outrage and disbelief that Paula was experiencing, both of which are common symptoms of the self-absorption that transformative theory presumes is central to the experience of conflict. Outrage indicates at least some vilification, and disbelief ("How could you possibly say that?") suggests that the party is unable to see things from the other's perspective.

When parties communicate heightened emotion around disbelief of what the other party has said, I try to reflect it, if possible. I want to make sure the parties have every possible chance to make choices around what to do about this aspect of their interaction. When they hear my reflection, they have another opportunity to pay attention to how they are reacting. In that moment they tend to become more aware that they have a choice and could respond differently if they wished. Sometimes the person who expressed outrage elaborates on their outrage. Sometimes they adjust their attitude a bit and ask a more precise question. Sometimes the other party responds in a way that makes their perspective more understandable. Regardless of how they respond, they have had another opportunity to make a choice, and perhaps reclaim some agency.

Paula responded, "Yes! And that you can't do anything about your dealer, lying to me about that certification?! I just can't believe it."

Dave responded, "Look, I can understand why this is so frustrating, and I'm really sorry about what the salesman told you, and that you had all those bad interactions with customer service. But here's how we're looking at it—we think that if there were a trial, we could show that you had the chance to save the engine by pulling over right away. We can prove that the temperature gauge didn't fail, so you should have seen that the engine was overheating. We just aren't responsible for you continuing to drive while your engine was overheating. That being said, we understand that you had a bad experience, and we would rather not deal with the expense of a trial, so we're willing to offer you $4,000."

Paula and Peter continued to look angry.

I said, "Paula and Peter, it seems like this conversation has been very frustrating for you . . . Would it be ok with everyone if I summarize what you've talked about so far?"

Everyone appeared okay with it.

I intended to accurately describe the entire conversation and also to organize it according to the themes that had arisen. Peter and Paula seemed overwhelmed. I hoped my summary would give them the opportunity to gain more clarity and greater awareness of their ability to make choices about what to do next. Perhaps this would make the situation seem less overwhelming and more manageable. I'm also aware that when I speak for a minute or more in a mediation, it gives participants a break, which may also help them think more clearly.

"One thing you've talked about is what happened on the highway when the car broke down. Paula you described how you were driving along and noticed the Check Engine light and called Peter right away. And within two minutes of when the light came on, the car lost power so you pulled to the side. And you pointed out that Dave wasn't there so he has no way of knowing what happened. And Dave, you've said that you'd be able to prove that the temperature gauge didn't fail so it must have shown that the engine was hot and so Paula should have known to pull over sooner."

"You've also talked about the dollars involved. Paula and Peter, you said you paid $15,000 for the car, including $1,000 for what you understood to be certification. And you were told that it would cost $9,000 to replace the engine, so you sold the car as is for $3,000, and you're suing for $15,000. Dave, you said you're willing to offer $4,000 because you understand that Paula and Peter have had a bad experience with Acme, and it would cost you to defend a lawsuit, but that Acme doesn't believe it's actually responsible for what happened. And you also said, regarding that $1,000, that all used cars Acme sells are certified so that was either a misrepresentation by the salesman or a misunderstanding."

"And you also talked about the frustration you've had, Peter and Paula, in communicating with Acme, and Dave you seemed to acknowledge that that didn't sound good."

"So what's next? Would now be a good time to take a break, or . . ." Since I had been controlling the conversation during my summary, I wanted to return control of the conversation to them so they could decide what was next . Although I suggested a break, I tried to do so in a tone that made it clear that taking a break was just one option. Any time I make a suggestion, I try to do it as gently as possible and I usually list several options to further indicate that I do not know what should be next—it is up to them. I hope to make it clear that my list of suggestions is in no way exhaustive and that any other ideas they have are completely welcome. I hope my suggestions are simply reminders to them that options exist and that it is their role to make the decision to pursue one of their own or one that I suggested. In this situation Paula and Peter spoke up before I could list other possibilities.

Paula and Peter said, "Yes, let's do that."

Dave stood up and walked out into the hall while Paula and Peter remained seated in my office, commiserating with each other about how difficult and frustrating this was. Peter said to me, "I just can't believe they don't care more about their reputation than this." And Paula said, "We at least need to get $12,000, because that's how much we really lost. I paid 15 and I sold it for three. It's still a shitty deal for us because of all of the hassle, but at least that's a fair number." I reflected what they both had said.

When Dave returned, Peter said, "We'd be willing to accept $12,000. That's how much this cost us. We paid $15,000 for the car, and we sold it for $3,000. At least $12,000 will allow us to buy something else." Dave took in what Peter was saying, and responded with "I follow your math. I know you were out $12,000, but you have to remember that we really don't believe we're responsible for it. I can offer you $5,000 but I really can't do much more than that. I totally feel for you guys, but you know, I've got a boss and I have to justify this to him based on our actual risk."

Peter and Paula still appeared frustrated and disappointed, but they seemed to seriously consider what Dave was saying.

Over the course of the next hour, Paula and Peter gradually moved from being frustrated to more accepting. They also seemed to relate to Dave more fully as a person. At one point, Peter said to Dave, "I understand you're just doing your job, man, but you've gotta see that this feels like we got screwed."

And Dave said, "Yep. I get that."

The parties finally agreed on an amount of $7,000. Peter and Paula's rationale for accepting the $7,000 was that they just wanted it to be over. They certainly were never going to buy an Acme car again. Although Dave wasn't as talkative about his rationale, I'm guessing that he figured that was the lowest amount he could settle the case for or the highest amount he could justify to his client. When they shook hands at the end, the tone was respectful and free of obvious animosity.

Although it is possible to look at this conversation simply as a negotiation or a transaction, we can also look at it in terms of the interaction between the parties. Both sides gained clarity about the possibilities and what each side would be willing to offer. Peter and Paula came to terms with the reality that Acme believed, or at least would argue, that the damage to the engine had been Paula's fault. Dave came to understand that Paula and Peter had strong feelings and would need some compensation in order to dismiss their lawsuit. The conversation gave all of the participants a clearer understanding of the situation they were in and what the possibilities were. As discussed above, that greater understanding of the situation and the possibilities, according to transformative theory, is called an empowerment shift.

There ain't no good guy, there ain't no bad guy— There's only you and me and we just disagree.
—Bill Krueger

The parties also appeared to experience "recognition shifts," the increased ability to empathize with and relate to each other. Looking at the interaction through that lens, we would say that Paula and Peter initially saw Dave as simply the representative of a heartless corporation. As they interacted with him, they became more aware of him as a person who was doing his job without malice—someone they could relate to. They got a better sense of his perspective and where he was coming from when making his offers. Similarly, Dave shifted from seeing Paula and Peter as merely an appointment on his calendar to likable people who had experienced an unfortunate series of events and who had legitimate complaints about how his client had treated them. These shifts helped both sides engage more effectively in the conversation, with both having the genuine intention of finding a solution that would work for everyone. The result was a settlement that felt to each side like it sufficiently honored their own perspective and needs while also allowing them to treat each other with a level of respect and consideration that felt good to them.

Dan supported the parties in making these empowerment and recognition shifts. He did this by holding up a mirror to them as he reflected what they said in their own terms. He also did this by shining a light on their conversation with his summaries. And he illuminated their opportunities to make choices about the conversation itself by checking in with them about what they wanted to do next. His intention behind all of his interventions was to honor the choices the parties were making and to create opportunities for them to make more choices. In this way he enhanced their self-determination, allowing them to increase their agency and to reverse the vicious circle.

As the stories above suggest, there is an emotional aspect to conflict interactions that affects the quality of the conversation. When people are trapped in the vicious circle, they are less able to have the sort of conversation that leads to understanding and are less able to work together to solve their problems. After all, people are generally not inclined to help their enemies get their needs met or solve their problems. Therefore their attitude toward each other needs to shift a bit before they can solve problems together. A supported conversation can remind them of their agency, which allows them to lower their defenses and engage more constructively.

Using *public goods* experiments, the field of behavioral economics has confirmed that feelings about others play an important role in people's decision-making processes. One version of a public goods game allows participants to contribute points (redeemable for actual money) to a common account in varying amounts. The more each player contributes, the more all participants benefit. Individual players may also choose to take a portion of the points for themselves without contributing to the common account. Other players notice the free-riders and do not take kindly to such behavior. They report feeling angry with these selfish players and explain that they reduced their contributions in later rounds of the game to punish the selfish participants.[4]

People will invoke punishment even at a cost to themselves by paying to place a fine on a transgressor.[5] As with altruism, there may also be a group-level evolutionary advantage when the members *punish* others at a cost to themselves. Fear of punishment may encourage cooperation when individuals may otherwise be especially tempted to compete.[6] These innate inclinations to both hurt and help each other fit with our understanding of conflict. In conflict, our intentions can go from wanting revenge to wanting reconciliation or from wanting to sue to wanting to talk.

People's emotions, particularly about fairness, influence their decisions. People care where their money goes, and why. They may feel good about donating money to charity but resist giving the same amount of money to someone who they believe is taking advantage of them. When litigants say "It's not the money, it's the principle," they mean it (at least sometimes). They willingly give when their self-determination is supported and they are making choices for their own reasons. Often clients would rather pay more to their friendly lawyer than to the noxious opposing party. The following story is from Dan's previous professional life as a practicing litigator.

I'D RATHER PAY YOU GUYS

A former employee, Edward, sued his ex-boss, Roberto, for wrongful termination based on a whistle-blower claim. Edward alleged that he had discovered that Roberto was committing tax fraud and had fired him out of fear that Edward would report these allegations. Roberto hired my firm to represent him. He thought the lawsuit was ridiculous and said he fired Edward exclusively because of his incompetence. Roberto also said he had not committed tax fraud, that he had no fear whatsoever of being reported, and Edward simply did not understand normal accounting practices.

I told Roberto that answering the complaint, conducting discovery, and then making a motion for summary judgment would cost around $30,000. I also said that, while it's possible we could get an order for Edward to pay the attorney fees, it was unlikely. So I recommended that he offer Edward $10,000 since that would be less expensive than our fees. Roberto said, "No way. I'd rather pay you guys $100,000 than pay him a dime." We said, "Okay, we'll continue with discovery."

Soon after came a traditional shuttle-diplomacy mediation. The mediator, an experienced and respected employment law litigator, tried to persuade Roberto to compromise, pointing out that juries do crazy things and might find in favor of Edward. He also pointed out that regardless, the costs of litigation would be significant and so forth. Roberto remained clear that as a matter of principle, he would not submit to what he considered extortion. Over the course of the day, Edward lowered his demand from $250,000 to $75,000 but Roberto wouldn't budge beyond $5,000, continuing to say he'd rather pay us. Several months later, after Roberto had paid us around $30,000, the case settled for $10,000.

Roberto ended up paying a total of $40,000 to end the lawsuit. It's possible he could have spent only around a total of $12,000 if he had been willing to negotiate earlier (the $2,000 he'd paid us at that point plus a $10,000 settlement). It's also possible that in a different sort of mediation, one where Roberto and Edward had a direct conversation and their agency was supported, their interaction could have shifted and a deal could have been reached more quickly at lower cost to Roberto. But Roberto was very clear that he much preferred that his money go to his lawyers as opposed to this person he currently viewed as an enemy.

Motivations unrelated to financial compensation are common in the world of lawsuits as demonstrated by plaintiffs' reports about why they're bringing the suit and what they want from the defendant. In medical malpractice cases, plaintiffs have reported goals that included receiving an explanation of what happened to them or their loved one, an apology, dignity, and respect in addition to the altruistic motive of wanting to prevent harm to others.[7]

Each mediation party needs to sort out for themselves their best path out of the vicious circle. This chapter has looked at the vicious circle as well as some ways that mediators can help with it. In all of the above stories (except "I'd Rather Pay You Guys" where the mediator tried to persuade the parties to compromise), the parties found their way to a greater experience of agency, or strength (that is, a sense of clarity and self-control), and connection, or responsiveness (the ability to see the other person as a fellow human rather than an enemy). With the help of the mediator, they overcame their sense of being victimized and instead came to feel they were taking good care of themselves. They also overcame their sense of hostility and distrust of the other party to reach a place where they could respond meaningfully to them. In those three stories, Dan's method of helping the parties was to support them in making their own choices throughout the process and to amplify those choices. Dan put the parties' words back in the room—even when those words could be seen as hostile or inflammatory. Dan did not try to sugarcoat the parties' feelings or nudge them in any particular direction (except for the slip when Dan told Phil's lawyer what the case was really about). The parties' progress came from their own choices throughout the process.

When mirrors and lights enhance the parties' view, those parties can see the path to a better place and gain confidence in their capacity to make it there. In conflict, that better place usually means acting with greater confidence and clarity and with greater consideration of the other. The lights and mirrors, which illuminate and reflect each party and their surroundings, provide clarity and therefore enhanced agency. With agency comes greater capacity to be open and responsive to the other, creating a virtuous circle of strength and responsiveness.

As we see it, at the core of parties' conflict experience is a sense of powerlessness, and a process full of party choice can ameliorate that. Once people begin to regain a sense of strength, they also regain their ability to connect with each other as humans rather than obstacles. Connection, like autonomy, is a basic human need. We will explore connection in detail in Chapter 3.

Notes

1. Robert A. Baruch Bush and Joseph P. Folger, *The Promise of Mediation: The Transformative Approach to Conflict* (San Francisco: Jossey-Bass, 2005), ch. 2.

2. Bush and Folger, *The Promise of Mediation*, ch. 2.

3. Bush and Folger, *The Promise of Mediation*, ch. 2.

4. Herbert Gintis, "Strong Reciprocity and Human Sociality," *Journal of Theoretical Biology* 206, no. 2 (September 2000): 171.

5. Elinor Ostrom, James Walker, and Roy Gardner, "With and Without a Sword: Self-Governance Is Possible," *American Political Science Review* 86, no. 2 (June 1992): 411.

6. Gintis, "Strong Reciprocity," 178.

7. Tamara Relis, "'It's Not About the Money!'" A Theory on Misconceptions of Plaintiffs' Litigation Aims," *University of Pittsburgh Law Review* 68 (March 2007).

CHAPTER 3

Self-Determination and Our Desire to Connect

If you want others to be happy, practice compassion. If you want to be happy, practice compassion.

—Dalai Lama

If you haven't been living under a rock, you are aware of the human tendency toward aggression. Wars, genocide, and Twitter battles are just a few examples of places our darker side can take us. Noticeably in the United States, political polarization has rarely been worse.[1] However there are also indications that humanity has been moving in a nonviolent direction as wars, genocide, homicide, and nearly all forms of violence have generally trended downward over the years, going back millennia.[2] And even in the midst of the darkness, one can find examples of selflessness and kindness breaking through. Soldiers have put themselves in danger to rescue injured platoon-mates, and entire battalions have dropped their weapons to connect with the enemy as fellow human beings,[3] reminding us of who we are as well.

Despite the human propensity for competition and destruction, people prefer, whenever possible, to feel positively connected to each other.[4] They want to treat others well and to be treated well by others. A disrupted or negative connection is part of what people say they hate about being in conflict,[5] and a desire to improve the connection can motivate them to work through it. As mediators, we have seen many examples of people shifting from a negative, defensive, angry interaction to one that is positive, open, and accepting. These shifts happen at the parties' initiative under conditions where they feel supported in acting as they wish. We feel inspired and uplifted when we see these shifts.

Sometimes these shifts happen only for a moment, fading into the distance as a new point of contention arises. Other times they lead to the ultimate resolution of the conflict, with the parties shaking hands and in some instances laughing and chatting as they walk out the door. No matter the specific outcome, we have witnessed a recognition of the other's humanity, seemingly out of nowhere. These moments are a big part of why we do this work. We recognize the human motivation to treat others with kindness and compassion and believe in the capacity of our clients to do so even in the midst of conflict. This belief about human nature motivates us to remain supportive of people when they are at their worst. We assume they want to be in a better place and are trying to figure out how to get there.

Human beings seem unable to live without war, but they are also unable to live without love. —Arundhati Roy

Especially dramatic expressions of compassion, kindness, and recognition often happen in divorce mediations, where the relationships are close. (Of course, especially dramatic expressions in the opposite direction also happen in divorce mediations.) Here is an example we chose as a particularly powerful demonstration of the need and ability to connect even in the midst of conflict.

WILDER PARENTING

Wilder is three years old and his parents are divorcing. Dad is devastated by the divorce and is afraid he's also going to lose his relationship with Wilder so he is insisting on a 50-50 schedule. Mom believes that equal parenting time might work when Wilder is a few years older but certainly not yet. After both exchange angry words about this issue for a few minutes, Dan offers a summary of the parties' conversation including their emotions surrounding the divorce, each of their perspectives on Wilder's needs, and what type of parenting schedule would be best for him. Following the summary, Dan asks the parties what they would like to do next.

Dad takes a deep breath and says, "Wilder is ALL I'VE GOT now. I can't lose him too." Dan looks at Dad and says, trying to match Dad's intensity, "You CAN'T lose Wilder. He's ALL you've got." Mom stops, looks down for a moment and turns her chair more fully to Dad. Then she says, "Wilder loves you SO much. He needs you. I will NEVER prevent Wilder from seeing you." Dad tears up, and quietly says, "Okay."

Dad's choice to reveal his vulnerability, followed by Mom's choice to respond compassionately, were not prompted by the mediator. Dan did not try to guide the conversation but instead did his best to accurately reflect the choices they made. While Dan needed to choose what to reflect and where to shine lights throughout the process, he attempted to keep the mirror as undistorted as possible, and to shine the lights on where the parties were rather than where he thought they should be. Providing this support allowed the parties to restore the connection that they both seemed to value.

Although these sorts of deep shifts may seem unique to divorce mediation, dramatic moments can also occur in business mediations as relational aspects of the conflict are often at play there as well. We chose the next story because it is especially inspiring—mediations do not always include these touching moments of connection.

STUCCO

Homeowners become concerned that their contractor (a former in-law) is mismanaging their renovation after hearing that he hasn't been paying the subcontractors. They notify him that they are terminating the contract and that he owes them a refund for unfinished work. The contractor threatens to sue the homeowners for breach of contract. At the mediation, both sides start out sounding hostile and accusatory but seem calmer and clearer after telling their story and having their perspective reflected by Dan.

While we can't know what is happening internally for the contractor, it's possible that he absorbed the homeowners' sense that he had treated them without consideration and he wanted to correct this misunderstanding. After a long pause, the contractor turns to one of the homeowners and says, "Jim, I agreed to do this job because I knew about your cancer diagnosis. I turned down a good, regular gig, and I was only going to make about $20 an hour to do this for you. With you firing me from this, I'm screwed." Dan: "You heard about Jim's cancer diagnosis, and turned down a regular gig to work for them, and now you're screwed." Jim looked surprised when the contractor was talking, and then his face softened. "I didn't realize that, but appreciate it. We'll figure something out."

As with Wilder's parents, the important shift arose from the parties. Dan contributed an atmosphere of openness and nonjudgment, allowing space for the parties' expressions of anger as well as vulnerability. Dan shone a light on the choices the parties were making and their opportunities to continue to do so. The parties responded by passionately asserting their own perspectives, becoming more aware of their power and getting back in touch with their desire to connect.

We remember these moments fondly. They evoked an emotion in us that social psychologist Jonathan Haidt has termed "elevation," which he describes as "a warm, uplifting feeling that people experience when they see unexpected acts of human goodness, kindness, and compassion."[6] Witnessing such acts of kindness leaves us feeling inspired and optimistic about human nature.

As the parties reestablish a sense of agency, becoming clearer, stronger, and more centered, these moments happen naturally. Humans are social animals, and how we relate to others matters to us. In fact, research shows that people have a basic psychological need for connection, which they can meet both by caring for, and being cared for by, other people.[7] And people can even meet this need through interactions with strangers.

Our desire to help others, which is closely related to our need for connection, seems to be rooted in our distant evolutionary past. It has been demonstrated across cultures, ages, and species.[8] For example, toddlers seem happier when giving treats to others than when receiving treats themselves.[9] Children this age also spontaneously help adults who are pretending to have trouble accomplishing a goal, such as reaching an object.[10] Even chimpanzees offer help to humans in these situations.[11] Similarly, rats help each other when there is no clear benefit to the helper,[12] which suggests that our ability to empathize with others runs deep as does our desire to offer help when needed.

When we practice loving kindness and compassion we are the first ones to profit. —Rumi

While we undoubtedly have beneficial competitive tendencies, cooperative behaviors have long provided benefits to humans and other animals as well. Prosocial behaviors aid in group functioning, increasing the survival of individuals and groups.[13] Some theorists have taken these explanations further, positing a single consciousness, or will, that connects our seemingly separate points of consciousness.[14] These theories suggest that the compassion and empathy that people (and animals) have for each other stems from the (perhaps unconscious) understanding that what happens to you, happens to me.[15]

Given the human tendency to prefer cooperation and connection, why do hatred and violence persist? Philosophers, theologians, psychologists, and political scientists explain the origins and purposes of the ugly side of human nature in a variety of ways. These theories range from the selfish gene[16] to economic systems[17] to original sin. As we discussed in Chapter 2, we believe that insufficient agency drives the human propensity for destruction.

We all are one, we are the same person.
—Jimmy Cliff

The aggressor feels like a victim for real or imagined reasons. The fear of being victimized leads the aggressor to victimize the person or people they fear. A vicious circle of action and reaction can emerge.

This fear-based aggression occurs when an abusive husband views himself as the victim of a controlling wife or when a powerful country invades a weaker one out of fear of terrorism (perhaps after being attacked by someone else). The harmful actions come out of a sense of desperation, of being threatened, of feeling stuck, or of not having many options. We cannot explain why people do all the destructive things they do, but the sense of being victimized and experiencing diminished agency seem to be a big part of it.

Since people prefer to help others and feel good when doing so, should mediators strongly encourage people to help each other out? Would that accomplish the same goals? Probably not. In a study of college students completing a joint task, helping only yielded benefits when the helper gave it freely.[18] Pressuring the students to help made both the helper and the person being helped *worse* off than they were in the control condition, suggesting that no help is better than pressured or forced help. As we saw in Chapter 1, people have a basic need for autonomy, and pressure to change others' attitudes or behaviors can backfire. Genuine connections, and the benefits that flow from them, require self-determination.

These findings pertain to mediation in a few ways. People care about their interactions with each other—how they are being treated, and how they are treating the other. They want to treat each other with consideration, or at least fairness. Parties struggle to reconnect with and honor this aspect of their nature when they are in conflict. Parties often say that they are "trying to do the right thing" but that the other party is misunderstanding their intentions. That is, parties are often clear that they don't intend to harm each other and even that they'd like to make the other person happy but it seems impossible under the circumstances.

Other times parties *are* clear that they want to hurt each other, at least at the start of mediation. While they may not use the word "revenge," we have heard parties use expressions that convey similar intentions such as "I want to teach them a lesson" or "I'd like to show them what it feels like." They may also say "It serves them right" or "What goes around comes around." This desire to harm *also* supports the idea that connections matter to people. Instead of being solely concerned with their own bottom line, people also want to have a certain impact on each other. If we feel like we've been disrespected, we want to make the other party take us seriously. If we've lost faith that the other person will treat us kindly, we may lash out simply to let them know that our feelings matter.

While the research we've cited, and our experience in mediation, support this optimistic view of human nature, we don't mean to minimize the other side of the coin. Selfishness, violence, and cruelty are real. People often desire revenge at the height of conflict. The motivation to unite with one's tribe to defeat the opposing tribe also runs deep into our evolutionary past.[19] The sort of mediation we've been discussing can tip the scales, helping people find their way to the joy of peace and helping them turn away from the thrill (and anguish) of battle.

Because mediation can give the parties room to make thoughtful, voluntary choices, it is well positioned to help them access their giving nature and apply it even to their enemy. When mediation offers an opportunity for people to choose to listen to each other and help each other, it has the potential to work with, and not against, the deep-seated need to connect. It is essential, though, that these are true choices. Attempting to nudge people in that direction—for instance by asking them to acknowledge the other's interests or to speak to each other respectfully—is not only unnecessary, it is likely to be counterproductive.[20]

Mediation also provides an opportunity for at least one other person in the room (the mediator) to offer nonjudgmental support to each party. Since even brief interactions with strangers can satisfy our need to relate to others, the parties' connection to the mediator matters. Although the parties' conversation is with one another, our practice of listening and supporting each party nonjudgmentally can meet their need to connect.

The vignettes shared earlier in this chapter illustrated how the mediator's support for each party's self-determination seemed to increase their sense of agency, which then led to a moment of connection. While the moments of connection led to agreements in each of these cases, as they often do, the parties' gestures toward each other did not appear strategic. Instead, they seemed to be motivated by compassion and a genuine desire to connect.

Of course, some actions may have multiple motivations that are hidden even from the person who made the choice. Has a connection been established (or reestablished) or are the parties simply accommodating each other's preferences as a strategy to get their own needs met? These different motivations and actions may ebb and flow throughout the conversation.

The following story of a conversation Dan mediated illustrates the path parties may take through the thick of conflict to an agreement, with moments of apparent understanding and accommodation along the way. If we assume that people are primarily self-interested, the moments of acknowledgment may seem like means to an end: strategic moves to get a desired outcome. If we assume people are motivated also by the desire to connect, these moments seem like ends in themselves.

TEXAS KIDS

Bart and Cindy, the parents of two-year-old James and four-year-old Jackson, were divorcing. I conducted the mediation via videoconference. Bart and I were in Los Angeles and Cindy was in Texas.

When everyone arrived on screen, I gave a brief introduction to the process and asked them how they'd like to start. Cindy said to Bart, "Why don't you go ahead?"

"Okay, so we got married 10 years ago. We were both very young and we had serious ups and downs. We both behaved badly at times."

I thought the conversation was off to a good start. Cindy's invitation for Bart to speak first seemed like a genuine demonstration that she wanted to hear his perspective; at the very least, she was okay with hearing what Bart had to say and with having me hear it. And Bart's acceptance of the invitation to speak seemed genuine as well. I didn't detect any suspicion of Cindy's motivation. Instead, it seemed to me that he trusted Cindy's intentions to simply give him the floor. The fact that they were able to make this small decision together—of how they'd begin—suggested that there was some goodwill between them. Because I'm committed to trusting the choices parties make in their conversation, I would have accepted any way they chose to start the conversation—but I still find it reassuring when I see parties collaborate in this way.

At this point, I saw a blonde head appear at the bottom of the screen as a little kid climbed into Bart's lap. I said, "Oh, who's that?"

Bart said, "I've got my son here."

Jackson poked up his head and said, "Hi Mommy." Cindy's face lit up and she said, "Hi, Baby."

Jackson's arrival raised a question. Family mediators often seek to protect children from their parents' conflict. At the same time, mediators believe that parents are in the best position to make choices about their kids. Although I had a brief thought that I should suggest that Jackson not be in the room, it wasn't clear to me that this was a high-conflict situation. It also seemed like it might be a nice moment for Jackson—sitting in his dad's lap and exchanging loving smiles with his mom. I also believe that keeping the decisions in the parties' hands as much as possible supports their ability to gain a sense of agency, improve their connection with each other, and have a good conversation. So I decided not to comment other than to wave and greet Jackson.

Bart continued, "So yeah, toward the end of our relationship, it wasn't good. And Cindy moved out last October [10 months earlier]. Then in January, this accident happened with my girlfriend's dog. It was a total accident. The dog is not vicious, he just got startled. James got bitten in the face. I was totally on top of it. I disinfected it. It was under control." Cindy rolled her eyes at this point.

I noticed that by saying "We both behaved badly at times" and "It wasn't good," Bart had acknowledged his role in their troubles—he wasn't purely blaming Cindy for them. On the dog incident though, Bart was opposing Cindy's story. My purpose for noticing both of these tones from Bart (conciliatory and critical) was to keep myself focused on the quality of their interaction. That is, I had no intention to encourage the conciliatory tone, for example, or to discourage the critical tone. I only intended to pay close attention so I could effectively support Bart right where he was. While I believe that this kind of support is conducive to shifts, I never know whether or when those shifts will occur so my commitment is purely to be ready to shine a light on or hold up a mirror to exactly where the parties are.

Bart went on, "So Cindy freaked out. And two days later, my boys were gone. I thought maybe she took them to Texas but I had no way of knowing, and she did it totally by surprise. So right now they're back out here for two months, which is great, but I am not looking forward to saying goodbye to them in two weeks, but I've agreed to it. And I get it that Cindy is back there trying to get on her feet financially, but I don't want my boys to stay there. That was never the plan . . . My main thing is I don't want my kids to become residents of Texas. They have me and my whole family here. They have friends here. They have a huge support system here. The only thing they have in Texas is Cindy and her sister."

Again, I noticed that Bart's story was a mixture of dismissing Cindy's perspective and acknowledging it. He was dismissing it by saying "Cindy freaked out," and acknowledging it with "And I get it that Cindy . . ." The part of his statement that was dismissive energized me with the awareness that I had some work to do to help him get to a better place. The part of his statement that accepted her perspective reassured me that Bart had the capacity and the preference to acknowledge Cindy when he could. As always, I was paying close attention not with the intention to strategize about how to move the parties but with the intention to understand the parties clearly and deeply so I could reflect them accurately when the time came.

Bart paused and I reflected back to him what I heard. Then I said, "So I'm not sure if you want to say something at this point, Cindy, or if you have more to say, Bart?"

Bart said to Cindy, "Go ahead."

Again, I took the invitation from one party for the other party to speak as an important, constructive bit of interaction.

Cindy unmuted herself and said, "Okay, so first of all, this was an abusive relationship."

"Okay, here we go," I thought. "Here's evidence of high conflict. This might be tougher than I had been guessing." I was also aware that many family mediators would hear the word "abuse" and wonder if a private conversation with Cindy might be necessary at this point. While I might suggest a private conversation if I had immediate safety concerns, for many reasons (including that the parties were mediating from separate states), I had no such concerns in this situation. (We address the issue of domestic violence and other potential power imbalances in Chapter 7.) Nonetheless, I also knew that I wanted to support Cindy in saying whatever she wanted, including things that might insult or enflame Bart. Here's where my commitment to party self-determination needed to stay firm as I'm sometimes tempted to try to suppress intense conflict.

Bart muted his audio as soon as Cindy began speaking, but I saw him laughing and rolling his eyes through much of what Cindy said next.

Cindy continued, "But anyway, when I took the boys to Texas, I was legitimately concerned for their safety. Bart did NOT take good care of James after he got bitten. I had to be the one to insist that they take him to urgent care. When I saw him, his face was all swollen. Bart was worried that something would happen to the dog if it got reported. And that incident was not the only thing. Just a few days before that, I had asked Bart where the boys were. They were with some woman he had met two weeks earlier on the Internet, and he wouldn't give me her name or number."

I noticed that although Cindy was differing with Bart on important elements, she seemed mostly calm and clear. Again I noticed both that there was enough conflict in the air for me to feel like I had some work to do but plenty of reason for optimism.

Bart shook his head and looked to the sky demonstratively at this point but he was still muted. I said, "I see you're having a lot of reactions there, Bart, but I guess it's working out okay that you're muted." He gave me a thumbs up. If we had been together in person, I might have simply reflected Bart's body language either by doing a version of it myself or by saying, "I see you're shaking your head." My purpose for reflecting it would be the same as for reflecting words: to give both parties the chance to notice it and decide how to respond to it. In this case, I reflected both that Bart was reacting but also that he was choosing to stay muted.

I was impressed at this point with Bart's and Cindy's ability to restrain themselves while the other was talking. Cindy too clearly felt Bart was misstating the story but she managed to allow him to say everything he wanted before she replied.

Cindy went on, "The other thing was that the boys were staying with Bart's mom, who was certifiably mentally ill and had to be hospitalized. I came over there one day and she was standing on the bed yelling at the air conditioner! Meanwhile I had been laid off and had no money so I had to come to Texas where I could stay with my sister, and the boys were not safe out there in L.A."

I reflected Cindy's story back to her. She nodded, and then Bart unmuted himself and said, "Can I say something?" I nodded to indicate that it was fine with me, and I shrugged to indicate that it was not really my call. Cindy said, "Go ahead."

Bart said, "Well first of all, I HAD NO IDEA WHERE MY KIDS WERE! FOR TWO FULL DAYS! For all I knew the three of you drove into a river! THAT WAS NOT COOL! And you wonder why I've sent you some harsh texts?! Please. That's nothing compared to what I went through!"

Bart's voice was strong and clear at this moment. He appeared to be in full control of himself while also being very focused on what he wanted Cindy to understand and acknowledge about his perspective. This statement was his clearest expression yet of the core of his frustration with Cindy. This appeared to be a textbook empowerment shift from weakness to strength as described by Bush and Folger.[21]

Because empowerment shifts often precede recognition, it was not a surprise that Bart was still somewhat self-absorbed ("And you wonder why I've sent you some harsh texts?!"). As Bart shared more details of his story and Cindy listened, his voice softened. The conversation continued with both parties talking—talking over each other occasionally but also generally acknowledging each other's perspective and sharing their own.

At one point, Cindy said to Bart, "I get it that you were genuinely worried when you didn't know where the kids were for those two days."

This comment struck me as a significant moment of acknowledgment and it appeared to be a continuation of the constructive cycle that may have started when Bart asserted himself so clearly.

Bart said, genuinely, "Thank you." He seemed to appreciate her acknowledgment of how difficult that time was for him. He then reciprocated by saying, "And I know that you actually believed the kids were in danger when you took them."

And Cindy said, "Thank you."

Bart said, "And you know what, this is a little bit off topic, but I think you and I could actually be good friends again at some point."

And Cindy said, "That's what I've been saying, but you've been so fucking harsh in those texts!"

Bart said, "Yeah, I know."

Bart and Cindy had gotten in touch with their strength as they described their frustrations in dealing with each other. Along with that increased sense of strength came greater capacity to focus on each other. Once Bart and Cindy started to open up to each other's perspective, it didn't take long for them both to acknowledge that they actually wanted to be good friends again. Cindy's choice to follow her comment about friendship with a strong statement about how harsh Bart had been revealed both her strength and her clarity that their connection mattered to her. It seemed, in that moment, that Cindy wanted Bart to know how his texts affected her and for him to acknowledge that his texts affected her, which he did.

Next they discussed their differing perspectives on the importance of finances to the kids' well-being. Cindy talked about the cost savings of staying with her sister. She pointed out that if she lived in Los Angeles, she'd have to stay near Bart in what she called the "ghetto" of Los Angeles.

I reflected occasionally, and after about 40 minutes I summarized the conversation: "You two have covered a few different aspects of your situation, may I summarize what you've talked about? [They both nodded.] Just now you were talking about your perspectives on how finances affect the boys. Cindy, you said that if you lived in L.A. now, you'd have to live in the ghetto, which you don't think would be good for the boys. Bart, for you, it would still be preferable for Cindy to live in L.A. You said the boys being physically close to you is more important than how nice a place they live in. You two also talked about how the two of you are relating to each other, and you both said you'd like to improve that. Bart, you said that, first of all, Cindy taking the boys without telling you was really messed up and that since then she's been putting a negative spin on your behavior when she talks about it. And Cindy, you said you've felt very attacked by Bart's text messages, they've been very harsh, and you don't find that helpful. But again you both have hope that you can change how you relate to each other and be good friends at some point. And you've also talked about what the plan is for the boys, both for the next year, and after that. And for this coming year, Cindy you're saying that you need to stay in Texas and that the boys should be with you there. Bart, you've said that that's not your favorite plan but that you're willing to go along with it. And you both also talked about what happens after this year. And Bart you feel strongly that the boys need to come back to L.A. next year. You do not want them to become residents of Texas; they have so much family and connection here; you really insist that the boys come back here and you hope that Cindy will come back and live nearby at that point. Cindy, you've said that you're not sure if one year in Texas is going to be enough to get you on your feet financially but you're not ruling out that you and the boys would come back to L.A."

I was attempting with this summary to be as true as possible to what each party had said. I repeated the expression "messed up," which Bart had used, even though it could be seen as insulting. I even used the word "ghetto," which Cindy had used, even though it occurred to me that someone might find that word offensive. Whether someone outside the mediation would be offended by it though was beyond my focus. It was the word Cindy chose so it's the word I used. I wanted to help them consider precisely their current situation, including the words they were using. I structured my summary according to the different topics or themes they had covered. I did so because I wanted to provide some structure so they could decide clearly whether to revisit any of the themes or to address something else. This was my effort to shine a light on their conversation.

When I finished summarizing, I said, "Is there more you two want to discuss about any of those topics? Or, what else do you want to talk about?"

Jackson had continued to slip in and out of his dad's lap periodically. The conversation between Cindy and Bart fluctuated from snippy to collaborative, punctuated by the occasional "Hi Mommy" from Jackson and "Hi Baby" from Cindy, with Bart giving Jackson a boost to make sure he and his mom could see each other.

As the conversation continued, in addition to increasing acceptance of the validity of each other's perspective, they became more open to the potential acceptability of each other's preferred outcomes. Bart became more accepting of Cindy's need to stay in Texas for a year and he accepted that the boys should be with her for this year. And Cindy accepted that, for the longer term, the boys would be better off if they and she returned to Los Angeles.

Toward the end of our three-hour meeting, Bart and Cindy agreed that they would share joint legal custody and joint physical custody of the boys. They also agreed that Bart would pay Cindy $400 per month for child support while they were in Texas. And Cindy agreed that after one year, she and the boys would return to Los Angeles. I checked to see if there was anything else they wanted to talk about. I noted that the court order mentioned property division and debt allocation, and Bart said, "No, we've got that figured out," and Cindy nodded. I noted that our three hours was almost up. I said, "So I could leave this Zoom meeting open for the two of you if you like but I'm going to log off." Bart spoke up and said, "Cindy, let's Facetime. You can just close the meeting, Dan." Bart said to Jackson, "We're going to call Mommy on Facetime now." Cindy nodded, we all waved, and Cindy and Bart logged off.

Bart's and Cindy's interaction fluctuated throughout this mediation. There was eye-rolling, headshaking, and blaming but there were also clearly articulated perspectives as well as acknowledgment and appreciation. Over the course of the mediation, they trended toward more acknowledgment and easier collaboration. While acknowledging each other's needs likely helped them reach satisfying agreements, it seemed that they were primarily motivated by the desire to help each other out when they could. Their desire to connect provided a natural momentum to the mediation without Dan needing to guide or push things in that direction. Dan's mirrors allowed them to see themselves more clearly and his lights allowed them to see each other more clearly, and then they made decisions that led to a restored connection.

Let's return to Ben and Lisa to see how their feelings about each other, along with their need to connect, play a role in their conversation. In the previous chapter, we paused their story with a summary from Dan. The summary was Dan's attempt to illuminate what the parties had shared thus far so they could make choices about what was next. His summary covered all the topics Ben and Lisa had touched on: whether the company was discriminating based on gender; Lisa's performance as an employee; why John got the promotion; and the relationship between Ben and Lisa. After the summary, Ben makes a significant choice about which topic he would like to address further.

Ben: Actually, coming back to that point, there is something I would like to add. I mean, Lisa, you said you feel disappointed in me. Now, I want to make . . . The thing is, I can't go into a huge amount of detail because of confidentiality and things like that, and I don't know to what extent you're going to believe me. But I do need to make you aware that I do actually take it . . . I spoke to the bosses about you, and actually, your name was short-listed, and you were considered for this promotion because I put your name forward. Okay.

I spoke out on your behalf, and I did my best. But the problem is, they saw John's leadership and management. And my personal feeling is that you probably would be better in this job than John. That's my personal feeling. But the decision wasn't mine.

Dan: You're saying you believe that Lisa would be better in that job.

Ben: Yeah, absolutely. That was my personal opinion. But you know, the decision was made above me to put John forward.

Dan: The decision was made above you to put John forward.

{When I've shown this video at mediation trainings, some group members at this moment have said things like, "Wow, Ben just threw the company under the bus." They feel Ben has revealed information that will help Lisa's discrimination claim against the company. I often counter that, on the other hand, Lisa may now be less angry and therefore less likely to sue. Next a conversation often breaks out about whether the company actually would be liable for discrimination. It's interesting how we all form opinions about what's really happening in a fictional situation.

The good news for me as a mediator who is committed to supporting the conversation is that I don't have to evaluate any of those questions—I'm fulfilling my role if I support Ben's and Lisa's decision making in their conversation. I'm holding up a mirror to what each of them says so they can see it more clearly and decide what is next. I'm shining a light on the choices they are making and on their opportunities to continue to make progress in their thinking and their communication. Whether Ben intends to undermine the company, intends to protect the company, is focused purely on himself, or is focused on compassion for Lisa, I get to support him as he gets clearer about what he wants to do; and I get to support Lisa as she decides for herself what to make of it.}

Ben: Yeah. I mean, as of right this minute, probably John would be best, because he's got the leadership and management, but my opinion is that Lisa's got more potential in the long term.

Dan: Okay.

Ben: But that's very much my personal opinion.

Dan: Your personal opinion is that Lisa has more potential in the long term, though at this moment, because of John's leadership and management skills, he's probably the best choice at this moment.

Ben: Yeah, absolutely.

{You may notice that I'm reflecting almost everything that Ben is saying, sticking very closely to his words. I'm noticing some significant recognition shift[22] opportunities for Lisa now that Ben is sharing new information about his role in the hiring decision. I'm repeating Ben's words to ensure that Lisa has a chance to hear them and react to them, if she chooses to, which she does.}

Lisa: Well, that makes me feel a little bit better about you, Ben. Because I feel like over the past eight years we did develop . . . You know, I really put a lot of trust in your leadership with me, and helping me along. And you always said, "Just take my advice, and be as productive as you can, and I will come to bat for you." And that's why I was so disappointed as to what had happened here.

Dan: So this information makes you feel a little better.

Lisa: I'm now kind of more angry at the company, if what Ben is saying is true, that he was looking out for me, and that the decision was made higher up.

Dan: So your anger is shifting a bit to the company, a little bit away from Ben.

Lisa: Yes. Yes. I'm still upset with the company, but now it's more with the company, and not really focused on one person, my boss, my immediate boss.

Dan: Okay. So, you're feeling . . . You said that, based on your relationship with Ben, the sense was that he was looking out for you. Hearing this from Ben, that he indeed did put your name forward, makes you feel better toward Ben, but still you're angry at the company about the decision they have made.

Lisa: Right. With the information I have right now, it still looks to me like they chose a man over . . . You know, they choose men over women, that's just what I can gather with the information I have here. And that's not right.

{I continued to stick closely to the words that each party said. At this point, Lisa's words and demeanor suggested that she was experiencing a recognition shift. She was beginning to see Ben in a new light with this new information, while also expressing her suspicion and anger toward the company. By reflecting Lisa's words, I gave both parties further opportunities to build on this shift and to address any other aspects of what Lisa shared if they chose to. Note that Lisa's recognition shift was in relation to Ben and not in relation to the company. That is, she understood and saw Ben more clearly but now, at the same time, she had new anger and distrust toward others at the company.}

Ben: I mean, the way in which the decision was taken, obviously they had a number of candidates and one of the people involved was myself. There was Adam and a couple of others, you know, senior management, and essentially they have the say over me. I can advise them, and I can give them my gut feeling, which I did. I think John was a good candidate, don't get me wrong, but I did make it clear that, you know, Lisa should be their priority one, followed by John.

But unfortunately, they took the decision that they did. And I really don't have that much information about why they made that decision, but I do know that it would have definitely had to be in line with their policies. Because when the company got to . . . You know, we've got 500 employees now. When any company gets to that size, it just can't get away with discrimination.

One, nobody really wins by discrimination. It's a very self-defeating thing to do, whether it's racial discrimination, or gender, or anything else. There is no point to it. Nobody wins from doing that. And when you've got so much to lose, from a company with 500 employees, you know, it's enough to sink the reputation for the company. And so, nobody is going to risk that.

Dan: So Ben, you're saying that you were in a position to advise those who made the decision, but it was Adam and a couple of others that were involved. And you aren't privy to their exact process in making the decision, but you do believe that, given the current size of the company, and given that it's just not good policy to be discriminatory, you're confident that they made the decision in a nondiscriminatory way, is what you're saying.

{My decision to reflect Ben here did not arise from an obvious need expressed by either party. I did it simply to add an opportunity for both parties to think about what Ben had said. Maybe hearing it again would raise more questions for Lisa; maybe it would help Ben think of what else he'd like to say; maybe it would simply confirm for them that the conversation was on the right track. Regardless, I believed it would contribute to their sense of control of the conversation. Note that my choices to reflect often arise not from any strategy to focus on certain things—I'm simply acting on my commitment to pay attention to and honor all of the choices that the parties make in the conversation.}

Ben: Yeah, yeah.

Dan: It just wouldn't be good policy to make the decision based on gender.

Ben: Exactly.

Dan: And you don't think they did it that way.

Ben: They wouldn't gain anything from doing that, other than, you know . . . I'm sure there are some people out there in some companies who do that out of a sense of macho pride, or whatever, but nobody is going to win from doing that. We're in this to make money at the end of the day. Nobody makes money from being like that, and you stand to lose everything.

Dan: So, for a variety of reasons, it just wouldn't make sense to make the decision based on that. Maybe there is someone out there who does it out of macho pride, but it sounds like your sense is that that's not what's happening at this company.

Ben: Yeah, absolutely.

{At this point, both Ben and Lisa were quiet. I decided to check in with them to make it clear to them that they had the opportunity to decide what happened next. I shone a light on their opportunity to make a choice.}

Dan: Well, so what are your thoughts about where best to focus the conversation at this point, you two?

Ben and Lisa's conversation revealed that their relationship mattered to them. Lisa shared that she had felt betrayed by Ben; Ben revealed that he thought of Lisa as a friend. Of all of the topics to return to after Dan's summary, Ben chose to focus on his relationship with Lisa. How Lisa felt about him mattered to Ben, and finding out that Ben had not betrayed her, as she originally believed, meant something to Lisa.

Parties, at some level, want to connect with each other as human beings, and they are usually more willing and able to do so when they have regained a sense of agency. In Ben and Lisa's case, they focused on their

> *Social connection is such a basic feature of human experience that when we are deprived of it, we suffer.* —Leonard Mlodinow

previous relationship as coworkers and friends, explicitly. In other cases, the desire to connect appears between people whose only relationship is a lawsuit. In all cases, the mediator can support parties' efforts at connecting by illuminating the choices the parties are making as well as their opportunities to continue doing so.

In Chapter 4, we'll turn to the topic of problem solving and how it also seems to benefit from a sense of agency. We'll explore parties' often inspiring ability and desire to rise to challenges, consider solutions, and solve what are sometimes complicated problems even in the midst of conflict.

Notes

1. Michael Dimock and Richard Wike, "America Is Exceptional in the Nature of Its Political Divide," Pew Research Center, https://www.pewresearch.org/fact-tank/2020/11/13/america-is-exceptional-in-the-nature-of-its-political-divide/.

2. Steven Pinker, *The Better Angels of Our Nature* (New York: Penguin, 2012).

3. History.com, "Christmas Truce of 1914," https://www.history.com/topics/world-war-i/christmas-truce-of-1914.

4. Richard M. Ryan and Edward L. Deci, *Self-Determination Theory: Basic Psychology Needs in Motivation, Development and Wellness* (New York: Guilford Press, 2017), 86.

5. Robert A. Baruch Bush and Joseph P. Folger, *The Promise of Mediation: The Transformative Approach to Conflict* (San Francisco: Jossey-Bass, 2005), 46.

6. Jonathan Haidt, "The Positive Emotion of Elevation," *Prevention and Treatment* 3, no. 1 (March 2000): 1–2.

7. Ryan and Deci, *Self-Determination Theory*, 11.

8. Lara B. Aknin, Christopher P. Barrington-Leigh, Elizabeth W. Dunn, John F. Helliwell, Justine Burns, Robert Biswas-Diener, Imelda Kimeza, Paul Nyende, Claire E. Ashton-James, and Michael I. Norton, "Prosocial Spending and Well-Being: Cross-Cultural Evidence for a Psychological Universal," *Journal of Personality and Social Psychology*, 104, no. 4 (February 2013); Felix Warneken and Michael Tomasello, "Altruistic Helping in Human Infants and Chimpanzees," *Science* 311 (March 2006); Warneken and Tomasello, "Altruistic Helping."

9. Lara B. Aknin, J. Kiley Hamlin, and Elizabeth W. Dunn, "Giving Leads to Happiness in Young Children," *PLoS One* 7, no. 6 (June 2012).

10. Warneken and Tomasello, "Altruistic Helping."

11. Warneken and Tomasello, "Altruistic Helping."

12. Inbal Ben-Ami Bartal, Jean Decety, and Peggy Mason, "Empathy and Pro-Social Behavior in Rats," *Science* 334 (December 2011).

13. See Ryan and Deci, *Self-Determination Theory*, 622.

14. Arthur Schopenhauer, *The World as Will and Representation* (Cambridge: Cambridge University Press, 1818) as cited in Larry Dossey, *One Mind: How Our Individual Mind Is Part of a Greater Consciousness and Why It Matters* (Carlsbad, CA: Hay House Publishing, 2013); also see Rupert Sheldrake, "Part I: Mind, Memory and Archetype: Morphic Resonance and the Collective Unconscious," *Psychological Perspectives* 18, no. 1 (1987).

15. Dossey, *One Mind*.

16. Richard Dawkins, *The Selfish Gene: Fortieth Anniversary Edition* (Oxford: Oxford University Press, 2014).

17. Charles Eisenstein, *Sacred Economics: Money, Gift, and Society in the Age of Transition* (Berkeley, CA: North Atlantic Books, 2011).

18. Netta Weinstein and Richard Ryan, "When Helping Helps: Autonomous Motivation for Prosocial Behavior and Its Influence on Well-Being for the Helper and Recipient," *Journal of Personality and Social Psychology* 98, no. 2 (February 2010).

19. Jonathan Haidt, *The Righteous Mind: Why Good People Are Divided by Politics and Religion* (New York: Vintage, 2013).

20. Robert A. Baruch Bush, "Taking Self-Determination Seriously: The Centrality of Empowerment in Transformative Mediation," in *Transformative Mediation: A Sourcebook*, eds. Joseph P. Folger, Robert A Baruch Bush, and Dorothy J. Della Noce (Institute for the Study of Conflict Transformation, 2010), 66.

21. Bush and Folger, *The Promise of Mediation*, ch. 2.

22. As we discussed in Chapter 2, recognition shifts occur when one party becomes more open to or understanding of the other party.

CHAPTER 4

Self-Determination
and Solving Problems

The only solutions that are ever worth anything are the solutions that people find themselves.

—Satyajit Ray

People regularly solve problems together without the assistance of a mediator. Married couples make small and large decisions together such as what to have for dinner, where to live, and how to parent their children. Coworkers, condo board members, and principals of large organizations sort out their competing needs and make plans and agreements. Pairs and groups of people talk, negotiate, and find solutions that work for everyone. They usually do so without any outside help. They have the information they need, or they know where to find it. Often their interaction remains constructive throughout the process of making decisions.

Challenges arise when their interaction degenerates and they descend into the vicious circle of conflict, as discussed in Chapter 2. The path to regaining that ability to solve problems involves reversing the vicious circle through reclaiming agency and re-establishing connection. A mediator can help by focusing mirrors and lights on the parties' choices as they make decisions about both the process of mediation and the outcome. Once they return to interacting constructively, they regain the ability to sort out their differences themselves. In this chapter, we will tell stories of people solving their own problems in mediation. We will also cite research that suggests that the best solutions happen when mediators provide support through mirrors and lights but do not guide or direct the parties' problem-solving efforts.

For an illustration of parties solving their own problems, let's return to the story of Ben and Lisa. You'll recall that when we last saw Ben and Lisa, Dan had just posed the question "Well, so what are your thoughts about where best to focus the conversation at this point, you two?"

Ben: Well, Lisa, what do you want out of this? Do you want to stay with the company? Do you have any plans elsewhere? What would you like out of this?

{Ben responded to my question by asking Lisa what she wanted. Notice that there was no need for me to direct them toward discussing their needs or interests. I stuck with my intention to give them the opportunity to decide what to talk about, and Ben asked the question he wanted to ask. His question happened to be "What would you like out of this?" It would have been okay with me if either of them had asked or stated anything else as well. The important thing was that they made the decision.}

Lisa: I really enjoyed working my eight years here. But to work for a company that I believe has this ceiling here for women, I'm not sure if I can continue. We'll have to see if there's another management opportunity that comes up, and what happens with that. But at this point, gosh, to think that I could continue to work years and years and not receive a promotion is very, very frustrating.

Ben: Well look, this is just my opinion again. This is just very much you and me. I get the impression there is a glass ceiling, but I don't think it's anything to do with gender. I mean, I'm getting the impression that I'm pretty much where I'm going to be. I don't think I'm necessarily going to go any higher than where I am now. There is a ceiling on promotion, but I honestly believe—and please believe me when I say this—I honestly don't think it's anything to do with gender.

I think the company, particularly this external company that bought 51% of the shares, I think they've got their own agendas and their own people that they want to put into place. So I don't think any allegations of discrimination is going to work. Because, to be honest, I empathize with you. I feel I'm in the same position.

{Ben's disclosure to Lisa about his uncertainty about his own career at the company might have been completely genuine, or it might have been a manipulative tactic. I didn't know. I also didn't know how Lisa would take it. I was also aware that I didn't need to know the answers to these questions and that it was their place to continue to make decisions.}

Dan: So you feel there is a . . .
Lisa: How is that?
Dan: . . . I'm sorry.

{Here I started to reflect Ben but backed out when I saw that Lisa wanted to say something. As always, I'm trying to keep every possible choice about the conversation in their hands.}

Lisa: Oh, okay. Because there is a glass . . . You sense there is a glass ceiling for yourself?
Ben: Yeah. yeah.
Dan: Your sense, Ben, is that there is a ceiling for those of you who have been with the original company, that the corporation that's bought the

company has its own people that they intend to put into the higher positions.

Ben: Yeah. I mean, when an organization gets this big and is sort of Stalinist with the way they approach HR and promotions, it's very difficult to see exactly what the criteria are. I could be wrong. They might make me CEO tomorrow, but my feeling is, hell, I would like to go and set up my own shop to be honest, and go it alone. But unfortunately, that's not a luxury I could afford at the moment.

Dan: So you empathize with Lisa's frustration and kind of doubt about potential advancement, based on the new corporation having taken over. And you would ideally like to start your own shop, but it's not possible at this time.

Ben: Yeah.

Lisa: Well, I appreciate hearing that, Ben. I just feel like I . . . Could I be provided an opportunity to talk to some of the upper-level people and express my frustration? I kind of feel like that's something I need to let be known, that I didn't appreciate what had happened. I could speak for myself. I won't include you in it because what we talked about is just between you and me. It will be my frustration in that I sense there's limited potential for me, and for others, because other people are really . . . There's a few people towards the top that are really controlling things, and those at the bottom have little voice.

Dan: So you would like to express your frustration to the higher-ups, and you would keep confidential the things that Ben has shared with you about the process.

Lisa: Yes.

Dan: But you feel like they need to hear the voice of people like you, who have this sort of frustration.

Lisa: Yes, yes.

Ben: Yeah, absolutely. I can do my best to try and get you an appointment. Certainly with Adam, I could see that working. I can try my best to try and get you an appointment. As I understand, you do have the right to—you know, you've got a grievance—you've got the right to take it to me, as your direct supervisor. You can then take it above me, and above him, and above him, and above him, to the person on top.

Lisa: Mm-hmm. Okay.

Ben: So, you can always do that as well. And it may be, I mean, I've got to be honest, I would like to know what they would say. I mean, obviously, that would be for your eyes and your ears, but I would be very interested to see what they say to you. But I would really appreciate it, obviously, if you could keep what I've said to you—I really said that as a friend—about my own concerns.

Lisa: Sure.

Ben: About promotion. But you know, the thing is, I certainly couldn't guarantee that if there was another promotion in six months' time, or a year's time, then that might not be given to somebody else. Hell, they might get somebody in from Europe, someone completely new, and just give it to someone random.

Lisa: Mm-hmm. I understand.

Ben: But, yeah, absolutely, a meeting, no problem.

Dan: So you're saying that you could arrange a meeting with Adam for Lisa. Also, she could continue with a grievance process. And I guess I'm not clear whether this grievance process has started with this meeting yet, but you're saying she could make a grievance to you. And if she's not satisfied, make a grievance the next step up the chain. And you would have some curiosity about how they would respond, yourself.

{As always, my intention here was to shine a light on what they were doing, which at this point appeared to be collaborative problem solving. I was aware that if my reflection distorted what Ben said, I would be undermining their choices. I did my best to be true to what Ben said and not to spin it in any direction—I tried to hold up an undistorted mirror.}

Ben: Yeah, and . . .

Dan: And you would . . . Sorry.

Ben: I was just going to say, I think probably at this stage it would be more productive if we just arranged a friendly chat with Adam. I mean, I can just say to him, "Look, we've got this problem. You need to meet Lisa, and you need to talk to her, and you need to explain to her what's going on." I think he'll probably listen to me on that one. If he doesn't, then obviously, you've got the grievance process, and can escalate it from there.

Dan: So at this point, you're suggesting a friendly chat between Lisa and Adam.

Ben: Yeah.

Lisa: Okay. That sounds acceptable to me.

Dan: That is acceptable.

Lisa: Mm-hmm.

Ben: I mean, one thing that I do think we should probably try to address is that he may very well just fob you off. He may say, "Yeah, that's just the way things happen. Deal with it." I would say about 80% of me thinks that's probably what he's going to come out with, because he's not . . . I don't know if you've spoken to him much, but you know, he's not the most tactful of men. He's not exactly diplomatic. So I just wanted to make you aware there's a very good chance he may very well do that.

Lisa: Okay. But I'm sure that he wouldn't want, you know, legal action taken against the company, and for me to go to the press and everything. So, if he gets some advice from in-house counsel, hopefully he'll just have a listening ear.

Dan: You're thinking that might motivate him to be more responsive, the possibility of legal action and going to the press.

Lisa: Yes.

Ben: I would agree with that. Or what I would say—and this didn't come from me—is don't push him too hard, because otherwise, if you push this guy he pushes back. And there comes the point when he just goes, "All right. To hell with it. See you in court." And you know, it's not really good for anybody.

Lisa: Right. Okay.

Dan: So pushing too hard could be counterproductive,

Ben: Yeah.

Lisa: Okay.

Dan: Well, can I just summarize what you've talked about in the last few minutes here? Just to kind of make sure we're all on the same page about what's been covered?

{Since I'm suggesting that I take over the conversation for a minute, I make sure they are okay with it. My hope, again, is to shine a bright light on what they've discussed so they can make clear choices about what's next. Notice that my decision to summarize and my choices about how to do so are my decisions. Any time I make decisions about the conversation, I am potentially violating my commitment to party self-determination. There is a paradox here. The best way to manage this paradox, as far as I know, is to make sure that my summary serves the parties' decision-making process by remaining as true as possible to the choices they have made. I also remain ready to stop my summary the moment they indicate the desire to say something. This solution is not perfect as the parties may defer to my summary.}

Lisa: Sure.

Dan: So, most recently you've been talking about some next steps, and Ben, you suggested, and Lisa, you said it would be acceptable that . . . It sounds like, Ben, you will help facilitate a meeting happening between Lisa and Adam. You're saying you're not so sure, 80% of you thinks he might not be particularly receptive, but you're not sure. And Lisa, you're saying that you're prepared to have that conversation, and it may help to the extent that he's aware there's the possibility of legal action or going to the press. And Ben, you suggested, "Be careful not to push too hard, because that could lead to a backlash that won't be helpful."

In terms of kind of what I heard you both say, the last time I heard you say it, about the company and the company's policies, it sounds like, Lisa, you still have some concern that there may be some gender discrimination happening, based on your experience with John getting this promotion. And Ben, your sense is that it's not about gender discrimination, that there may indeed be other things going on, such as, for example the company having a preference for its corporate people coming in, that leads to your own kind of mixed feelings about where your career might be going there.

Ben: Yeah.

Dan: So there are still some different perspectives on what role gender discrimination plays in all this. Is there more to talk about within that? Or something else to talk about at this point?

Lisa: That sounds comprehensive to me, thank you.

Ben: I would agree with that. I don't, yeah. I mean, it's really difficult for me to say exactly what's going on, because quite frankly, I don't know. But yeah, I think that's a good summary of the way things are going.

Dan: Okay. Well, I'm kind of sensing that maybe the conversation has come to an end for now, but I don't mean to assume that if you feel like there's more to say at this point. I'm also available. You know, we just set up one hour. It looks like we've only used about 40 minutes. No need to use a full hour, as I mentioned.

Also, if a time comes where it would help to have me around for any further conversations, by the way, including, if anyone thought it would be helpful for me to be present for the conversation between Lisa and Adam. I would of course be happy to do that.

{It was self-serving for me to mention the possibility of helping with future conversations. I decided it was okay to mention that I'd be happy to, as long as I didn't go so far as to *recommend* that I be involved.}

Lisa: Mm-hmm.
Ben: Yeah. Yeah, that actually might be quite helpful. As I say, this guy responds to—I'm not going to say legal threats, or anything like that—but when something went . . . We've had to get a third party involved here. It's not just a sit-down chat, and I think that might encourage him to take it a bit more seriously.

I mean, Lisa, did you want to talk now about what happens if this meeting goes nowhere? Or do you want to leave that for some other time? Or do you want to take that up with Adam?
Lisa: I think we'll take it as it goes along. At this point I want to focus in on getting the meeting and seeing what he has to say first.
Ben: Okay.
Lisa: Before I decide on options. Yeah, I think that makes sense.
Ben: Sure.
Lisa: Because see, I have no idea what's going to come about from that meeting.
Ben: Yes. So you can make an informed decision, yeah. Okay.
Lisa: Yes.
Dan: Is there more that you two want to say about plans to be in touch with each other about all this? Or is that kind of self-evident? That apparently Ben is going to talk to Adam and try to set up this meeting. Is there more that you want to clarify about what's going to happen next?

{This question might have been a slight deviation from my commitment to being nondirective. I decided this question was already in the air and since the meeting was winding down it wouldn't do much harm to check on it.}

Ben: Well, I'll have a chat with Adam. And hopefully, I mean, yeah . . . I'll have a chat with him and try and convince him that a discussion is the way to go. And I'll also mention to him, you know, Dan, how helpful you've been, and I'll suggest that we should maybe set up another meeting.

Lisa, don't take this the wrong way, because obviously we've been in constant contact, you know, for many years now. But I probably won't be as chatty with you until after this meeting because Adam is going to want me to be on the side of the company. I'm representing the company and I should have their interests at heart. And if he sees me talking to you, he might think that you and I are conspiring, or something like that. So I think it would be helpful if I remained a little bit independent, but I will get in contact with you. And then, once we've got the time and date for this meeting . . .

Lisa: Okay.

Ben: . . . get that set up.

Dan: So Ben, you're saying that after you propose this meeting, or from now for the near future, you're going to want to keep a bit of a distance from Lisa, just for the purpose of reassuring Adam that you are not taking Lisa's side necessarily. You think it will be helpful if he sees you as kind of being part of management, and kind of being helpful to him in letting him know that he has something that he should deal with with Lisa. Is that . . .

Ben: Yeah. Yeah, absolutely.

Dan: Yeah.

Lisa: Okay.

Dan: That makes sense to you, Lisa?

Lisa: Yes.

Dan: Okay. What else, if anything?

Ben: Personally, I think that's probably it. Let's bring on Adam and see what he's got to say.

Lisa: Okay. That sounds good with me.

Dan: Okay. Keep me posted if I can be of help in the future, you two. It was a pleasure to meet you, and I wish you both a lot of luck. And I would love to be kept in the loop if it seems helpful.

Ben: I'll cc you in on email conversations between Adam, Lisa, and myself.

Dan: Oh, great. Okay. All right. Take care.

Lisa: Okay. Thanks a lot, Dan.

Ben: Thank you very much.

Lisa: Bye bye.

Ben: Take care, Dan.

Ben and Lisa arrived at a mutually satisfying plan of action, relying on their own awareness of what they wanted and of the situation they were in. Dan's summaries shone a light on their conversation, and his reflections gave each of them a better view of themselves, but Dan did not add outside information. In that bright and clear environment, Ben and Lisa were able to regain their pre-existing capacity to solve their own problems. It seemed as if their agency and connection had been enhanced, and they were able to use their inside knowledge of the situation and of the people involved.

Just as Ben and Lisa needed to find their own way to their next steps, the parties in the next story arrived at a solution that the professionals involved did not anticipate. To the lawyers and mediator, the solution seemed to come out of the blue, but it likely did not appear out of the blue to the parties. The parties, as always, knew more about their own needs, preferences, and overall situation than anyone else. Support for their conversation was all it took for them to find a solution.

FINE, I'LL MOVE

I wouldn't have predicted that Carolyn, the mother of five-year-old Jakey, would agree to move back to the suburb she had just left. She and Jakey's dad, Victor, were caught in the notoriously challenging situation where each parent wanted the child to go to school in the neighborhood closest to them.

This was all I knew about this case before it began but I had a feeling that there would be some strong emotions involved. I knew that relocation cases are often the most challenging—sometimes with no good solutions—because the parents often have very good reasons for moving, but their child cannot be in two places at once. During the first hour of the session, I learned a bit more.

Carolyn shared that she had moved 30 miles away to the suburb where her new boyfriend lived with his child, which was in a perfectly good school district, and that Victor had no business telling Carolyn where she needed to live. Carolyn's lawyer added that at Jakey's age, if he were going to be with one parent more than the other, that parent should be the mother; therefore, he should go to school near her home.

Victor, on the other hand, said that it did not make sense that Carolyn's choice to leave him for someone else and to move out of the suburb where they had lived together could possibly mean that Jakey also had to spend school weeks in a strange new town. He also mentioned that Jakey had close relationships with both sets of grandparents, who continued to live in Victor's suburb as well.

Those are the parts of the story I knew after an hour of conversation but I suspected that those facts were only a tiny part of the story and that they may have been nearly irrelevant to the question of how I could help Carolyn and Victor with their conflict. I did not know what outcome would be best for all involved, what topics they should discuss, or how they should discuss them. Instead I focused on supporting their efforts to do what I assumed they most wanted to do, which was escape the vicious circle of conflict.

I'd been doing my best to hold up mirrors and reflect what I was hearing. My goal was to give each participant an opportunity to gain agency as they heard their own words reflected back to them. Hearing their own words gave them the chance to determine if that was what they had meant to say. They could then elaborate on, retract, or clarify what they had said.

My reflections also gave the other party (and the lawyers) a chance to hear the words again—perhaps more clearly than they had the first time. Because I paused after each reflection rather than asking a question or making a suggestion, all participants were free to decide where to go from there. In my view this was the path most likely to lead them out of the vicious circle of conflict and to a satisfying solution to their problem, if there was one.

I had the opportunity to see what happened when their lawyers jumped in to do the sorts of things I used to do when I believed it was the mediator's job to guide the parties toward a solution.

"Have you looked at schools that are halfway between each of you?" asked Victor's lawyer.

Victor and Carolyn both rolled their eyes. One of them said, "That's ridiculous."

Carolyn's lawyer suggested, "What about just agreeing on a summer schedule now and revisiting the school question in August?"

"No, I want this done today," said Carolyn.

The tension in the room seemed to rise after both of these suggestions.

At this point in the conversation, I was thinking that it might be helpful for the parties to hear a summary of what they'd been talking about so far. I had heard them cover a number of different points, and thought that having the topics, and their different takes on them, organized a bit might help them figure out where they wanted to go next—maybe they would want to go back to a topic they had already touched on or maybe they would realize that there was something else they wanted to discuss. Either way, focusing a spotlight on the conversation they had had thus far would honor the choices they had already made, allow each of them to think about their own perspective, and help them see each other's. My summary might add clarity about themselves, each other, and the situation.

I said, "So you've talked about a few different aspects of the situation. Is it okay if I summarize what you've said? [All nod.] As for the school itself, you've both said that either school is fine in terms of quality but that location is what matters. As for location, Victor, you've said that you'd like to keep Jakey in Golden Prairie because that's where all the grandparents are and that's where you went to school. You also said that since you work near there, you'd be available to Jakey during the school day if needed. Carolyn, you've said that since the Apple Park schools are also fine, it makes more sense for Jakey to go there so he can spend most of the week at your home. Given his age, you feel like it's especially important that he have a lot of time with you. You've also both talked about what to do next about this disagreement. Carolyn, you've said that maybe the guardian ad litem would be willing to make a recommendation. And Joe [Victor's lawyer], you said you don't think that's likely but that a custody study will be necessary instead. Carolyn, you also said that you'd like to be done with this today. Another thing you all talked about was the parenting schedule. You all agreed that, except for the problem with the school location, a 50-50 schedule would be fine." I added a few more details of what I'd heard the parents and the lawyers say. All agreed that that was pretty much the gist of it.

After my summary, Carolyn said that she would like to take a smoke break. Victor's lawyer asked if there were any vending machines, and Carolyn's lawyer said he could also use a snack. Both lawyers headed toward the door together while Victor and I remained seated. As Carolyn and the lawyers walked out, I asked, "Is it okay with everybody if I chat with Victor while you're gone?" "Sure," said Carolyn, and the lawyers nodded.

"So how're you doing?"

"Fine. You know, we actually got along fine before these schmucks [gesturing to the lawyers] got involved."

"Yeah?"

"Yeah, and I didn't want to say anything to her, but I've heard from my other kids [I had not even known that there were other kids—apparently Victor had kids from a previous marriage who continued to spend time with Carolyn] that Carolyn and her new boyfriend get in fights all the time, right in front of the kids. I don't want to bring that up here, because that'd really piss her off."

"I see."

Carolyn returned after a few minutes followed by the lawyers who had been eating their snacks and chatting in the hallway.

I noticed that Carolyn now appeared calmer and more centered. She wasn't fidgeting as much as she had been before and her facial expression was more relaxed. I figured that her break and a bit of nicotine helped her gather herself in some way. Although I saw that change in Carolyn, I was surprised when she announced, "Okay, here's what I'm thinking. I'm looking for a new job up in Golden Prairie. If that comes through, I'll move back up to Golden Prairie, and Jakey can go to kindergarten there. But I want the schedule to be fully 50-50, and I want it to be understood that Jakey will not see my parents during my time with him."

Although this change was surprising, her tone suggested that she was at peace with it. And although I hadn't heard her mention her parents before, Victor nodded at that point as if he were fully aware that this would be important to Carolyn. Carolyn's clarity that arrangements needed to be made regarding her parents confirmed that she had thought through at least some of the implications of this move.

"Fine," said Victor. "But if they want to see him during my time, they're gonna."

"Fine," said Carolyn. "But you know I can't stand my mom, so you better let her know that when Jakey's with me, she doesn't get to see him."

Carolyn and Victor then ironed out the details of a plan that satisfied them both, including a commitment from Carolyn to move back to Golden Prairie in August regardless of whether she got the job. Carolyn offered this commitment, with no prodding from Victor, the mediator, or either of the lawyers in the room.

Carolyn's surprising choice to move back to Golden Prairie, with or without a job, arose from Carolyn. Dan had no way of knowing that returning would be a good choice for Carolyn and hadn't suggested such a thing. When the lawyers offered suggestions, they were quickly rebuffed by both Carolyn and Victor. Even Victor had not suggested that Carolyn return to Golden Prairie; the best outcome he had hoped for, or at least suggested, was that Jakey be allowed to stay with him.

Had anyone else suggested to Carolyn that she return to Golden Prairie, she would have been deprived of the opportunity to come to that solution herself and for her own reasons. Instead of gaining the ability to meet her needs for autonomy, competence, and connection through her decision, she may have instead experienced a reduction in all three. Moreover, psychological reactance[1] (as discussed in Chapter 1) might have been activated, leading her to resist the solution in an effort to maintain a sense of autonomy.

When parties make their own choices, they may defy convention. They may even disagree with what a judge orders them to do. When Dan mediated the following case, he noticed that the outcome was unique, but he remained committed to supporting the parties' choices.

SPLITTING THE KIDS

Susan and John had decided to divorce and had already found a house nearby for John to move into when they called to schedule a mediation. During the session they explained that their main challenge was how to manage the care of their seven children (four boys and three girls) while living in separate homes. I did my best to reflect what I was hearing, including all of the options they were considering, and to support their conversation without offering suggestions or advice; nor did I offer my opinion on any of the options they were considering. Over the course of their conversation, Susan and John became clear that logistically, it made sense for the boys to stay together and for the girls to stay together; the boys had similar sports schedules, and the girls had similar activities, such as dance. Because Susan and John wanted all the kids to have quality time with each parent and knew that neither had the bandwidth to care for all seven children at once, they agreed to have the boys and girls alternately; one week Mom would have the girls while Dad had the boys, and the next week they'd switch. On Sundays the whole family would get together so the boys and girls could stay connected.

I knew that this plan was unusual and that family mediators tend to believe that children should not be split. However, I also knew that the situation—seven kids—was itself unusual, and there were pros and cons to any choice the parents made. John and Susan had discussed these pros and cons at length. More importantly, I knew that Susan and John were in the best position to know their needs and capacities as well as those of their children.

Several months later, Susan emailed to tell me the judge had rejected the schedule they came to in mediation. Instead, the judge ordered a schedule that kept all of the children together, moving as a group from one parent to the other every week. Susan explained that, despite the judge's order, the family had been following the original plan. Life was hectic, she said, but they were happy.

In this case, the parents arrived at a plan that worked for them. Dan had not suggested what their plan should be, and when the judge made a suggestion—or an order, to be more precise—the parents smiled, accepted it, and then disregarded it, fully aware by that point that they were in control of their parenting.

It's so much easier to suggest solutions when you don't know too much about the problem.
—Malcolm Forbes

Ben and Lisa, "Fine, I'll Move," and "Splitting the Kids" exemplify parties making their own surprising decisions about the *outcome* of their mediation. Dan's next two stories illustrate what can happen when parties have the opportunity to make their own (sometimes surprising) decisions about the *process*.

SPITE FENCE

Myrna and the Smiths, owners of neighboring properties, had a dispute related to their property line. The Smiths' lawyer, Bob, called me after hearing from a partner at his firm that my unique approach (meaning I don't separate the parties and try to hammer out a deal as other mediators sometimes do) might make sense since the dispute was between neighbors. Bob asked if I wanted pre-mediation submissions. I said that as far as I was concerned there was no need but if anyone thought there was something I needed to know, they were welcome to share it with me as well as with the other side.

Lawyers often ask about pre-mediation submissions or simply send them. To many lawyers, it's essential that the mediator have this information as they see the mediator's role as evaluating each side's legal claims and then helping parties understand the weaknesses of their cases. I see my role as doing what I can to help the parties have a good conversation knowing that I will never have as much information about their situation as they do, so I don't ask for pre-mediation letters or briefs.

I reminded Bob that I'm neither a decision maker nor an evaluator so communicating with the other side was what mattered. I also told Bob that it was the parties' choice whether their lawyers attended the mediation. Bob made no comment on that question but told me that he and the other lawyer agreed that they would submit summaries of their arguments to me and to each other before the mediation.

Mediators often have preferences about whether lawyers attend. As I see it, the parties should decide, both because making the decision can increase a sense of agency and because the parties (perhaps in consultation with their lawyers) are in a better position to know what is right for them. In Chapter 9 we'll talk more about the opportunities and challenges that arise when working with the parties' attorneys or other representatives.

Several days before the mediation, Myrna let me know that she was disappointed to hear that the Smiths would be bringing Bob, their lawyer. Myrna had decided to leave her lawyer out of it. She wondered if I could arrange for her to be in a separate room from Bob and the Smiths. Her lawyer told her that was usually how mediations were done anyway. I told her I'd be happy to conduct the mediation in any way that all the parties were comfortable with but I don't generally pass messages between parties because I'm not capable of communicating anyone's message as clearly as they are. Myrna said that she'd think about it.

Two days before the mediation, I received a call from Myrna saying that she planned to bring a friend for support but was not sure if she'd want to meet in the same room with the Smiths. She seemed comfortable playing that by ear.

I also received both legal summaries, along with some photos from Bob. The most striking part of Bob's submission, to my eyes, was a photo of the fence that Myrna had erected. The fence appeared to be about 12 inches from the Smiths' door. From those photos, I could understand the Smiths' frustration.

On the day of the mediation, I was glad I had reserved the big conference room. I hadn't known that both of the Smiths would be there, and I hadn't known that Myrna would bring two friends. I asked the group, paying special attention to Myrna's response (since she previously stated a preference for separate rooms), if it would be okay for us all to gather in the big conference room to start so that I could briefly introduce myself and the process.

If Myrna had been clear that she did not want any contact with anyone from the other side that day, I would have made her wishes known to the other side prior to the meeting. If they were still willing to participate, I would have made arrangements to keep them separate from the beginning (in Chapter 8, I tell a story of a mediation that proceeded this way). However, since there was no clear message from either side about needing this, I chose to suggest having everyone in the same room to begin. This way I could leave it to the parties to share any preferences about how the mediation would be conducted, if they wished.

Myrna quickly and convincingly said that meeting together would be fine, as did everyone else. So Bob, Dave Smith, Angie Smith, Myrna, Myrna's two friends, and I sat down around the big conference table. I gave my standard introduction where I told them that I was there to support their conversation and let them know that they would call all the shots about how the conversation unfolded. Then I said, "How would you like to start?"

After a brief pause, Myrna turned to Dave Smith and said, "I'd like to know what your favorite outcome would be." Dave said, "Okay, I'd like you to remove the fence, give us an easement so we can walk around our house, remove the trees that you've planted that obstruct our view of the river, and pay us $25,000 for all the hassles we've been through with you." I reflected what Dave had said.

Although Dave's opening comments were in no way conciliatory, and could be seen to be getting things off on the wrong foot, I remained comfortable. Myrna had had the opportunity to start the meeting the way she wanted, and Dave had spoken up and asserted himself. As far as I knew, this was exactly what needed to happen. Some mediators may believe that getting things off on the right foot is important and that they know how to make that happen. They may suggest, or even insist on, ground rules in an attempt to ensure respectful communication between the parties. In contrast, and given our beliefs about the importance of party decision making about the process, I do not suggest ground rules. I remain open to supporting any discussion of ground rules that the parties suggest, but I do not raise the topic.

Myrna said, "Okay, well, I can tell this isn't going to go anywhere. But let me get a few things off my chest."

Dan: You can tell this isn't going anywhere . . .
Myrna: Right.
Dan: . . . but want to get some things off your chest.
Myrna: Yes.

My intention here was to reflect and illuminate Myrna's sense that this process might be futile and to fully support that sentiment. It was not clear (as it never is) where Myrna was in her experience of strength versus weakness or recognition versus self-absorption. The timing of her statement, which directly followed Dave's, suggested that she had little hope of being able to see things from his perspective. Myrna also may have been experiencing a lack of faith in her own ability to communicate effectively in this process, at least with Dave. So my sense was that Myrna was at some level caught in the vicious circle of conflict.

And because Myrna might have anticipated that I would resist her suggestion that the process was futile (she might assume I would want her to continue), I wanted her to know that she had my support in expressing that sentiment and in any decisions she might want to make based on that feeling. My reflections also provided an opportunity for everyone else in the room to know where Myrna stood at that moment. Additionally, Myrna made it clear that she wanted to get a few things off her chest. So even though Myrna expressed a lack of faith in the process, she hadn't given up on communicating with the other participants. I wanted to illuminate her desire to communicate.

The others in the room listened quietly as Myrna told the following story, which she directed to the Smiths. "So here's some background, which I thought you knew, but maybe not. I had an understanding with the previous owners of your place, the Johnsons. I had given them permission to walk on my land all they wanted, including along the side of the house, where the fence is now. But I was always doing that as a favor to them. I had sold them that lot and that was part of our informal understanding. When they told me they were selling, I agreed to grant them a full-fledged easement so they could pass on to the buyers (who turned out to be you two) the right to walk around the house. We agreed on a price of $10,000 for that easement. They backed out on that deal, so there is no easement. As you know, the arbitrator agreed with me on that. The fence is on my land. So despite your lawyer's arguments, I have every legal right to have that fence there. What's more, I was very careful to put that fence on my side of the property line because I didn't want any more confusion with you two. Since I'm not living there, I didn't want my tenants to have to deal with this. Your lawyer's argument that this is a 'spite fence' is simply not true. I am not a spiteful person."

Throughout Myrna's telling her story, I offered some short reflections so that she would feel heard and supported as she told the story, increasing her sense of agency and confidence, and allowing her to tell her story more clearly. These reflections would also illuminate what Myrna was saying, giving others in the room an opportunity to more easily hear and absorb Myrna's perspective. From there, everyone involved could make choices about how to interpret Myrna's story and what to do next.

Dave and Angie both chose to challenge Myrna's perspective, and share their own. "Oh really?" asked Dave. "When we first moved in, the first thing we heard from you was that we owed you $10,000. That wasn't exactly the most neighborly way to welcome us."

"Yes," said Angie. "Demanding $10,000 . . . I don't know if spiteful is the word, but it didn't really get our relationship off on the right foot. And the Johnsons have a whole different story about what your deal with them was. They told us we already had the easement. That $10,000 issue, as far as we could tell, was between you and them."

Bob chimed in, saying, "'Spite fence' is the legal term for a fence that is raised with no legitimate purpose other than to annoy the neighbors. No one was necessarily calling you spiteful; we're just saying that this was a spite fence."

"I'm calling her spiteful," Dave said. "Why else would you put that fence there? It doesn't add to your tenants' privacy—it's chain-link. Nor does it add to the beauty of the yards. Part of the appeal of that neighborhood was its openness. And planting those trees down at the end of the yard—that does nothing but block our view of the river. Yes, I believe you did all of this out of spite."

"I'm spiteful? You're the ones who are suing me now even after an arbitrator told you you were wrong!"

"We've always been willing to talk about this with you, Myrna."

"No you haven't—you absolutely refused to talk about this."

"We refused to talk about paying you $10,000, but you're the one who said you didn't want to talk last time."

"Well, at that point, I wasn't interested in talking with you and the Johnsons. The Johnsons are your friends—they're on your side. And then you wanted to talk with your lawyer there. I wanted to talk like normal people do."

Throughout this conversation, I frequently reflected what each person said. I made sure to follow the heat and capture the accusations the parties shared. For example, I reflected Dave's accusation that Myrna was being spiteful along with Myrna's accusation that Dave and Angie had refused to talk like normal people. The parties were caught in the vicious circle of conflict. My goal was to reflect them accurately and nonjudgmentally, giving them opportunities to shift their interaction, if they chose.

At this point, I thought it might be helpful to raise the spotlight and illuminate the conversation as a whole—to shine a light on the topics the participants had discussed and the perspectives that they had shared on each topic. To keep the decisions in the parties' hands, I asked permission to summarize what they had been discussing as a group.

"You've talked about a few different aspects of this situation. May I summarize what I've heard? [All indicated that would be fine.] One topic has been what you see as the ideal outcome of this conversation. Dave, you said you'd like the fence and trees to be removed, an easement so you can walk around your house, and $25,000 for the hassles you've been through. Myrna you've suggested that you're happy with the status quo and with the arbitrator's determination that the fence is legal and that there is no easement. You also talked about the history of your interactions. Myrna, you said Dave and Angie have refused to talk to you about the $10,000 unless they had the Johnsons or their lawyer with them. Dave and Angie, you both said that Myrna demanded $10,000 from you as soon as you moved in and that got things off on the wrong foot but that you were willing to talk about it with her. Is there more that you want to clarify about those topics? Or what else would you like to focus on?"

By following the summary with a question about where the participants would like to go from there, I was attempting to remind the parties that this was their process and to shine a light on the opportunity they had to make a decision about next steps. At this point, Angie suggested that we all take a break, and everyone seemed to agree that now would be a good time. I pointed out that my office had coffee and other beverages, and I said that I would check in with everyone to see if they wanted to talk to me about anything. After spending a few minutes with Myrna and her friends in the conference room, I told them I'd check on the others, who had gathered in my office. When I arrived there, Angie asked, "Would it be okay if just the three of us talked—you, me, and Myrna?" I said that that would be fine with me if it's okay with everybody else. Angie added, "I just think I might be able to get further with her, because she and Dave have too much bad history." Dave nodded.

I do not know how Angie and Dave arrived at this strategy of Angie having a private conversation with Myrna. I often don't know where parties' insights come from. I believe they arise when I allow space for them and when I consistently communicate that the parties can and should take responsibility for thinking about what they need and want.

"Sounds good to me," I said. "Would you like to suggest it to her?"

Angie and I walked back down the hall, and I poked my head in the room to say, "Angie's here and wants to make a suggestion—is that okay?"

"Sure," said Myrna.

I held the door open for Angie, and she said, "I'm wondering if I could just talk to you alone, with Dan,"

Myrna asked, "And without your lawyer either?"

Angie said, "Right—just you, me, and Dan."

Myrna said, "I think that's a great idea."

The others filed out of the room and Angie, Myrna, and I sat down. The conversation between Angie and Myrna took about 45 minutes. It included Angie saying, "I had no idea how hard this has been for you. But I want you to understand that it's been hard for us too." And Myrna said, "I do understand that now. I still don't like your husband's attitude, but now I at least know that you're a decent person." And Angie said, "Dave really isn't as bad as he seems—a lot of people think he's absolutely great—it's just the way this whole thing happened . . . He does think you're just being spiteful."

Essentially, Angie and Myrna had a good old fashioned heart-to-heart. In that 45 minutes, they agreed that Myrna would move the fence far enough from the Smiths' house so they could walk around comfortably. They also agreed that the Smiths would pay to move the fence and, perhaps, for a nicer fence. Myrna agreed to keep her new trees on the border trimmed to under five feet, and Myrna and Angie decided to meet in a couple days to figure out exactly where the fence would go. They agreed that this would be a license, as opposed to an easement, so that Myrna could reconsider her options if either of them decided to sell their property. And they agreed that they'd work with Myrna's lawyer on the language of the license.

After Angie had a chance to explain the understanding to Dave, the whole group gathered again.

Perhaps, after all, the most beautiful words in the language are I'm sorry.

—Christopher Buckley

After the group had reviewed Angie and Myrna's understanding, and Dave had also agreed to it, Myrna said, "One more thing . . . I'd like an apology from Bob. Bob, the things you wrote in your letters to me and to the mediator were unnecessary and very hurtful."

Bob, who had been pretty quiet throughout the mediation, said, "Myrna, I'm sorry. In my role as advocate I do things with the intention of protecting my clients' rights, and I'm aware that those things can be offensive. I'm sorry about that."

Myrna said, with genuine appreciation, "Thank you."

Angie's and Myrna's choice about the process—to have a conversation with only the two of them and Dan—came first from Angie and then from Myrna's enthusiastic agreement to it. That choice led to a better conversation and an outcome that satisfied everyone. And they made that choice without even subtle direction from Dan, who had not considered the idea before Angie suggested it. This story illustrates that for the parties to have control of the *outcome*, they may need to have control of the *process* as well. In this case, the process question was who should speak with whom and who should be out of the room. We suspect that the parties would not have arrived at this outcome had Angie and Myrna not been given the space to choose to have a private conversation. And Angie may not have had the insight to suggest the private conversation if she had not first had the opportunity to participate in a free-flowing conversation with the group as a whole. Dan's consistent attitude that all of the parties' choices were fine with him may have added to her awareness that she was free to make process suggestions.

Even before Angie's and Myrna's decision to meet one on one, Myrna had made decisions about the process. She decided not to bring her lawyer but to bring her two friends instead. She also considered asking to be kept separate from the Smiths and their lawyer, thought about it, and then decided to go ahead and meet with them face to face. Her shift, from preferring to be separate from the Smiths to boldly starting the conversation by asking Dave what his favorite outcome would be, suggests that her sense of agency was increasing. Her opportunity to make those process choices appeared to be an essential part of her increased agency.

It was also helpful in this case that the mediator wasn't attached to getting all the participants to connect with each other. Although positive connection can and does occur, we have no way of knowing *whether* or *how quickly* it will happen between any two people. The parties in this case made the apparently helpful decision that it was better simply to separate Dave and Myrna so that Angie and Myrna could work things out.

One reason mediators think they should evaluate the parties' conversation and nudge it toward certain solutions is the belief that doing so will lead to better, more durable agreements. The available research suggests otherwise.

Parties are more likely to adhere to mediated decisions than to judicial ones.[2] That adherence likely arises from two characteristics of party decision making: autonomy and specificity. First, the parties' autonomy matters to them—if they are free to make their own decisions, they experience a greater sense of ownership and therefore commitment to the decisions. Second, when parties make their own decisions, they are free to tailor them to their own situation, making them more workable on a practical level than those they did not craft. When compared to lawyer-led negotiations or a judge's decision, nearly all forms of mediation provide some level of these benefits. However, it is likely that these benefits exist on a continuum and that benefits due to both autonomy and specificity can be maximized when support for party choice is maximized.

As for autonomy, the parties' sense of ownership over their decisions will likely vary with their level of engagement in the problem-solving process. The experience of generating ideas, crafting agreements, and making choices about how and what information to gather can all contribute to the parties' ownership of, and commitment to, their decisions.

Regarding specificity, sometimes mediators attempt to help the parties tailor their agreements by directing the parties to think about particular needs they might have or by suggesting solutions that the mediator believes will meet the parties' unique needs. As the stories above illustrate, though, when the mediator stays out of the way, parties often make choices that appear perfectly tailored to their unique needs. Moreover, this engagement can generate a sense of accomplishment, which is intrinsically rewarding.

While it may be clear now that neighbors can and should make process choices in their mediations, divorces present a more complicated situation. Completing a divorce can be overwhelming simply due to the red tape involved. The process can get especially confusing if the couple is in conflict while they manage it. On the other hand, it is possible for parties to remain in control of the process and make their own decisions about many aspects of it. In the following case mediated by Dan, the parties came to their own agreement about disclosing their assets. Even though their solution was likely similar to what a judge would have suggested, their agency around it probably served them well as they completed the process.

DISCLOSE YOUR ASSETS

Kumar and Prisha were getting divorced. Before their first joint mediation session, each had a private phone call with me. On her call, Prisha told me that she believed Kumar would not be forthcoming about his financial situation as he had always been secretive about it during the marriage. On his call, Kumar said that he still very much loved Prisha and that he wanted to be generous to her in the divorce but that he resented the money she spent during the marriage while he had saved so much.

In the first joint session, Kumar laid out his financial proposal and mentioned that he would not be disclosing the details about his separate (non-marital) assets. Kumar shared that these assets were in the form of a trust from his parents, which named only him as the beneficiary. I was aware that the legal divorce process would require Kumar to swear that he was disclosing all of his assets, including non-marital ones, but since I was focused purely on supporting this conversation, I did not share that information with the parties. It was only after the meeting that Prisha called me and told me that she wanted to know the value of Kumar's separate assets, including the trust he mentioned. Without asserting anything about my own understanding of the law, I reflected what Prisha said and continued to do so as she expressed her intention to tell Kumar that she needed that information.

Kumar and Prisha next exchanged a series of emails, copying me, in which Prisha insisted that Kumar share detailed information about his separate assets. She told him that it would be necessary, as part of the legal process, for him to disclose that information so she preferred that he do it now. Kumar also asserted in those emails that he would not be distributing any of those assets to Prisha as part of the divorce. Prisha acknowledged that those assets were non-marital but said that she nonetheless wanted to know what they were while she considered the big picture of their settlement.

Kumar and Prisha also negotiated the timing of the exchange of this information. Kumar wanted the entire process to move quickly, while Prisha had work obligations for the next several weeks that led her to request some time to complete her side of the disclosures. They arrived at an agreement to share all of the information within a month.

Prisha and Kumar made decisions together about what information they shared and when they shared it. No guidance from Dan was necessary for them to meet their respective needs around the process despite their initial differences. In fact, Dan's nondirective support may have helped them get clear about what mattered to them, increasing their sense of strength and agency. This increased clarity and confidence may then have led them to take responsibility for getting their needs met.

In all of these cases the parties arrived at solutions that worked for them, for their own reasons, and in their own ways. During the conversations, they took the initiative to do many of the things some mediators might suggest—gather information, define the issues, identify their interests, consider the law, brainstorm, evaluate options, and decide on solutions. They appeared to enter those stages of the process seamlessly at the moment that felt right to them. When they received unsolicited input from professionals (whether the input came in the form of a suggestion or an order), they simply disregarded it. Sometimes such input might be helpful, at least in the short run, but parties often arrive at satisfactory solutions, in ways that they can feel good about, without such guidance.

It is also likely that the parties in each of these cases felt a sense of accomplishment. This sense of accomplishment matters to people. In addition to the basic psychological needs for autonomy and connection, discussed in previous chapters, humans need to experience a sense of competence. People are intrinsically motivated to learn skills and solve problems, and they actively seek out opportunities to increase their capacities.[3] People want to rise to challenges and they feel good when doing so.

This motivation to master one's environment is apparent from very early on. Toddlers seem to be intrinsically interested in exploring new environments and interacting with toys or other objects they find.[4] In fact, when children are reluctant to explore a new environment, this is viewed as evidence of a problem—specifically, an insecure attachment to their caregiver.[5]

Even our nonhuman cousins like to experience a sense of competence. For example, rats seem to prefer exploring new environments rather than returning directly to their nests[6] and have even walked across an electrified grid, subjecting themselves to pain, in order to reach an unexplored maze on the other side.[7] Similarly, rhesus monkeys choose to solve puzzles without needing a reward outside of the inherent satisfaction of engaging in the task.[8] Taken together, this research suggests that our need to experience competence is hard wired.

> Well-being is a combination of feeling good as well as actually having meaning, good relationships and accomplishment.
> —Martin Seligman

So not only are people often *capable* of solving their own problems, they are *motivated* to do so. People want to rise to challenges, master their environment, and experience a sense of competence.

Research on the effects of different mediation practices is consistent with the research on people's basic psychological needs, including their need to experience and express competence. Two studies conducted in Maryland[9] showed that in general, practices that supported people's choices and gave participants the opportunity to generate their own solutions, although not overlapping completely with the mirrors and lights approach we advocate, worked better than directive ones.

In family court mediations, reflecting strategies, which included "frequent use of reflecting back the participants' emotions and interests, and clarifying with participants the topics to address,"[10] were associated with a variety of positive outcomes. In the short run, reflecting strategies increased the likelihood that parties would report that the other party listened to them and that they could work with the other party. Reflecting strategies were also associated with a lower likelihood of rejecting the other party's perspective. These strategies did not decrease the parties' chances of arriving at a consent order, and they led to agreements that were more personalized (although they were associated with fewer agreements reached within the mediation).[11] Six months later, reflecting strategies (which, for long-term outcomes, also included offering summaries and asking open-ended questions[12]) were associated with the ability to share concerns with the other parent, work together as a team, prioritize their child's needs, and consider each other's perspective.[13]

In district court mediations, "reflecting back to the participant what the participants themselves expressed, with a focus on the emotions and underlying interests"[14] was associated with an increase in self-efficacy from before to after the mediation although it was not associated with any long-term outcomes. And "asking participants what solutions they would suggest, summarizing the solutions being considered, and checking in with participants to see how they think those ideas might work for them"[15] (considered together) were associated with a greater likelihood of reaching a lasting settlement (i.e., with parties being less likely to later request an enforcement action against the other party[16]) without decreasing the parties' satisfaction with the mediation process, the outcome, or the other party. In fact, these practices appear to increase the likelihood of underlying issues coming out during the session, the parties becoming clearer about what they wanted out of the situation, the parties listening to and understanding each other during the session, and the parties becoming better able to work together.[17]

The stories in this chapter and research from Maryland point to the value of parties receiving support for their own process of decision making. The stories and research suggest that party self-determination is far more than merely a characteristic of mediation; it is *the* characteristic that makes mediation so potentially valuable. We have described our process as being defined by the mirrors and lights that we use to illuminate and clarify the parties' experience. In the next chapter we will describe in greater detail how we use those tools.

Notes

1. Stephen A. Raines, "The Nature of Psychological Reactance Revisited: A Meta-Analytic Review," *Human Communication Research* 39, no. 1 (January 2013).

2. See Roselle L. Wissler, "The Effectiveness of Court-Connected Dispute Resolution in Civil Cases," *Conflict Resolution Quarterly* 22, nos. 1–2 (December 2004).

3. See Richard M. Ryan and Edward L. Deci, *Self-Determination Theory: Basic Psychological Needs in Motivation, Development, and Wellness* (New York: Guilford Press, 2017), 11. Also see Robert W. White, "Motivation Reconsidered: The Concept of Competence," *Psychological Review* 66, no. 5 (1959).

4. Annie Bernier, Celia Matte-Gagne, Marie-Eve Belanger, Natasha Whipple, "Taking Stock of Two Decades of Attachment Transmission Gap: Broadening the Assessment of Maternal Behavior," *Child Development* 85, no. 5 (September–October 2014): 1854.

5. Bernier, Matte-Gagne, Belanger, and Whipple, "Taking Stock," 1854.

6. K. C. Montgomery, "The Relation Between Fear Induced by Novel Stimulation and Exploratory Drive," *Journal of Comparative and Physiological Psychology* 48, no. 4 (August 1955), as cited in Ryan and Deci, *Self-Determination Theory*, 110.

7. Henry W. Nissen, "A Study of Exploratory Behavior in the White Rat by Means of the Obstruction Method," *Pedagogical Seminary and Journal of Genetic Psychology* 37, no. 3 (1930), as cited in Ryan and Deci, *Self-Determination Theory*, 110.

8. M. J. Gately, "Manipulation Drive in Experimentally Naive Rhesus Monkeys" (Unpublished Manuscript, University of Wisconsin, 1950), as cited in Ryan and Deci, *Self-Determination Theory*, 110.

9. Maryland Judiciary, "What Works in Child Access Mediation: Effectiveness of Various Mediation Strategies on Short- and Long-Term Outcomes," 2016a, https://mdcourts.gov/sites/default/files/import/courtoperations/pdfs/familyfullreport .pdf; Maryland Judiciary, "What Works in District Court Day of Trial Mediation: Effec-

tiveness of Various Mediation Strategies on Short- and Long-Term Outcomes," 2016b, https://mdcourts.gov/sites/default/files/import/courtoperations/pdfs/districtcourt strategiesfullreport.pdf.

10. Maryland Judiciary, "What Works in Child Access Mediation," 61.

11. Maryland Judiciary, "What Works in Child Access Mediation," 61.

12. Maryland Judiciary, "What Works in Child Access Mediation," 61.

13. Maryland Judiciary, "What Works in Child Access Mediation," 61–62.

14. Maryland Judiciary, "What Works in District Court Day of Trial Mediation," 53–54.

15. Maryland Judiciary, "What Works in District Court Day of Trial Mediation," 54.

16. Maryland Judiciary, "What Works in District Court Day of Trial Mediation," 54.

17. Maryland Judiciary, "What Works in Child Access Mediation," 62.

CHAPTER 5

The Art of Using Mirrors and Lights

There are two ways of spreading light: to be the candle or the mirror that reflects it.

—Edith Wharton

In the first four chapters, we explained why self-determination matters, especially for people in conflict. While we believe supporting party self-determination is valuable in itself, we made the case that it also increases the likelihood of enhanced agency, genuine connection, effective problem solving, and reversal of the vicious circle of conflict. Using the metaphor of mirrors and lights, we illustrated ways mediators can support party self-determination without interfering with it. With these tools, mediators can illuminate the parties' path as they work through conflict and move to a better place. In this chapter we will explain the practices in more detail, using the metaphor of mirrors and lights and revisiting previously discussed cases.

Leaving Every Possible Choice to the Parties

The act of making choices can enhance party agency—the psychological dimension of self-determination. Therefore, we leave as many decisions as possible to the parties. We are careful not to suggest we have any ideas that might be better than theirs. We don't say, "It's your choice, but if it were me . . ." Instead, we do our best to remain clear that it is not our place even to have an opinion about what the parties should do. With that attitude, we keep our lights focused on their ability to make the choices in question.

The opportunities to support party choice begin before the first mediation session. When we talk to the parties or their lawyers before the first session, the parties have the opportunity to make a number of decisions about their participation. In "Spite Fence" (Chapter 4), the parties or their lawyers raised questions about who would attend the mediation, whether there would be pre-mediation submissions, and whether they would meet in the same room. Dan told the Smiths' lawyer that he took no position on whether the lawyers should attend the mediation or whether they should provide a pre-mediation brief. He said these decisions were up to the parties and their lawyers. When Myrna told Dan that she was not sure she would be comfortable meeting in the same room with the Smiths and their lawyer, Dan reflected her concerns and gave her the opportunity to decide whom to bring, if anyone, and whether or not to meet in the same room with the Smiths and their lawyer.

Sometimes the parties (or their lawyers) disagree about some aspect of how the mediation should be conducted. Other times we, as mediators, have needs that conflict with the parties' choices. We will describe these situations, and how we handle them, in Chapter 8.

We make clear to the parties from the first point of contact that mediation is voluntary. Even when the parties have been ordered to mediation, we support their choice about whether or not to comply with that order. In his first conversation with Ben and Lisa, Dan stressed voluntariness in the following way.

> This process is voluntary, as far as I'm concerned. And I really mean that, that we should only do it for as long as each of you feels like it's worth doing. We have up to an hour to do it today, but there is no obligation as far as I'm concerned that we use that whole hour. We really only should do this for whatever period of time both of you feel like it's helpful.

Even before describing his view on the voluntariness of mediation, Dan gave the parties an explicit opportunity to forgo his introduction: "Would it make sense for me to say a few words about how I see this conversation going at this point? Would that be okay?" He shone a light on the parties' opportunity to make a choice even about whether he would share his perspective on the nature of the process. If a party said that they needed to say something first or that they had no need for his explanation, Dan would have honored that choice. Although the vast majority of participants say yes to this question, Dan asked the parties for permission as a way of setting the tone that this was truly the parties' process and he was there to serve them. Any time we talk during the mediation, the parties are welcome to stop us.

Dan continued to set the tone by telling Ben and Lisa that what happened would be up to them. He shone his light on their ability to exercise choice by describing the multiple opportunities they would have to decide how, and whether, to participate. He described the mediation process as an opportunity, not a requirement, to have a conversation. He chose the word "conversation" to make it clear that they need not treat mediation like a formal or rule-bound proceeding. This was a chance to talk to each other. After his introduction, Dan made it clear it was the parties' choice how to proceed, including who would speak first.

Dan intervened throughout the mediation by reflecting the parties and summarizing their conversation (practices described in more detail below). Dan tried to strike a balance between actively helping and allowing space. Sometimes he explicitly put choice in the parties hands ("What would you like to do now?"). Other times he stayed out of the way. Before starting a long summary, he asked the parties' permission; for quick reflections, he jumped in without asking. When a party continued to speak over Dan's reflection, Dan respected the party's choice by ending his reflection. While Dan had a consistent goal of supporting the parties' choices and their efforts to gain agency, being supportive without interfering is more of an art than an exact science.

Finally, Dan followed the parties' lead on when the conversation should end. When it appeared they were winding down, he tentatively said, "Okay. Well, I'm kind of sensing that maybe the conversation has come to an end for now, but I don't mean to assume that, if you feel like there's more to say at this point." They talked for several minutes after that, with Dan reflecting and summarizing along the way.

Paying Attention to the Parties

Each moment presents an opportunity for the mediator to support party self-determination. Sometimes the moment calls for an active intervention, such as a reflection, to support a choice the party just made. Other times, the moment calls for the mediator to refrain from interfering with the parties' self-determination and to silently attend to the choices they are currently making. The parties may choose to speak or remain silent, to look at another party or look away, to lean forward or lean back. The participants are never *not* making a choice. The same can be said for us. Paying close, nonjudgmental attention to the parties in each moment is a choice. By paying attention, we shine the light of our consciousness on the parties. Our focus on the parties enhances their sense of agency by reminding them that they matter and that their choices matter. If agency is "the self-aware and reflective assertion by an individual of the intentional choice to make decisions,"[1] our attention contributes directly to the parties' agency.

When paying attention to the parties, we focus on their interaction. We watch for cues, such as strong emotions, that indicate how the parties are relating to each other. We also pay attention to the flow of the conversation so we can intervene in a way that supports, and does not interfere with, the parties' process. And if we do intervene, we pay attention to whether a party speaks over us so we know when to back out and support their preference to speak at that moment.

Paying attention to the parties also means noticing when we are *not* paying attention to them. For instance, we are not paying attention to the parties when we are thinking about what they *should* be doing or saying instead of what they *are* doing or saying. We also monitor ourselves for impulses to contain the conflict or nudge it down a different path. Noticing these judgments and directive impulses can help bring us back to the present and remind us of our intention to fully attend to the parties in each moment.

Microfocus

If we want to support party self-determination, we have nearly unlimited opportunities to do so. Party decision making happens in every moment of the process, and each time a party makes a choice, they can enhance their agency. The parties' options are many: whether they mediate, who attends the mediation, where they sit, whether they speak, when they speak, what they say, and how they say it. Nearly everything that happens provides an opportunity for the parties to make choices and for the mediator to support their process of choosing. Every time we draw attention to a choice they have made, point out an opportunity to make another choice, or decline to usurp their opportunity to make a choice, we have supported their self-determination. We do not think about the big picture of what the potential settlement will be nor do we evaluate the strengths of a party's legal case. Instead, we microfocus[2] on what we see happening in each moment.

Life is choices, and they are relentless. No sooner have you made one choice than another is upon you. —Atul Gawande

Actively Supporting the Conversation with Mirrors and Lights

In addition to putting as many choices as possible in the parties' hands, we support their choices by acknowledging them, which often means repeating their words—we tell them what we heard them say or what other communication we observed (including body language, tone of voice, or the choice to remain silent). Supporting parties' choices this way gives them room to consider their choices as they make them. This further consideration can lead to greater clarity, a greater sense of competence, and a greater sense of agency. Throughout the book, we have used the terms "reflecting," "summarizing," and "checking in" to describe the mediator's interventions. Now we will describe, in more detail, how we use these practices in ways that are consistent with our intention to support party self-determination.

Reflecting

The metaphor of the mirror is well-suited to the practice of reflecting. When we reflect the parties, we genuinely strive to give them a clear, accurate, undistorted view of themselves. We do so by engaging directly with a party immediately after that party has spoken. We essentially repeat what they said, using many of the same words, without reframing or embellishing and without softening any negativity. The speaker hears their own words, and the other participants hear what the speaker said, but in a different voice. This repetition slows the conversation down, giving everyone another chance to think about what the speaker said and consider what they would like to do next.

In conflict, there is often misunderstanding. When people are caught in the vicious circle, feeling weak and self-absorbed, it is difficult for them to take in the other person's perspective. A reflection or summary provides space for the parties to clarify their own perspectives, hear each other's perspectives again, and make a conscious decision about their next move. We support the parties in ways that we believe will put them in the best position to make empowerment shifts (toward strength) and recognition shifts (toward responsiveness).

In the example presented in Chapter 2, Dan used many of Lisa's words in the following reflection, without softening her sentiments.

> Lisa: Well, we can see, you know. I mean, if I pursue this further, and take legal action, I could go to the press. I could really make a big stink out of this and expose the company. Then you'll have to really prove that you're not discriminating against women.
>
> Dan: You're saying, "We'll see about that. We'll expose . . ."
>
> Lisa: I'm so frustrated that that makes me . . . I just feel like I could pull that lever at any time right now, because I am so angry.
>
> Dan: You're so angry you could go to the press. You could make a big stink about it.

The intensity of Lisa's frustration and anger signaled that she was caught in the vicious circle and that some support might be helpful at this time. While we never know, with certainty, how much weakness or self-absorption a person is experiencing, there are cues we look for when trying to gauge the parties' experience and what we can do to help.

One clue we look for is a high degree of emotionality, particularly frustration or anger. Frustration suggests the person feels stuck—they would like to change the situation but don't know how. We see the expression of frustration as an indication that the person is experiencing weakness. Anger (which is often tied to frustration) suggests the person is experiencing self-absorption—they're having a hard time understanding the other person's perspective or seeing the situation through their eyes.

Recognizing the signals of weakness and self-absorption, Dan started to reflect Lisa and then stopped when he noticed she had more to say. As soon as the next opportunity arose, Dan continued his reflection. In addition to potentially helping Lisa become clearer and calmer and helping her to regain strength and agency, Dan's reflection gave Ben an opportunity to hear, perhaps more clearly than the first time, how strongly Lisa felt about the situation. While holding up a mirror to Lisa, Dan was also shining a light on Lisa's frustration for Ben.

Dan did not know if Ben was experiencing weakness or self-absorption at that point but he knew that having the opportunity to hear Lisa a second time would, at the very least, buy Ben some time before responding. In addition to holding lights and mirrors for the parties, Dan was adding space to the conversation—his interventions provided room for the parties to gather their thoughts and make more conscious decisions about what to do next.

> True empathy is always free of any evaluative or diagnostic quality.
> —Carl Rogers

Finally, as discussed in Chapter 3, the mediator is also providing empathy to the parties. Listening and supporting each party nonjudgmentally can meet their need for connection.

Summarizing

We use mirrors and lights when we summarize as well. A summary helps parties get clearer about what they have discussed so far. We organize summaries into themes the parties discussed, specifying where they differed and where they agreed. We seek to be accurate, above all else, and often include direct quotes from the parties. To the extent the conversation feels overwhelming or confusing to the parties, summaries may help them see that their situation is less complicated than they thought. Summaries afford the parties opportunities to see and consider the choices they have already made and, with those in mind, decide what to do next.

> A little light dispels a lot of darkness. —Rabbi Schneur Zalman of Liadi

We generally offer summaries after the parties have each commented on at least one topic, there is a pause in the conversation, and it appears the parties are not sure what to do next. We also might offer a summary when there's been a rapid back-and-forth between the parties and a reflection would feel one sided.

Before Dan summarized a portion of Ben and Lisa's conversation (in Chapter 2), he asked for their permission. Asking for permission reminds the parties that Dan is there to serve them and this is their conversation. It also signals that he's about to do something a bit different from what he had been doing when reflecting each party, one at a time. As always, Dan would defer to the parties if they gave any indication that they preferred to speak at that moment. Dan suggests a summary with awareness that he, and not the parties, has suggested it, and he must heed any sign that the parties prefer something different.

Dan: I wonder if it would make sense for me to . . . You've covered a few different aspects of this situation. Can I just kind of summarize what I've heard? In case that helps clarify where you want to focus at this point? Would that be all right?

Only after they both said yes, did Dan summarize as follows.

Dan: Okay. So, you talked about the overarching question of the company's discriminatory policy, or not. And Ben, you've stated that you do not feel the company has been discriminatory, and in particular, recently policies have been put in place where equality is an important priority of the company. And you say that that's evidenced by the fact that 60% of the workforce are women, and that goes to show that the company is not discriminatory in general.

    Lisa, you're saying that, well, yes, 60% of the company workforce are women, and yet in terms of management positions, your sense is that in fact women are under-represented. And certainly in this particular instance of John being selected over you, that feels to you like an instance of discrimination.

Lisa: Yes.

Dan: Another thing you both talked about is basically Lisa's performance up till this point, and you both agreed that Lisa has been very productive. Ben, I think you said "the best," in terms of productivity. Or "one of the best."

Ben: Yeah. I did.

Dan: And I guess there's no disagreement about that. You've also talked about how it came to be that John, instead of Lisa, was given this promotion. And Lisa, you're saying that, given your productivity, it really doesn't make sense other than that John's a man. And to the extent that John may have done some networking, you see that as an old boys thing. They're out, you know, whatever, drinking scotch and smoking cigars, and you were never invited to that sort of thing, so you didn't have the opportunity to do that.

    Ben, you're saying that the way that John earned this position was that he took a lot of initiative, worked a lot past his paid hours, past the workday, did a lot of networking. That he took his own initiative, you're saying that he made those opportunities happen. And you also say that, from your standpoint, productivity is not really the criterion that determines who should have this job, but it's management skills. And your sense is that John was the person with those types of skills.

    And one more thing that you discussed was your relationship with each other. And Lisa, you said that you had trusted Ben to basically be a mentor to you in the company, and you had sought his advice on how to advance in the company. And you felt like you had a relationship where you could trust that he would advocate for you and would at least let you know about this opportunity coming up. And you feel incredibly frustrated that he has not lived up to that relationship. And Ben, you also acknowledged that the two of you have been friends.

Dan used a specific structure for the summary. First, he named the topic that Ben and Lisa had discussed. Then he described each party's perspective, essentially reflecting them again. He spoke to Ben when recapping Ben's perspective, and he spoke to Lisa when recapping Lisa's perspective. While the purpose was to allow them to hear their own and each other's perspectives, he was not translating for the parties by telling Ben what Lisa said or telling Lisa what Ben said. He was speaking directly to each party (using the second-person "you") so they could correct or confirm immediately and so the other party could listen from a safe distance. Lisa and Ben both chimed in with "Yes" or "Yes, I did" after he summarized their perspectives.

The goal of the summary was to increase each party's clarity about what they had discussed so far so they could make a conscious decision about what to do next. As with a reflection, a summary provides an opportunity for parties to confirm, clarify, or correct the mediator's interpretation of their communications. It also adds space to the conversation, which gives the parties an opportunity to collect their thoughts and consider their next move.

Checking In

Immediately after the summary, Ben spoke up to say more about one of the topics Dan had included. When the parties do not immediately speak up after a summary, we generally check in with them about what they want to do next. We shine a light on the decision point and their opportunity to make a choice. We might say, "What would you like to do now?" If the parties appear stumped, we might add, "We could take a break, either of you could talk privately to me, we could revisit one of the topics you touched on earlier, or we could call it a day. I'm sure there are many other possibilities . . . It's up to you."

We also use the check-in to ensure that each party is comfortable with their level of participation as well. For instance, if a party has not spoken for a while, we may say, "Jane, how are you doing? Just checking if you want to say anything." We provide a gentle reminder that they have options while making it clear that their current choice to remain silent is also totally acceptable to us.

The Effects of Mirrors and Lights

Conversations supported with mirrors and lights tend to move in the direction of parties gaining clarity about their situation and what they want from it as well as gaining a deeper understanding of each other. However, the mediator avoids nudging the parties in those directions. Tempting though it may be, the mediator does not push parties to stand up for themselves. Nor does the mediator suggest that the parties should be more open to each other's perspectives. To nudge in either of those directions would be to supplant the parties' decision making about the most important aspect of their conflict: how much to focus on themselves and how much to focus on the other.

In addition to supplanting the parties' decision making, nudging would likely be counterproductive. As mentioned previously, people value autonomy and resist pressure,[3] so pushing the parties may lead to resistance. Moreover, *genuine* strength and openness can only come from the parties themselves.[4] In upcoming chapters, we will address many of the situations where we deviated from this supportive, nondirective approach (for better or for worse).

Once Ben and Lisa gained some clarity and confidence, they also began to hear and understand each other's perspectives. They connected on a deeper level and related to each other as friends who were now aligned in solving a problem. Ben took risks and demonstrated that he trusted Lisa by revealing his own struggles with the company. Lisa responded to Ben's trust in her by assuring him that she would honor his confidence when speaking with upper management. Ben and Lisa appeared to reverse the vicious circle of conflict. Throughout the conversation, Dan continued to reflect, summarize, and check in with the parties, following and supporting them as they made their choices.

What Ben and Lisa Thought of the Experience

The Ben and Lisa mediation was an unscripted simulation with mediators acting as the two parties. These role-players, who labeled their own mediation approach facilitative, had enacted the same scenario with a mediator who practiced facilitative mediation. Ben and Lisa were therefore able to compare that experience with Dan's mirrors-and-lights approach. After Dan's mediation simulation, Ben and Lisa described the experience from their perspectives as parties and as mediators. You can view the entire post-simulation discussion in this video.[5] The following are highlights from their discussion.

Lisa

Lisa appreciated that Dan did not lead the process. She noted that "he let the parties control it, yet there was something about the strength in his presence, that I didn't feel alone or that I wasn't being supported . . . I felt like his role was supportive for me . . . but I also sensed that he was listening to Ben's side of the story as much as he was listening to mine."

Dan's mirrors and lights felt helpful to Lisa. "I very much appreciated that Dan was actively listening and actively reflecting back . . . And less than half-way into the mediation, when Ben was expressing his empathy, I really felt better about the situation and was thinking more constructively." Lisa's comment suggests that she experienced both a greater sense of clarity and a greater sense of connection to Ben as a result of the conversation and that Dan's interventions played an instrumental role.

Ben

When Ben compared having Dan as a mediator to the other mediation he experienced for this case, he said, "The result we got was totally different . . . It was far more productive." Ben explained, "If you can address the personal problems between the parties, then you enable them to resolve their own technical problems." Ben went on to discuss the parties' creative solution to their problem. "Looking forward, maybe if Lisa goes up to this Bruce guy and says, 'I've got a claim on you for gender discrimination,' he may very well go, 'Oh, well, as it happens, there's a new position opening up somewhere else.' And so it really does foster that collaborative approach rather than just chucking money at a settlement." Ben's comment is consistent with our discussion in Chapter 4 noting that people are generally able to solve their problems once they have shifted out of the vicious circle of conflict.

Ben also shared how surprised he was by Dan's description of the process. "Going into a mediation and not hearing 'We're here to settle, we're here to resolve the dispute' . . . was really really weird, and *worked* . . . It really let Lisa and I repair our relationship . . . I'm astonished—I really am, how effective it was."

One interesting aspect of Ben's reaction was that he attributed to Dan a strategic agenda that Dan did not intend. Ben noticed that in one of Dan's summaries (used as the summary example above), Dan had mentioned Ben's and Lisa's friendship as the last topic. Ben, in role, had then addressed that topic. In the debriefing after the session, Ben said he assumed that Dan intentionally placed the matter of friendship last because he knew that it was especially important for Ben and Lisa to discuss that topic. Dan explained that he had not intended to emphasize that topic—he had simply addressed the themes in the order they occurred to him. While Dan's accidental placement of the topic may have influenced Ben, it's also possible that Ben chose to address his relationship with Lisa because he (immersed in his role) became aware that his friendship with Lisa was a priority.

It is not always that easy. Because the Ben and Lisa mediation was a recorded role-play, it may have been easier for Dan to remain consistent with his principles. Because he knew others would view the mediation, he was especially motivated to practice what he preaches. Also, because their dispute was not their own, Ben and Lisa may not have experienced or presented the same investment in the dispute as actual parties. Finally, we cannot rule out the possibility that Lisa and Ben were being polite rather than fully honest when giving their feedback since Dan was listening to their remarks. In the next four chapters, we will demonstrate what can happen when the real-world pressures (e.g., to settle a case, protect a party, or satisfy lawyers) interfere with our ability to fully support the parties. In Chapter 6, we will explore a common impulse that interferes with our ability to support parties in their own process: the desire to nudge the parties toward an agreement.

Notes

1. Robert A. Baruch Bush and Peter F. Miller, "Hiding in Plain Sight: Mediation, Client-Centered Practice, and the Value of Human Agency," *Ohio State Journal on Dispute Resolution* 35 (2020): 597.

2. This term was coined by Robert A. Baruch Bush and Joseph P. Folger in *The Promise of Mediation: The Transformative Approach to Conflict* (San Francisco: Jossey-Bass, 2005), ch. 6.

3. See Richard M. Ryan and Edward L. Deci, *Self-Determination Theory: Basic Psychology Needs in Motivation, Development and Wellness* (New York: Guilford Press, 2017).

4. Baruch Bush and Folger, *The Promise of Mediation*, 72.

5. Dan Simon Mediation, "Transformative Mediation in Action: Workplace Discrimination Case Example," September 29, 2014, https://www.youtube.com/watch?v=Cq0upTnMbVc.

CHAPTER 6

The Temptation to Nudge Parties Toward Agreement

> Honest disagreement is often a good sign of progress.
> —Mahatma Gandhi

Supporting self-determination involves accepting the parties where they are and honoring *their* process of deciding *for themselves* where to go next. We have made the case that supporting parties in this way, without guiding or nudging, is the process most likely to help them escape the vicious circle, make strong and compassionate decisions, and reach an agreement that satisfies them in the short and long term. Nonetheless, despite our commitment to honoring parties' choices, even we are sometimes tempted to cut corners in the process and push toward a settlement. When we focus on settlement in this way, we have disregarded our knowledge that the path to a satisfying agreement may take twists and turns that may feel discouraging to them and to us. And we have disregarded the possibility that ending mediation without an agreement may, in any particular case, be the best option for all involved.

Despite our commitment to party self-determination and our belief that this approach generally leads to the best outcomes, we also need to contend with the pervasive idea that success means an agreement. Mediation trainers and writers often imply that settlement is the goal. Judges, lawyers, and program administrators suggest, or directly state, that they would like a case settled. And often the parties themselves say they would like the case to be over. They even ask for our success rate (or more explicitly, our settlement rate). To the extent mediation is considered a form of alternative dispute resolution (ADR), *resolution* is part of its definition. The first sentence of the Model Standards' Preamble implies that resolving the dispute is mediation's purpose ("Mediation is used to resolve a broad range of conflicts within a variety of settings").[1] It is difficult to escape the feeling that it is our job, as mediators, to help parties get to an agreement.

But reaching an agreement is not always the parties' top priority. The details of both the process and the outcome matter to the parties. Tara, in a blog post[2] "Settlements Are Like Sex," used an analogy to illustrate the problem with a mediator viewing the agreement as the main, or only, goal.

> Many mediators say their goals are the parties' goals. According to these mediators, if the parties begin mediation saying they hope to reach an agreement, then it's the mediator's job to get them there. But what does it mean to hope for an agreement? Does it mean any agreement, by any means?
>
> In my view, hearing someone say they hope to reach an agreement is like hearing someone say they hope to have sex. If you heard such a thing, would you assume the who and the how did not matter? Clearly, there are implied conditions, such as mutual desire, and these cannot be forced. Moreover, goals are not static but often change over time as experiences and information accumulate. If the proper conditions are not met, a person would probably rather not have sex than have sex with someone they're not attracted to or who is not attracted to them. Or they may find they simply have something better to do.
>
> Likewise, there's a mutual psychological state implied by the word "agreement." People who hope for an agreement are hoping to find themselves on the same page, willingly accepting the same outcome. Even if they are merely settling rather than enthusiastically agreeing, no one enters mediation hoping to be pressured, manipulated, or misled into a settlement. And while a mediator might not be able to prevent the parties from pressuring each other, the mediator can serve the parties well by understanding they each might prefer no agreement to one that was reached through misinformation, manipulation, or the mediator's heavy hand.
>
> Settlements, like sex, require self-determination, and the details matter.

Of course, the details matter to parties to differing degrees. As with sex, people will vary in how choosy they are. For some, a deep sense of connection must be part of the picture. For others, coming to an agreement is worth doing even if it means continued resentment or a sense of unfairness. Often the parties are not on the same page about their goals, including how important it is to reach an agreement in mediation. As we see it, it is not the mediator's role to prioritize the goals of one party over the other.

We have all heard stories of people saying, "I just wanted out of that marriage so badly, I gave my ex everything. I didn't even care!" And a mediator who sees something like that happen in a session may want to protect the party from giving away the farm. Of course, if the party *truly* didn't care, they would not need a mediator—they could simply leave the other party with everything. Since the parties have chosen to enter mediation, they must want something more than for the negotiation to be over. At the very least, they care about the specifics of the agreement. They want to pursue the negotiation in a way that leads to terms they prefer. Often, though, they have relational needs such as for an apology, acknowledgment, or improved interaction.[3] As we have discussed, people in conflict also want agency, connection, and the opportunity to solve their own problems.

You can't separate peace from freedom because no one can be at peace unless he has his freedom. —Malcolm X

The urge to nudge parties toward agreement is based on the mistaken notion that the last moment of the mediation, when agreement has been reached (or not) is the only moment that matters. A written agreement surely has significance to the parties, and potentially to a judge. Yet how the agreement was reached, and what happens after the agreement, also matter. The parties' lives continue after the mediation, and any agreement reached may change over time. In addition to the possibility of an agreement that is durable and works well for the parties in the long term, other potential post-mediation outcomes include increased self-confidence and self-respect, a better understanding of the other party, the ability to work with the other party in the future, and improved communication and conflict resolution skills. The end of the mediation need not be considered the only moment that counts. One mediator expressed the limited temporal nature of our roles as follows.

> I'm stepping into the river of their lives, and hopefully that will change the current a little, but it's their life and there's a lot that came before and there's a lot that's going to go after that has nothing to do with me and my stepping in. So I step in and I step out. And that's another image that I think I keep with me.[4]

We mediators sometimes forget we are a relatively small part of the parties' story. We have a limited view of the parties, their relationship, what this conflict means to them and where it fits into their lives. Our ideas about what it would mean for their situation to improve are necessarily oversimplified. Yes, settlement of a lawsuit often seems like it would be an improvement, but we never even know that with certainty. In the big picture, our well-intentioned encouragement that they, for example, listen to each other could interfere with them doing something else more important for them at that moment such as asserting themselves. The river metaphor puts our contributions in perspective and helps us let go of the belief that we know which way things should flow.

In the following mediation, Dan couldn't help himself. He thought he knew which way things should flow. He tried to make one of the parties see things differently. As always, Dan meant well, but his efforts to nudge the party did not actually move the party in Dan's preferred direction, and they were likely counterproductive.

MANIPULATING THE SYSTEM

I couldn't help but think the postal employee, Joe, was paranoid. He believed management had intentionally damaged his reputation with the people who reported to him. As far as I could tell, he had imagined it, but it wasn't my place to say that.

According to Joe, it all started when he saw an email in which one of the higher-ups said the supervisors at Joe's facility had been "manipulating the system." The system in question was the one employees use to request certain days off, and Joe was the supervisor primarily responsible for that system. The email HAD to be referring to him. But the only manipulation he had done was to enter the information on behalf of some of his employees — in their presence. He was helping them because he was more familiar with the system than they were.

After Joe explained what he had done, Bari, author of the email, said, "Yes, exactly! YOU entered the information. Supervisors aren't supposed to be in there manipulating the system."

I held a mirror to Bari, and said, "That's what you meant! JOE entered the information for the employees, and he wasn't supposed to manipulate the system like that."

Bari had simply meant supervisors shouldn't be entering the information for employees — she had never meant to imply Joe had done something dishonest or corrupt. She meant "manipulating" in the sense of getting in there and handling it. Joe didn't seem to hear Bari say that, and my reflecting Bari's words didn't seem to help Joe hear it any better.

Joe went on without acknowledging Bari: "And when you came to this facility you never met with me — you only met with the supervisors on other shifts, and I heard that you were smearing me in those meetings, and that Dennis [Bari's supervisor, who was also present at the mediation] was saying stuff about me behind my back, as well."

Bari: I honestly don't know what you're talking about. I did not mention your name in those meetings. And I assumed you chose not to attend those meetings because you no longer wanted to be involved in the process.

Joe: You didn't have to mention my name. Everyone knows the guy responsible for that system here was me.

Bari: I was here to update everyone on the new way we were doing it. I was not here to badmouth you. I didn't mean to badmouth you. I've never worked with you before. I have nothing against you. I don't know how you got that idea.

The conversation continued, with Dennis saying, "I don't smear people. That's not how I operate. I find it a bit insulting that you're suggesting I went out of my way to disparage you."

In summarizing what Joe and Bari had said about the meetings Bari had with other supervisors, I said, "So, on the topic of what was said at the meetings, Bari, you're saying you did not badmouth Joe in those meetings. You had no intention to do that. You had no reason to do that. You were just there to train people on the new aspects of the system. And Joe, you're saying it's not possible Bari didn't smear you in those meetings. You've heard about those meetings from other people and you have no doubt whatsoever about what happened."

Once the words were out of my mouth, I realized "not possible" and "no doubt whatsoever" were exaggerations of what Joe had said. I was trying to nudge Joe toward acknowledging he wasn't at those meetings and it's possible he was mistaken. That sort of nudging is not consistent with the pure support of parties I aspire to. If Joe had been open to contemplating the possibility he was mistaken, he had the opportunity to do so based on what Bari and Dennis had said and on contemplating what he himself was saying. After my summary, Joe could probably sense my doubts about his perspective. If anything, my nudges made Joe less open to adjusting his viewpoint. I saw Joe look away from me when I said those things as if they didn't quite hit the spot.

What's more, the other two parties did not show the sort of frustration with Joe that I did. At one point Bari said, "I've never had anything against you and I still don't." And Dennis said, "Okay, Joe, I'm hearing that you have different perceptions about things. That's okay. That's natural." As the mediator, I felt like I was the one who should have the greater capacity to be nonjudgmental and to accept contrasting viewpoints as being valid, and that's what I aspire to do. But in this case, the parties were the ones who demonstrated less judgment of Joe and more acceptance.

Perhaps because the other parties offered Joe nonjudgmental acceptance, my slip-up *seemed* not to do any harm. It wasn't clear whether Joe ever changed his view that Dennis and Bari had been smearing him to the other employees. But when Dennis agreed that, in his next two meetings with supervisors, he would make it clear Joe had been doing a fine job and Bari's visits had been only for the purpose of updating the system, Joe agreed to withdraw his complaint.

While the basis of the Joe's complaint was sex discrimination, that issue did not come up at all during the meeting. If I had entered the mediation with the idea that I needed to help them focus on that issue, I would have interfered (even more than I did) with the conversation they wound up having. This conversation led to resolution perhaps because I did not imagine that I knew where the conversation needed to go. Perhaps, paradoxically, my lack of attachment to settlement helped them reach a settlement.

Even if we could know what decisions the parties should make throughout the process or where they should arrive in the end, nudging them in a particular direction is unlikely to get them there. As we discussed in Chapter 1, people value their autonomy, and pressure to move in one direction can create resistance, leading them to move in the opposite direction of the nudge.[5] In contrast, supporting the parties' autonomy helps them get clearer on what they need to do. If the mediator's preferred direction is actually the right direction for the parties (not that the mediator should have a preference), supporting their autonomy can help them arrive at that conclusion by themselves.

In addition to autonomy, people have the basic psychological needs of relatedness (connection), and competence, which we discussed in Chapters 3 and 4. The three needs are actually mutually reinforcing, as explained by Ryan and Deci.

> These three needs, while to some degree independent, are nonetheless mutually supportive of each other. When people experience competence, they tend to feel that they have the skills and ability necessary to get their other needs satisfied; when they experience autonomy, they tend to feel authentic, to more openly communicate with others, and to explore ways of getting their other needs satisfied; and when they experience deep relatedness with others, they tend to feel. . . [the] security that is necessary for them to venture out into the world in pursuit of greater confidence and agency.[6]

Although all three needs can reinforce each other, autonomy provides the greatest entry point for mediators. As we see it, supporting party autonomy is, essentially, supporting party self-determination. While this support can naturally lead to a greater willingness and ability to connect with the other party, any attempts on the mediator's part to direct the parties toward increased understanding—no matter how much we might secretly hope this will happen—would necessarily interfere with the parties' autonomy, reducing the likelihood of a genuine connection between the parties.[7]

As discussed in Chapter 4, research specifically focused on mediation also suggests mediators can best serve their clients by supporting them as they make choices. Although the studies were not randomized controlled experiments, the findings suggest that the more autonomy support the mediator offers, as opposed to direction and control, the better the results.

It's not easy to provide constant support for party choice above all else. In the following case, Dan slipped up at least twice and gave in to urges to nudge the parties along.

CHARLES'S ESTATE

Charles was almost 80 when he died from a heart attack. He was survived by his second wife Linda and his daughter from his previous marriage, Julie. Julie was almost 50 at the time he died and had always had a tense relationship with her step-mother Linda.

Charles's will left his house in equal shares to Linda and Julie. Two years after Charles died, Linda—who had been living in the house—received an offer to sell it for $1.1 million. She wanted to accept that offer and split the proceeds equally with Julie. Julie felt she was entitled to more than half of the proceeds (because of other disputed assets), and she believed they could get a higher price for the house.

Before the mediation, both Linda and Julie told me they did not want to see each other that day and preferred the conversation be conducted through their lawyers. I made arrangements for them to have access to separate rooms and to arrive at different times. I also told them that although I would generally not pass messages between them, I would make an exception for information about what they would require in order to have a face-to-face conversation.

At the mediation, I spent much of my time facilitating the conversation between the two lawyers, with Linda and Julie occasionally receiving updates from them. After the mediation had been going on for several hours, Julie asked me to let Linda know she would like to speak with her directly. She added that the reason she wanted to talk to Linda was she was incensed by the lies Linda had been telling, and she wanted me to pass this message along to Linda as well. I jokingly said, "I see—you want to start off on the right foot."

I immediately regretted saying that. Although Julie's lawyer laughed, I realized my comment was not supportive of Julie at that moment. In fact, that probably *was* Julie's idea of starting out on the right foot so my sarcastic joke was misplaced. Julie didn't laugh at my joke and probably noticed I was making light of her anger. I quickly resumed being supportive of Julie by genuinely reflecting what she'd said. I also clarified that I hadn't heard Linda was open to meeting directly with Julie but I'd tell her Julie was now open to it.

When I told Linda that Julie would talk directly to her, I left out the part about Julie being incensed. I probably would not have withheld that information had Linda shown any sign she'd be open to meeting with Julie, but I assumed if I started with "Julie wants to meet with you because she's incensed about your lies," that would have eliminated any possibility of them meeting.

Even though I am committed to supporting and not supplanting all of the choices parties make, I screwed up here. I made a strategic choice about what part of the message to convey. I wanted to maximize the chance the parties would talk face to face so I intentionally omitted something Julie had asked me to convey. This sort of urge, which I succumbed to here, is one reason carrying messages is problematic—the temptation to spin the message is strong.

Linda remained clear that she preferred not to talk directly to Julie. When I shared this news with Julie, she was surprised. Julie had assumed *she* was the one preventing the face-to-face meeting. It's hard to know the exact impact on Julie of Linda's refusal to meet with her. I was hoping it led to some awareness for Julie that she herself had not been so easy to deal with, but more likely, Julie continued to believe Linda was mistreating and disrespecting her. After a moment, she nodded her head and raised her eyebrows as if to say, "Do you see how she disrespects me?"

Next I facilitated another conversation between the two lawyers. Linda's lawyer said Linda would be willing to give Julie $10,000 in addition to Julie's half of the proceeds of the sale of the house. Julie's lawyer explained that Julie would need to pay significant capital gains taxes (approximately $40,000) on the proceeds from the house, which Linda would not have to pay. It seemed this was Julie's lawyer's way of making a counteroffer without committing to it. (I suspected he really could not commit to such an offer as Julie was still hoping for much more.)

At this point I offered my own suggestion.

I hesitate to do this sort of thing because I want to honor the parties' and their lawyers' choices about what's being suggested—I assume they might be aware of whatever possibility I'm about to suggest but they're choosing not to raise it for reasons of their own, which I intend to respect. However, in this case I thought it might not hurt for me to offer a suggestion.

I said, "I know Linda wants to accept the offer of $1.1 million, and I know Julie believes the house is worth more and also that she should receive more than half. What if Julie guarantees Linda she'll receive half of $1.1 million ($550,000) and Julie takes the risk or reward of holding out for more? That way Linda gets everything she wants and Julie has the opportunity to get the higher amount she believes she can get as well as the higher proportion she believes she deserves?" Julie's lawyer responded as if he thought that was an interesting idea he hadn't thought of. While his reaction may have been genuine, it's also likely he was motivated to flatter me in an attempt to cause me to lean to his side. Linda's lawyer seemed to dismiss the suggestion as raising too many questions such as, exactly when would Linda receive the $550,000? And what would happen if the market took a significant turn for the worse or the house burned down before being sold? And how would Linda feel if Julie DID wind up receiving a lot more than 50%?

My decision to deviate from my approach and offer this suggestion did not seem to do any harm, as far as I could tell, but it also didn't seem to help. It's possible my real motivation for making the suggestion was impatience I was feeling toward Julie—I wanted to call her bluff and reveal to her that her resistance really wasn't about wanting a certain amount of money; it was about something no settlement could achieve. It was about grief, loss, and existential truths that required acceptance more than negotiation. If that was my motivation—to cause Julie to see she was being unreasonable—it was doomed to fail. I was having the sort of directive impulse we transformative mediators aspire to let go. At the same time, Linda's sense that there was no reason Julie should be entitled to anything more than 50% of the proceeds of the house kept *her* from wanting to offer much more than she already had. My suggestion, though clever in an interest-based, problem-solving way, did nothing to ease Linda and Julie's struggle.

In this case, in an attempt to get the parties to an agreement, Dan deviated from his goal of purely supporting the parties' choices and instead suggested a solution. He succumbed to the temptation to nudge. His idea seemed to him like such an elegant, win-win solution because it responded to what they had shared about their priorities and what mattered to them (in problem-solving parlance, their *interests*). Dan seemed to have lost faith in the parties' ability to make good choices for themselves. It's also possible Dan, feeling particularly sympathetic to Linda, was trying to protect her from the ongoing distress of the situation.

> *You must trust and believe in people or life becomes impossible.*
> —Anton Chekhov

There's no way of knowing the impact of his deviation, but it certainly didn't lead directly to a settlement. There's reason to suspect it may have diminished the quality of the conversation as it was a distraction from the parties' and the lawyers' own process of gaining clarity. Among the possibilities that Dan's suggestion precluded was that one of the parties or one of the lawyers themselves could have come up with the same or a similar idea. In that case, the idea could have been experienced as empowering for the person who came up with it, and it could have appeared to the other party as a meaningful gesture toward them as it would have taken their needs into consideration. Since Dan suggested it, it could not have brought with it that level of meaning in terms of empowerment and recognition.

Dan's earlier joke about starting off on the right foot also revealed his impatience with Julie and may have caused her to continue to feel embattled. Dan hoped the joke would serve as a subtle suggestion to Julie that being gentler with Linda might be more conducive to an agreement. Even at this point, Dan deviated from his commitment to being supportive, and that deviation was likely counterproductive both in terms of transformation and in terms of a possible settlement.

Transformative mediators consider it a core part of their practice to monitor themselves for directive impulses—to notice them when they arise, make sure not to act on those impulses, and return to supporting the participants' process. When Dan made the suggestion and when he made the joke, he was not supporting party self-determination but was indulging his urge to nudge the parties toward agreement.

We mentioned in Chapter 4 that Maryland studies showed a correlation between supportive mediator moves and positive outcomes. Conversely, those studies also show a correlation between directive mediator strategies and negative outcomes. A mediator's use of directing strategies (e.g., introducing and enforcing guidelines or explaining one participant to the others) in child access mediations was associated with a greater likelihood the participants would return to court within 12 months to file an adversarial motion.[8] Similarly, in district court mediations, the more the mediator offered opinions, advocated for their solutions, and provided legal analysis, the less likely the participants were to report, at the three- to six-month follow-up, that the outcome was working, that they were satisfied with the outcome, that they would recommend alternative dispute resolution (e.g., mediation as opposed to litigation), and that they had changed their approach to conflict.[9] This research suggests, among other things, that even if a mediator sees settlement as the main goal, nudging parties in that direction, either directly or indirectly, may have significant drawbacks.

Parties who want to focus on the bottom line, talk about their interests, or listen to each other nonjudgmentally should be supported in doing so, but if the mediator hopes to support the parties in making their own choices, the mediator must support *whatever* they may choose to do. These choices could include insisting on being heard, giving ultimatums, storming out of the mediation, threatening to storm out, accommodating the other party, apologizing, offering a hug, or recommitting to litigation. Each choice must have some value to the parties, since they made it—at the very least, the choice is an assertion of their autonomy. And that, itself, matters.

> To go wrong in one's own way is better than to go right in someone else's.
> —Fyodor Dostoevsky

Supporting parties' choices means doing nothing to inhibit the parties' freedom, and it means actively supporting the parties in making their own choices. This nondirective support seems to increase the parties' sense of agency so they can make better (clearer, more thoughtful, and less likely to be regretted) choices. From this perspective, party self-determination is not merely a characteristic of mediation but is, instead, its essence.

In the following story, yet again, Dan succumbed to a directive impulse. He imagined he could, with a leading question, help one party understand the other's perspective.

FORCING RECOGNITION

In a separate meeting with a wife before her divorce mediation, she told me why she felt she should receive spousal support. She said she had spent the past 15 years moving from city to city because of her husband's career. Because of the moves, she had not been able to establish her own career and was now earning half as much as her husband. While it was true that she had been earning as much as he was earning in the year before the divorce, she had hated that job and the city where it was located. Since she was no longer tied to that city, she had moved back to her hometown, where the best job she could get paid much less than her previous job.

Next I met separately with the husband. He said he was willing to give his wife half of his pension because it had accumulated during their marriage. However, he did not think paying her alimony was appropriate because though she currently earned less than he did, that was her choice—she chose to take a more fulfilling but lower-paying job. He thought he should not have to pay for that choice.

I asked him what he thought her rationale might be for believing alimony was appropriate. I was hoping he would say something that acknowledged the reasoning the wife shared in her private conversation with me. I imagined hearing, "Well, for her, the fact that we moved often for my career meant she never had a chance to get established, and the well-paying job she left was one she genuinely hated and in a city she never wanted to live in, so I can see the truth that our marriage did hurt her earning potential." Instead I heard, "My wife has a victimy personality—nothing is ever her fault, and everyone is always doing her wrong."

Dan probably should have known the husband wouldn't articulate the wife's perspective as she had but would instead reveal he was having trouble empathizing with her. Dan's question to the husband had been his attempt to force recognition despite his belief that any shift the husband made toward empathizing with the wife would likely only result from his own increased agency. Dan's greatest contribution would have been to help the husband feel free and supported in making his own choices rather than nudging him toward taking his wife's perspective.

When meeting separately with a party, it is especially tempting to ask them what they think the other party is thinking. The mediator hopes this question will lead to some empathy and help the party respond more effectively based on a deeper understanding of the absent party. However, if the party is not already thinking that way, this question tends to have the opposite effect, pulling them more deeply into the vicious circle and reducing their empathy for the other person. On the other hand, if the party initiates that question ("I wonder what she's thinking?"), it reveals the party may be open to changing their perspective on the other party. Supporting that thought process by reflecting it, as opposed to directing the party a certain way, is more likely to lead to meaningful shifts.

In "Charles's Estate" and "Forcing Recognition," Dan started out philosophically committed to being present to the parties' experiences and abstaining from doubting, questioning, or nudging. But in both cases he pushed ahead of the parties in a direction he thought would be helpful. That is, he nudged. He also deviated from his commitment to impartiality. In the case of "Charles's Estate," Dan's impatience with Julie, along with his desire to protect Linda, affected his actions. In "Manipulating the System," Dan's skepticism of Joe's perspective influenced his summary of the parties' conversation. In all three cases, Dan's deviation from following and supporting the parties did not seem to be helpful. While this book focuses on the value of party self-determination, one additional justification for following the parties, as opposed to leading them, is that leading them often favors one party more than the other.

Here's one more instance where Dan got directive. At least this time he had to be pushed.

APOLOGIZE TO YOUR WIFE

Henry and Lois had been separated for six months when I met with them, and they were experiencing extreme conflict. They had been financially devastated when their investments had disappeared in a Ponzi scheme, and they blamed each other. Henry also believed Lois had committed tax fraud, and he threatened to report her to the IRS unless she complied with his demands around the financial aspects of their divorce. Their mutual hostility was apparent.

My best efforts at attending to them, reflecting them accurately, and summarizing their conversation with the hope of adding clarity around the decisions they had to make did not seem to lead to any shifts. Although I only met with them once, at the end of the session both apparently felt their conflict was too intense for me to be of any further help.

Henry called to tell me they would not be working with me further but he wondered if I had any advice for him. I told him it wasn't my place to give advice but I understood he had hard decisions to make. He complained that he had paid for my time but I hadn't "added any value." Ouch. I felt criticized and defensive. Nonetheless, I held it together (for the moment anyway). I acknowledged that he felt I hadn't been particularly helpful but repeated that it wasn't my place to form opinions about what he should do. He continued to express frustration that I wouldn't give him advice, and I grew more frustrated. I decided maybe this was an exceptional situation—a client is asking for advice, and honoring his choice means giving it to him. So I said, "Okay, how about assuring your wife you're not going to turn her in to the IRS and apologizing for threatening her with that?"

He responded with "What?! Are you kidding me?!"

Instead of reflecting Henry's surprise and clear rejection of this suggestion, I doubled down at this point. "You said you wanted my advice. You said you don't want to have to litigate with your wife. How about apologizing for threatening her, and starting from there?"

The conversation ended shortly after. Later I received a call from Henry's lawyer, who told me she was surprised to hear that I had suggested Henry apologize to his wife. This lawyer had taken my mediation course and knew I didn't believe in giving advice. Embarrassed, and bearing in mind my confidentiality obligation to Henry, I did my best to assure Henry's lawyer that I do normally follow a strict no-advice policy but that I sometimes screw up.

Dan had a few factors working against him on the phone call with Henry. He had the disappointing sense he hadn't been helpful to this couple. He also had the fear they might wind up in one of those worst-case-scenario situations with a very expensive, long-lasting litigation. And finally, he felt criticized by the client who was suggesting he wasn't providing enough value. Succumbing to the pressure to give advice, particularly while feeling frustrated with the client (which may have come out in the delivery), was Dan's main mistake. The content of his advice though, was typical mediator-think: "You two should be nicer to each other" or "Why can't you just get along?" If only it were so simple. While apologizing can increase goodwill between people, especially when it is (or is perceived to be) genuine, the *advice* to apologize carries with it an implicit judgment of wrong-doing because it suggests there is something to apologize *for*, and this tends to raise defensiveness.

Notice Dan justified his choice by convincing himself he was honoring party self-determination! "The party has determined they want advice from me, so I'm honoring his self-determination by giving it to him." Mediators often use this sort of reasoning. "They hired me because they want to settle the case—I'm honoring their self-determination by pushing them toward settlement." Clearly we see party self-determination differently.

Not only was Dan's advice unhelpful, but he, in particular, should have known better—he once mediated a case where one spouse's threat to turn in the other spouse to the IRS actually led to their *reconciliation*![10] Exactly where a conversation, or relationship, will go is often unpredictable. Supporting parties' choices requires the mediator to let go of preferring a certain outcome and also to let go of the belief that the mediator knows how to get there.

> *Those who have knowledge, don't predict. Those who predict, don't have knowledge.*
>
> —Lao Tzu

The above stories demonstrate a range of ways mediators may attempt to nudge parties toward settlement. Mediators' attempts are sometimes direct (e.g., by suggesting a specific solution) and sometimes indirect (e.g., by recommending a party apologize or by reframing a party's statements to promote a different perspective). Mediators also often either nudge toward or explicitly recommend specific steps of the mediation process.

We understand (and sometimes succumb to) the temptation to nudge the parties closer together in an effort to protect them from what we see as their own stubborn natures. However, in this chapter we hoped to show these efforts are not only unnecessary, they actually interfere with the parties' ability to gain a sense of agency so they can solve their own problems (and often reach an agreement). In the next chapter, we will explore another way we may be tempted to steer parties toward a better place: trying to protect them from each other.

Notes

1. American Arbitration Association, American Bar Association, and Association for Conflict Resolution, "Model Standards of Conduct for Mediators," September 2005: Preamble, https://www.adr.org/sites/default/files/document_repository/AAA%20Mediators%20Model%20Standards%20of%20Conduct%2010.14.2010.pdf.

2. Tara West, "Settlements Are Like Sex," https://www.transformativemediation.org/news/12714992.

3. See Tamara Relis, "Consequences of Power," *Harvard Negotiation Law Review* 12 (2007): 490.

4. Judy Saul, spoken commentary in the Institute for the Study of Conflict Transformation, "What the Parents Know: A Transformative Mediation MP4" (2011), 1:14.

5. See our discussion of psychological reactance in Chapter 1.

6. Richard M. Ryan and Edward L. Deci, *Self-Determination Theory: Basic Psychology Needs in Motivation, Development and Wellness* (New York: Guilford Press, 2017), 302.

7. Robert A. Baruch Bush, "Taking Self-Determination Seriously: The Centrality of Empowerment in Transformative Mediation," in *Transformative Mediation:*

A Sourcebook, eds., Joseph P. Folger, Robert A. Baruch Bush, and Dorothy J. Della Noce (Association for Conflict Resolution, Institute for the Study of Conflict Transformation, 2010), 66.

8. Maryland Judiciary, "What Works in Child Access Mediation: Effectiveness of Various Mediation Strategies on Short- and Long-Term Outcomes," 2016a, https://mdcourts.gov/sites/default/files/import/courtoperations/pdfs/familyfullreport.pdf.

9. Maryland Judiciary, "What Works in District Court Day of Trial Mediation: Effectiveness of Various Mediation Strategies on Short- and Long-Term Outcomes," 2016b, https://mdcourts.gov/sites/default/files/import/courtoperations/pdfs/districtcourt strategiesfullreport.pdf.

10. See Dan Simon, "Transformative Mediation for Divorce: Rising Above the Law and the Settlement." in *Transformative Mediation: A Sourcebook*, eds., Joseph P. Folger, Robert A. Baruch Bush, and Dorothy J. Della Noce (Association for Conflict Resolution and Institute for the Study of Conflict Transformation, 2010), 253.

CHAPTER 7

Self-Determination
Is the Best Protection

No one saves us but ourselves, no one can and no one may.
—Poor translation of a quote from Buddha, but we like it.

None of us wants to facilitate abuse, trauma, coercion, or unfairness. If we limit our interventions to mirrors and lights, parties might harm each other. It is natural to wonder whether there are times when we should switch to other tools that might protect one party from the other. In this chapter we explore what we can do about the risks parties face from each other. We conclude the following: (1) The mediator is in no position to be either party's advocate or defender; (2) Forceful efforts by a mediator to protect parties are likely to do more harm than good; (3) When a party is at risk of being victimized, their self-determination is especially important; and (4) Our mirrors and lights are likely to reduce abuse, trauma, coercion, and unfairness. Therefore we believe, with a few exceptions, that extreme commitment to party self-determination leads to the best process and outcomes even in situations where a party is at risk. At the same time, the best way to act on that extreme commitment is unclear in some circumstances.

Domestic Violence

Domestic violence can make mediation risky for victims. One risk is that victims will be too afraid or intimidated to advocate for themselves sufficiently within the mediation. Another serious concern is that interactions within the mediation could trigger or intensify the abuse.

One of our fellow transformative mediators, Martina Cirbusová, handled a parenting case in which one party threatened the other with domestic violence within the mediation. Here is her story.

YOU'RE GONNA PAY FOR THIS

Adam and Anna, a former couple with one child, sought mediation to discuss parenting time and childcare arrangements. I started with a separate orientation meeting with each of them. Those meetings revealed no history of domestic violence. As always, I emphasized to both parties that mediation was entirely voluntary and they were free to end mediation at any time. Next I met with both of them for a three-hour session.

During the mediation, Adam and Anna discussed childcare arrangements as well as the history of their relationship, including their mutual sense of having been hurt by each other. From the start, Adam appeared more confident and determined than Anna and more able to express his demands clearly. Anna, on the other hand, was tearful and uncertain. She expressed doubt about what she was saying, and she several times simply gave in to Adam's demands, saying "Tell me what you want and I'll do it." I reflected her statements, including her uncertainty. I also checked in occasionally to see if she was still finding the mediation process acceptable. Anna insisted that the mediation continue, claiming that everything was fine, even though she was crying throughout the session.

During a break, I checked in privately with Anna while Adam was outside having a cigarette. I asked whether she was okay and if she needed anything. She said, in a matter-of-fact way, that she was okay and that she wanted to continue with the mediation. After the break, the interaction began to escalate. Several times after Anna made a request of Adam, she said something like "I'm going to pay for this, aren't I? This is going to turn out badly for me, isn't it?" She was clearly concerned that Adam would hurt her for what she was saying. I reflected what both she and Adam said and checked whether she wanted to continue mediating, take a break, meet privately with me, or adjust the process in any other way. Anna insisted on continuing the mediation. No matter how I checked in, Anna requested to proceed.

The situation became even more intense when Adam began to answer her questions positively. He confirmed that she was right that she would pay for it. Anna continued to insist that the mediation go ahead. She seemed very clear and strong in her responses to me, confirming that she wanted to continue the session. Although I felt uncomfortable with the situation, I honored her choice to continue.

The session continued for the scheduled three hours, with the threat of violence remaining in the air. When it was over, Adam left first. Anna stayed behind and thanked me, saying that this was the only way she could have a conversation with Adam and that it was the longest conversation they'd had in years.

I have never, before or since, participated in a mediation where the threat of violence was so explicit. I was not sure whether I wanted to continue to honor Anna's clear preference to mediate. I decided, though, that she was the best judge of what she needed, and she was clear with me—both privately and in front of Adam—that she wanted to go ahead. If I had decided to end the mediation, that would have been my choice and not hers. While I, as the mediator, have the right to end a session for my own reasons, in this case I decided it was important for me to honor Anna's choices and her possible empowerment. I do not know what happened next for this couple, but I am hopeful that this meeting helped them shift their interaction in a constructive direction.

Martina's choice to honor Anna's desire to continue mediating is consistent with a commitment to party self-determination above all else. Martina believed that the greatest hope for Anna's well-being arose from Anna's empowerment, whereas overruling Anna's decision to keep mediating would contribute to Anna's sense of weakness. Anna's private statement to Martina about her desire to continue confirmed for Martina that Anna genuinely wanted to continue. As is often the case, we do not know how things played out for Adam and Anna after the mediation.

As we see it, mediators cannot protect the parties. We do not have enough information to know what risks they are facing or what their options are. Determining where the balance of power lies, how each party should be behaving (e.g., standing up for themselves or treating the other with more consideration), and the identity of the *true* victim would be an impossible task. In the midst of the vicious circle, often both parties act like perpetrators and feel like victims.

Even when the dynamic seems fairly clear such as in "You're Gonna Pay For This," we mediators cannot truly protect the parties. Parties may be at risk of violence, coercion, or manipulation by the other party before, during, or after the mediation. While we clearly cannot control what happens outside the session, attempting to control what happens *within* the session has the potential to backfire. As we have discussed elsewhere, people value their autonomy, and efforts to guide or nudge are sometimes met with resistance. Even if a party complies with our nudges or overt direction in the mediation session, the aftermath could include retaliation against the party we were trying to protect.[1]

As "You're Gonna Pay For This" suggests, even if careful domestic violence screening has been conducted, we have no way of knowing with certainty whether abusive dynamics exist. This case was unusual in that the dynamics became very apparent during the mediation. We hope and believe that our focused attention on the parties, and support for their choices, allows them to shift their interaction in a way that includes victims standing up for themselves, abusers becoming less defensive and more compassionate, and interactions becoming more constructive. Essentially, we believe that this form of support offers the best chance for people to escape the vicious circle of conflict, but we can never guarantee it.

We cannot promise fairness, safety, or even a change in the dynamics in our process. We believe the approach that is most likely to enhance safety and fairness is one that promotes party agency. Still, if we see something that leads us to feel we cannot fully support one or both of the parties, we have the option to withdraw. And if we detect an immediate risk of violence, we can do our best to minimize that risk in the moment. We may meet privately with the potential victim to help them plan for their safety; we may walk them to their car to help them avoid a confrontation with the other party; or we may arrange for the victim to leave the site early without the other party's knowledge.

Beyond those rare moments when we might take action to prevent violence, and beyond our standard process that tends to decrease the likelihood of those moments occurring, we use a few additional practices to reduce the chances that people will be victimized during the process. When possible, we meet with each party separately before mediation begins. In that separate meeting, we create as much space as possible for each party to express any concerns or fears they have about mediation and the surrounding circumstances. We support each party in clarifying their concerns and in deciding how to handle them. We are especially careful to support them in exploring and acting on inclinations not to participate in mediation. If they feel mediation is not a good choice for them for any reason, we support them in pursuing other options. We also abstain from reassuring anyone that we can provide safety or fairness though we support each party in discussing how they want to address these concerns for themselves.

My job isn't to fix or rescue or to save. It's to accompany, see people, listen to them. —Greg Boyle

If mediation proceeds, we continue to pay close attention and respond when we see any indication that a party feels threatened. At the same time, we pay attention when a party expresses anger. We support them as well with our lights and mirrors. When parties are being acknowledged and seen, they tend to de-escalate. When they can see themselves clearly, they are far less likely to act aggressively. After 23 years of practicing mediation and doing as little as possible to contain or suppress conflict, Dan has never seen violence erupt in a mediation.

The possible presence of domestic violence reminds us of the importance of parties receiving support for their process choices and especially whether to start and whether to continue mediation. Since the parties are in the best position to assess the risks and consider the benefits, their perspectives on whether and how to proceed should be prioritized. While such risks provide a vivid example of why we should never nudge parties toward participation, the same rationale requires that we do not nudge parties *away* from participation—mediation may be their best opportunity to change the dynamics. Real, moment-to-moment party self-determination, whatever choice a party makes, is essential.

Other Power Imbalances

The dramatic example of domestic violence raises questions similar to those raised by other cases of potential unfairness. Most mediators care about fairness and justice. We hope our process does not perpetuate unfairness in any particular case or in society as a whole. Fortunately, our process has the potential to meaningfully change the dynamics between those with relatively more power and those with less. While advocacy for the less powerful party or group, or the intervention of a court or other venue, may help shift power dynamics, we mediators can help in a different way. By remaining committed to supporting each party's choices, we can support parties in accessing their own strength, clarity, and compassion.

A party may also be at risk due to their own cognitive or emotional limitations, which the other party knowingly or unknowingly uses to their advantage. We cannot claim to be able to diagnose such things nor do we believe these limitations necessarily prevent meaningful participation. As we see it, all mediation participants will differ in important respects. One will be more eloquent, another will be more logical, and another may have more emotional intelligence. These differences will likely persist after the mediation as well.

Regardless of their unique gifts and limitations, each person has the potential to become clearer, calmer, and more confident and to develop a greater sense of agency during the process. Each party also has the potential to become more responsive and see the other more clearly as a human being, which is particularly important when one party seems to be taking advantage of or dominating the other. That greater responsiveness can help in both directions. The stronger or more dominant party becoming more responsive is often the best path to a better outcome for the weaker party. The weaker party, becoming clearer and more realistic about the stronger party, can make better choices about how to deal with that power imbalance.

We don't even know how strong we are until we are forced to bring that hidden strength forward. —Isabel Allende

Self-Determination at Risk

Many mediators attempt to protect victims of domestic violence with the goal of preventing harm and promoting fairness. They may similarly attempt to balance the power between parties in less severe cases where the playing field seems uneven. In those cases, they are trying to protect one party from an unfair deal or perhaps to protect the process itself from being misused. Mediators justify using directive interventions, potentially interfering with the self-determination of one or both parties, to promote these other values.

Further, mediators may use directive intervention in an effort to protect one party's self-determination in relation to the other party. They may say that less powerful parties have no meaningful self-determination in relation to a party who is wielding power over them. Ellen Waldman, author of

Mediation Ethics: Cases and Commentaries, uses analogies to suggest that significant power imbalances might mean the weaker party has no meaningful self-determination in the situation. As Waldman puts it,

> If you agree to hand me all of your money because I put a gun to your head, can we say that you acted autonomously? If you haven't eaten in four days and agree to sign over the deed to your house in exchange for the rosemary-infused walnut baguette I'm waving under your nose, is that decision a true expression of free will?[2]

Waldman's examples demonstrate the roles that coercion and duress can sometimes play in motivating agreements. Being threatened with a gun or experiencing extreme hunger would certainly influence a person's choices. But does this mean that the parties' decisions are not self-determined?

As we discussed in Chapter 1, self-determination is both more and less than the absence of constraints. It is the experience of making one's own decision, with strength and clarity, for one's own reasons. The choice to take an unfair deal or succumb to coercion might be the most sound choice a person could make in a given situation. Both the choice to stand up and the choice to stand down can be made from a place of strength or weakness.

Waldman's examples are extreme but the same principles apply to real situations we see in mediation. If a richer party with a team of lawyers on retainer is threatening a poorer party who cannot afford to litigate, is the poorer party's choice to take the meager offer necessarily lacking self-determination?

One common situation where power imbalance could be a problem is when mediation is between a supervisor and an employee. We might assume that the employee, being dependent on their supervisor for their job, would not find mediation with the supervisor to be fair. Yet the greatest body of research on mediation, based on over 12,000 mediations conducted as part of the U.S. Postal Service REDRESS program, suggests that employees in the study did not feel mistreated. The mediators of these cases were expected to use the transformative model—the approach we have been describing as mirrors and lights—which entails a commitment to supporting all parties' choices rather than attempting to identify and protect the weaker party. In this environment, 96% of the employees (along with 97% of the supervisors) said that the mediator conducted the process fairly.[3] In all, 87% of employees (and 92% of supervisors) found the process to be fair overall; and 91% of employees (92% of supervisors) were satisfied with the process. While the employee's positive experience of mediation does not prove that the process was fair to them, at least it appears that the employees generally believed that the process was fair.

The process we have been describing as supportive rather than protective may ironically provide the best protection mediation can offer the parties from each other. It at least protects the parties from the good intentions of a mediator who believes they know which party needs protection and how to ensure it. But what if we find ourselves feeling a strong urge to protect one party from the other despite our commitment to supporting each party in the process?

Although we are not trying to identify victims or assess fairness when we mediate (and are actively trying to avoid making such judgments), we cannot help but form opinions about these things from time to time. While we do not accept our opinions as fact, if we have a strong sense that a situation is abusive or unfair, we may decide that we can no longer support one or both parties.

In this next story, despite his efforts to refrain from judging the situation or the parties, Dan believed one of the parties was being victimized. Although that party chose to continue to participate in mediation, Dan resorted to the standard move mediators sometimes make in these situations. He bailed. He decided that he had no way to protect one party from the other but that he could choose not to participate in what he perceived as victimization, and he could refrain from providing a venue for it to continue. In fact he felt it was *necessary* for him to withdraw because of the risk that his own behavior could harm the parties.

WEEKLY PHONE CALL

Bernice called to ask whether I could work with her and her coparent Erik over the phone. I said that was fine with me if Erik agreed. Erik called the next day to ask whether he was required to participate. He explained that their divorce decree said they must first attempt mediation of any "new parenting disagreement that arises." While Erik agreed they certainly had conflict around the parenting of five-year-old Daisy, he felt Bernice was creating new issues for the purpose of forcing him into mediation. He said Bernice knew it was hard for him to pay his half of the mediation fee, and she was trying to abuse him financially as well as verbally.

I told him that I could not answer the question of whether he was legally required to mediate as to do so would be to provide legal advice. I also told him that in terms of my involvement, mediation was voluntary, and if he did not want to do it for any reason, that would settle the issue for me, meaning I would not mediate. He replied, "Yeah, but our divorce decree says we have to." I said I would be happy to mediate if he wanted me to.

I hoped to support Erik's self-determination in this conversation. Regardless of the answer to the legal question (such answers are, of course, often debatable), he did have a choice about whether he participated in mediation at this time, with me as the mediator. While he may have been complying with what he saw as a requirement, his decision to comply was a choice.

In the first session, Bernice had harsh, angry words for Erik. Typical exchanges went like this.

Bernice: You are such a piece of shit!
Erik: I know you feel that way about me, but can we just talk about the plan
for Daisy?

Bernice: Oh, aren't you just such a caring father!

Erik: Can we please talk about Daisy?

Bernice: Yeah, we can talk about Daisy! We can talk about what a poor example of a father you are to her because you're such a piece of shit!

I reflected both parties frequently. While doing so often helps harsh-talking parties hear themselves and choose to speak differently, no such luck in this case.

The pattern of Bernice calling Erik a piece of shit, an idiot, a wimp, or an asshole while Erik pleaded to make a plan for Daisy persisted throughout the first one-hour phone session and two subsequent sessions. When I checked in with them in each session about how the conversation was going and whether they wanted to approach it differently, Erik generally responded with "I'd really like to talk about the plan for next weekend." Bernice generally responded by insulting Erik.

Occasionally I summarized their very different ideas about what to talk about. "As for what you want to talk about today, Bernice, for you Erik has a really messed up personality and bad character. You've said he's a 'piece of shit' and a 'wimp,' and so that's what you'd like to focus on. Erik, you've said that you know that Bernice feels that way and so you were hoping in this meeting to talk about the plan for next weekend. Is there part of that that you two would like to talk about now? Or something else?" At the end of the first and second sessions, when I asked whether they wanted to talk again next week, Bernice said, "Yes!" and Erik said, "I guess we have to."

By the end of the third session, I decided I was no longer interested in working with them. When I told them I needed to withdraw "because I didn't believe I was being helpful," they asked for a referral to another mediator, and I suggested a lower-cost mediator I knew.

My choice to withdraw was a deviation from pure support for party self-determination. Even though Erik felt coerced by a combination of the court order and by Bernice, I would usually assume that my job was to support him in deciding what he wanted to do about that while also supporting Bernice in her efforts. If he (and Bernice) chose to participate in another mediation session with me, that would ordinarily settle it. My main reason for deviating this time was that I was finding it too difficult to remain supportive of Bernice. I no longer believed it was helpful to anyone for me to try to do so. I could no longer be impartial so I could no longer mediate. Perhaps another mediator would be able to do so and Bernice and Erik would find their way to a better place.

I later heard from their new mediator that she had two sessions with the couple, experienced a similar dynamic, and chose to withdraw.

It is hard to see "Weekly Phone Call" as a success. Maybe doing no harm is the most we can say for what Dan did. And maybe doing no harm is a big deal in a situation like this. If Dan had acted on an impulse to contain or redirect Bernice's harsh words, it is possible, and we believe likely, that

Bernice's hostility toward Erik would have only increased. Instead, having her complaints about Erik heard may have *decreased* the amount of hostility Bernice directed toward Erik outside mediation.

At the same time, it is entirely possible that Dan was wrong about who the victim was. Perhaps Erik was abusive toward Bernice outside the session. If so, we are especially glad that Dan did not communicate any negative judgment of Bernice despite how unpleasant he found her behavior.

Given our commitment to being supportive of all parties, we try not to judge them. When that fails and we find ourselves thinking of one party as the problem, we try to return our focus to remaining supportive. We believe that both parties are better off if the one who seems more difficult also receives nondirective support. After all, being difficult is common in the vicious circle, and support for parties' choices can help them change the pattern. Nonetheless, there may come a time when we no longer feel we can offer nonjudgmental support to all parties. In these situations, we withdraw. In the next story, Dan attempted to mediate a conversation between spouses who were discussing separation. In this case, it only took Dan one session to realize he needed to withdraw. As with "Weekly Phone Call," Dan knew he could not protect one party from the other so he decided to protect the parties from him.

THE GUY I HATED

It was a typical divorce in many ways. Susan made the decision but Gary was still coming to terms with it. In the first session, Gary expressed frustration with Susan for disrupting his and the children's lives but he said he was ready to talk about the plan for the kids and the house. The conversation about the house went like this.

Susan: Do you want to stay in the house?
Gary: Do you?
Susan: I'm asking you, do you want to?
Gary: Oh, you're asking me? Why don't you just say what you want?
Susan: Okay, I'd like to keep the house.
Gary: No way!
Susan: Oh, do you want it?
Gary: Maybe.
Susan: That's fine.
Gary: Oh is it?

The pattern continued as they discussed other topics as well. Susan would express flexibility and Gary would oppose whatever Susan said, preventing any conclusions from being reached. I came to view him as a chronic victim who wanted only to make this process unpleasant for Susan. If I had been in a different frame of mind, maybe I could have summarized the situation in a way that would have been helpful such as "So as for the house, Susan, you're saying you're open to either you or Gary taking it. And Gary, you're feeling like Susan put you in this situation by wanting a divorce, and you don't see either outcome as desirable."

Or maybe I could have seen Gary and Susan as experiencing the common phenomenon where one spouse has yet to accept that divorce is happening and some time and patience allows them to get to a better place. But I couldn't stand Gary so after a one-hour session with them, I told them I did not think I could help. When Gary asked why, I said it just did not seem like I was helping them make any progress.

In both of the previous stories, Dan experienced strong negative feelings toward one of the parties. In "Weekly Phone Call," Dan thought Bernice was using mediation purely to abuse Erik and that Erik was submitting because he believed a judge would continue to require him to attend. Dan did not want to be used as a weapon by one party intending to harm another but he also did not want his efforts at protecting the victim to harm the apparent abuser. In either case, Dan's participation would be contributing to the vicious circle of conflict.

But maybe Dan was wrong about what was happening. Perhaps Erik was a willing participant who was using this ritual to work through his own guilt about ways he had treated Bernice in the past or perhaps he was using these calls to gather evidence to use against Bernice. Or perhaps this is just how the couple communicated with each other, and they were both comfortable with it.

In our view, it did not matter what was actually happening because we, as mediators, can never know with certainty what is happening behind the scenes or even in front of us. All we can know, with anything resembling certainty, is what *we* are experiencing and what *we* are willing to do. In "Weekly Phone Call," Dan had developed such a dislike of Bernice that he did not trust himself to be supportive of her.

In "The Guy I Hated," the situation was a bit less complicated. Dan was not actually concerned that he was being used as a weapon or that either party was there involuntarily. He realized he just did not like Gary and that his feelings were strong enough to interfere with his ability to be supportive.

In addition to the risk of being mistreated by each other, parties risk being mistreated by the mediator. That mistreatment is most likely to occur when we believe we are protecting one party from the other. If we believe one party needs our protection, we likely believe the other party needs to be opposed. We naturally have biases. Those biases can do the greatest damage when we mistake them for objectivity.

We have no way of knowing whether Bernice was officially an abuser or if Gary was a certifiable jerk. If we are having a negative reaction to a party, it could be because the party is behaving in an abusive manner (to us or to the other party) or it could be because they remind us of someone from our past. It could be a little bit of both or something else entirely. Further, hostility is to be expected in conflict, but at some point we might decide it's too much. At these times, we get to exercise our own self-determination by choosing not to mediate. As we see it, this choice is required, ethically. Once we've concluded that we cannot help or may even be harming the parties, we are obliged to withdraw.

On the other hand, if we *are* able to remain supportive of both parties, regardless of the balance of power, we might contribute to greater fairness and justice in the specific case and beyond. Bush and Folger have examined this possibility.[4] They argue that mediation may very well perpetuate injustice especially if conducted in a settlement-focused way. Such mediation runs the risk of pushing weaker parties into unfair agreements. And if the mediator attempts to balance the power, this may increase the risk of backlash toward the weaker party from the stronger party. On the other hand, Bush and Folger argue that mediation that considers the relational nature of conflict and supports party self-determination above all else has the potential to promote strength in the weaker party, compassion in the stronger party, and real, lasting changes in the power dynamics.

We share Bush and Folger's belief that transformative (or mirrors-and-lights) mediation can promote justice. More constructive interaction allows parties to live up to their capacity to act with both greater agency and greater consideration of each other. Also, when the mediator supports either party's choice *not* to mediate and to pursue another approach they believe will more effectively protect them, those avenues remain open and the risk that mediation will do harm is minimized.

This approach also reduces the risk of harm arising from cultural differences between participants and the mediator. The mediator may have culturally ingrained and unconscious habits, preferences, or biases that clash with the culture of other participants. While there is no foolproof way of preventing a mediator's biases from affecting the parties, applying mirrors and lights to the parties and their situation leaves less room for the mediator's biases to affect the participants. Instead, this approach prioritizes the participants' words, perspectives, and values.

There are many challenges facing mediators who seek to practice with this level of commitment to party self-determination. In the next chapter, we will describe some of the challenges we've faced when trying to apply this approach to some complicated procedural questions.

Notes

1. See Robert A. Baruch Bush and Joseph P. Folger, "Mediation and Social Justice: Risks and Opportunities," *Ohio State Journal on Dispute Resolution* 27 (2012): 31.

2. Ellen Waldman, *Mediation Ethics: Cases and Commentaries* (San Francisco: Jossey-Bass, 2011), 4.

3. Lisa B. Bingham, "Mediation at Work: Transforming Workplace Conflict at the United States Postal Service," IBM Center for the Business of Government: Human Capital Management Series (October 2003): 34, https://www.maxwell.syr.edu/uploadedFiles/parcc/cmc/Mediation%20at%20Work-%20Bingham%20IBM.pdf.

4. Bush and Folger, "Mediation and Social Justice."

CHAPTER 8

Self-Determination and Procedural Complications

Idealism increases in direct proportion to one's distance from the problem.
—John Galsworthy

Supporting party self-determination is more of an attitude than a list of rules. A list of rules could not respond to the infinite variety of situations we face. An attitude allows us to look for and highlight opportunities for the parties to make choices regardless of the situation. A variety of constraints (e.g., laws, mediation program policies, the other party) limit our clients' choices. In this chapter we will describe how we've accepted the *constraints* while maintaining the *attitude*.

For example, it can be particularly challenging to support party choice when

- the parties disagree with each other about aspects of the process such as who participates, whether you meet privately with any parties, or whether you share your notes after a mediation;
- the parties expect you to intervene in ways you think might harm them such as to carry messages between them, offer information or advice, or make sure they stay in line;
- you have taken on the role of drafting the parties' agreement, and issues regarding word choice or enforceability arise;
- you (or an organization you are working with) would like the parties to sign a specific agreement to mediate;
- you are working with a large group;
- you are mediating online and encountering the challenges inherent in these technologies; or
- you are mediating a divorce (or other family case) where expectations around drafting documents, providing information, providing protection (for children and victims of domestic violence) are in the air.

When parties express opposite preferences about an aspect of the process, they may expect us to tell them the right way to do it or at least the way we do it. But these situations are perfect opportunities for us to remain supportive of their choices as they sort it out.

Who Participates?

It is tempting for the mediator to control who participates in a mediation. In commercial cases, we might want to make sure the person with settlement authority is present or available. In family cases, we may prefer that the parties' lawyers are present or we may prefer they stay away. We may have our own views about whether parents' new partners should participate.

While some of us may make those decisions for the parties or at least attempt to steer them toward a particular decision, it is also possible to leave these choices entirely to the parties. When the parties are not on the same page about who should be there, it gets complicated. Challenging though it might be, maintaining a focus on party self-determination can still guide us.

For example, in Chapter 2 we told the story of Phil and Steve ("You Can Have the Couch), who showed up at Dan's office with different views about whether Phil's lawyer should participate. Shortly after they arrived, Steve, Phil, and Phil's lawyer were debating the issue while standing in the waiting room, unable to begin mediation until a decision was made about who would be present.

Dan, expressing no preference himself, told the parties they could start the session either with or without the lawyer in the room and then make a different decision later. By doing so, Dan ventured away from merely reflecting, summarizing, or checking in but he kept the focus on party choice by reminding the parties that the decision was in their hands—not just now but throughout the process. Knowing they were not locked into the decision seemed to lessen its significance, allowing one party to make a relatively low-stakes accommodation to the other.

And in "Spite Fence," discussed in Chapter 4, Angie Smith had the insight that she and Myrna might have a better conversation if Angie's husband, Dave, were not in the room. This idea occurred to Angie (apparently in consultation with Dave) while taking a break from the mediation session so she mentioned it to Dan, who said, "That works for me if it works for everyone else." After Dave made it clear that he was on board, Dan walked Angie down the hall to the room where Myrna and her friends were waiting, poked his head in the door, and asked Myrna if it would be okay if Angie made a suggestion. Myrna said "Sure," and then Angie stepped into the doorway and made her suggestion, which Myrna thought was a good one.

So in that case, Dan needed to open the door (figuratively and literally) to help the two people have a conversation about who would be present for the next conversation. Yet he gave the parties as much room to make their own choices as the situation allowed. He put every choice, and as much of the communication as possible, in the parties' hands. After getting Myrna's permission for Angie to make a proposal, he gave Angie the space to make her own choices about how she would communicate that proposal.

Finally in "No Non-Compete," Chapter 4, the parties started in separate rooms by their own choosing. Dan told them he would not pass messages between the rooms but that they had options for communicating with each other including via the telephone or through their lawyers. Dan told them that one exception he would make to his policy against passing messages would be to share messages about what conditions would allow them to meet in the same room. In the end, Bruce, Dave, and their lawyer proposed one condition for meeting with John and his lawyer: that John's CFO not be present. John and his lawyer agreed, and they all met together without the CFO.

Although the specifics of each situation were different, in every case Dan put as much choice in the hands of the parties as the situation would allow. He focused on helping the parties make their own choices about who would participate in the conversation. That process of making choices likely increased their sense of agency, putting them in the best position to continue to make choices throughout the process.

Separate Meetings?

Many mediators have their own policy when it comes to meeting separately with the parties (also called "caucusing" by those who wish to make it sound fancy). For instance, some have a policy of never meeting separately, others always meet separately, and others occasionally meet separately when the mediator has a question or concern they'd rather raise with a party privately. As with most decisions, we believe that the decision of separate meetings can and should be in the hands of the parties. If the parties agree, it's relatively simple. However, as with the decision of who participates, things get more complicated when the parties disagree about whether either of them should meet alone with the mediator.

We presented Prisha and Kumar in Chapter 3 and showed how they were able to resolve their differences about information sharing without directive input from Dan. Dan found himself in a tougher spot with them when discussing the question of separate meetings.

MEETING PRIVATELY WITH PRISHA

In my first meeting with Prisha and Kumar, Kumar did most of the talking. I checked in with Prisha periodically to remind her that she was welcome to speak up if she wanted, and she said that she wanted to hear what Kumar had to say. At the end of the meeting, Prisha said simply that she didn't like how Kumar was approaching things and she had to think about what her next steps would be.

In emails that the three of us exchanged next, we discussed whether we would all meet together or whether I would meet with each of them separately. I also told them that either of them was welcome to call me for a brief conversation. I would keep the content of that conversation private but I would let the other party know that we talked. In one email, Prisha said, "I'd like to request for the next mediation if we can be in separate rooms."

Kumar responded,

> Hey Prisha, I'm somewhat surprised by this. If we do this separately we then will likely need to spend more hours and time with Dan. Up to this point it has felt like we have communicated with goodwill so I'd like to ask what's behind this request and come up with a solution that makes us both feel comfortable. If we are to work with Dan independently we will of course need to both pay for his time together at least as part of this settlement. Before doing that we will need to exchange proposals and hammer out an agreement I guess with him meeting each of us separately. Dan can you let me know what you advise? Can we potentially set up a conference call if email doesn't help resolve these questions?

In my email response, here's what I said about meeting separately.

> I'm happy to do it any way you are both okay with. My spending alternating hours with each of you is one option. Some people find that these meetings give them a chance to think more clearly without a sense of pressure from the other person. Those meetings might result in written proposals, or responses to proposals. On the other hand, meeting together helps relieve anxiety about what might be happening in the private conversation that you're not part of. A hybrid approach would be to plan a meeting (of 2 or 3 hours) where we are all present, but we alternate talking separately and together, as needed. Your choice.

Kumar responded,

> I'm open to us meeting in separate rooms but at the same time with you, Dan, to support Prisha's request. I am willing to go along with this change. But I don't want us to set up fully separate meetings at separate times with you. Since this change was Prisha's idea, she should pay for the extra time that will be required.

Prisha replied,

> Regarding Dan's payment. I am open to spending as much time as reasonably needed to feel comfortable with how this is settled. We can split the costs in the settlement. Kumar, since you are the higher earner here and have expressed wanting to be financially generous, it would be great if you could shoulder this until we have the settlement reached. If your resources don't allow for it, we can discuss alternatives.

Over the course of the next month, they copied me on emails in which they requested and shared financial information with each other, with neither of them attempting to schedule another meeting with me. Their email conversation seemed to be going well, and it appeared they managed their divorce without the need for further help.

Dan was careful not to express a preference for or against separate meetings. He would proceed in any way they were willing. Each party thus had veto power: If one party insisted on doing things a certain way, the other party would have the option of declining to continue with mediation.

If the parties are on different pages about this issue, we treat it as any other issue and support their conversation about it. If the conversation is happening in person or over the phone, we can use our regular practices of reflecting, summarizing, and reminding the parties that these are their choices. When the conversation is occurring over email, our options are limited (we discuss that situation below).

If the mediation ends because the parties cannot agree on how to move forward, the mediator still needs to decide whether to meet separately with the party who requested the meeting after the mediation concludes. We have decided that we will meet with the person who would like to meet, just once, even over the other's objection. As we see it, while either party has the right to terminate the mediation, they do not have the right to terminate our communication with the other party. This separate conversation allows the mediator to help a party decide what to do about safety concerns, for instance, while preserving mediation as a process where both parties have choice. We would limit such meetings to one conversation to avoid any conflict associated with treating one party as an individual client (e.g., for conflict coaching) after having interacted with both parties together.

For some parties, there is no disagreement about meeting separately. In fact, they would like to remain in separate rooms throughout the process as is commonly practiced in many litigation-connected mediations (as discussed in Chapter 6). While we believe we can be most helpful to parties who are willing to communicate with each other directly, we can still support the parties in making choices around how they communicate from separate rooms. In the next section, we explain why we, as mediators, attempt to support party self-determination by generally refraining from carrying messages between the parties.

Carrying Messages

If we see our role as managing or containing the conflict for the purposes of reaching a certain result, carrying messages makes sense. This way we can adjust the messages in a way that we believe will maximize the likelihood that the parties will move toward the result we're seeking. However, if we see our role as, above all else, supporting parties' choices about what and how they communicate, we hesitate to carry messages because we fear we will alter the message and undermine parties' choices about precise content and tone. We generally only carry messages to the extent the message is very simple or pertains to what will be required in order to allow for a face-to-face conversation.

While we believe we are capable of reporting reasonably accurately what a party says (as we try to do in reflections and summaries), we prefer to do so with the speaker present so they can correct, modify, or enhance our restatement of what they communicated. Unlike messages carried by a mediator, direct communication between parties allows the opportunity to contemplate what one is saying while receiving immediate feedback from the other party if only from their facial expressions. It's easy to say to a mediator, "Tell them to go screw themselves!" without considering the reaction of the other party. When face-to-face with the other party, different choices emerge, often including more nuanced messages.

When a party hears a message directly from the other party, there is an opportunity to gather important information about just how serious the other party is, and the changing nature of everyone's perspectives becomes more apparent. A message the mediator carries, on the other hand, may appear static. There is little opportunity to correct negative assumptions. From separate rooms, assumptions on both sides can harden and intensify, leading to greater polarization. In person, more information can be exchanged, leading to improved understanding and, potentially, connection.

> The single biggest problem in communication is the illusion that it has taken place. —George Bernard Shaw

As we see it, carrying messages can drain the life from a communication, freezing it where it was when the party first said it or inadvertently infusing it with the mediator's agenda. Most importantly, carrying messages removes party choice from important aspects of both sending and receiving messages, putting those choices in the hands of the mediator. Although the decision not to carry messages is one that we both feel strongly about, in Chapter 9 you will learn about a time that Dan veered from this commitment and passed messages between the parties and their lawyers to facilitate their negotiation.

Drafting Post-Session Notes and Agreements

Just as we can get too involved in spoken communication between the parties, we can make similar mistakes in writing. When we participate in drafting agreements, we can undermine parties' choices. We can prevent parties from making important choices about precisely what they are committing to and just how firm those commitments are. Here, Dan screwed up in an even more basic way, and one party's response to his mistake demonstrated the weight parties can place on an informal memorandum simply because it was drafted by the mediator.

WHERE'S MY COPY?

Matthew and Amara's relationship had always been volatile and now, after three years of marriage, it was time to divorce. Each of them felt incredibly betrayed by the other, and each of them felt their own behavior had been the inevitable reaction to the other's. Also, Matthew's music career had taken off over the past few years, leading to an income of $500,000 in the most recent year, and he hoped it would continue to increase. Amara, on the other hand, had left a career with a financial services firm in London to be with Matthew in Los Angeles. Now she had no idea how she would support herself. For his part, Matthew was concerned about the possibility of Amara damaging his career by revealing and likely exaggerating potentially scandalous aspects of his past. Matthew wanted a non-disclosure agreement (NDA) while Amara was clear that she wanted to be able to speak freely about the relationship. The intensity of their conflict was part of what led to my dilemma.

At the end of our third meeting, they had at least superficially come to an agreement though Matthew clearly still felt that Amara was taking advantage of his need to keep his divorce out of the tabloids. At their request, I took dictation from them and typed up a one-page memorandum that listed the terms of their agreement. I made it clear to them that I did not see this document as legally binding[1] and that my understanding about the process was simply that they still needed to complete more detailed, formal, legal documentation. This was something that had been understood from the beginning as they were working with lawyers and not expecting me to draft any of the legal paperwork for their divorce.

I would need to walk down two long hallways to access the printer from the conference room in my office suite, but first I needed to email the document to a staff member and ask her to print it. She was busy, and after I mistakenly requested that she print a copy, I decided it was not worth bothering her again, or making the clients wait, to get additional copies.

When I returned to the conference room, I placed the document on the table where all could view it. Matthew and Amara read over the document and both said they still agreed to the terms, though the hostility between them, and Mathew's misgivings, remained. After some discussion, Matthew stood up and said to Amara, "You are completely taking advantage of me. You know what you're doing is wrong. I hope you feel good about yourself!"

Amara said, "Oh please. You've been mistreating me for years. I've been traumatized by you. And you're still doing much better than I am financially." Matthew took the document and left. I stayed and listened to Amara for a few minutes. She had more to say about how difficult Matthew had become and about how much she had given up to be with him. Then she thanked me and left.

Within a half hour, Matthew called to tell me that he no longer agreed to those terms. I listened, reflected, and said I would be happy to help him and Amara continue the conversation. He said, "Okay, possibly."

Later that day, I received an email from Amara asking me to send her a copy of the document that Matthew had taken. I assumed that her intention was to try to hold Matthew to the terms of that agreement.

I am clear with clients that I will not participate in any adversarial processes that arise after mediation. Amara's request, given my awareness that Matthew no longer agreed to the terms of the document, felt like a request for ammunition against Matthew. I believed that my providing a copy at this point would be, in a sense, advocating for Amara against Matthew, which would not have been consistent with my role.

On the other hand, Matthew, and not Amara, had already received a copy of the document so didn't my current position favor Matthew against Amara? After some back and forth with Amara, I realized that the right thing to do would be to send her a copy and put her in the position she would have been in had I followed through with providing the notes everyone had agreed that I would provide.

This specific situation is undoubtedly a rare one and could have been avoided by ensuring that both parties were given hard copies of the document during the session. However, this case illustrates the importance that clients sometimes attach to a document drafted by a mediator even when the mediator specifically refers to the document as nonbinding.

Drafting the parties' decisions, in any form, puts the mediator in a position where they are doing more than simply supporting a conversation. When doing so, the following issues may arise that could have implications for party self-determination.

- The clients are unaware or misinformed about the potential legal implications of the document drafted by the mediator (e.g., Is it legally binding?).
- Decisions made by the parties seem to lack clarity in the way that they are worded or raise additional questions (e.g., By what date must a sum be paid?).
- The mediator suspects that decisions of the parties will not be honored by the court.
- The parties differ in their apparent enthusiasm for a given decision (e.g., one party is pushing for it and the other is merely acquiescing).
- The mediator suspects that decisions made by the parties are misinformed or questionably informed.

Given these issues, does the mediator have additional duties to the parties when serving as a drafter or a drafting attorney? How can the mediator best support party self-determination while serving in this dual role?

Court-annexed mediations often include a standard procedure where the mediator or the parties fill out a court-provided form detailing any agreement that is reached. Putting the agreement into writing without putting words in the parties' mouths can be a challenge. Here's how a conversation might go after the parties have agreed on the basic outline of their agreement.

Mediator: So, it sounds like you've made some decisions here, and, as you know, we've got this form to fill out for the court. Would you like me to write down your decisions or would one of you like to do it?
Carol (Tenant): You can do it.
Susan (Landlord): Yeah, why don't you do it?

Mediator: Okay, how would you like me to word it? Do either of you want to give me the language you'd like to put in here?

Susan: Once Carol moves out, I'll refund half of the rent for this month.

Mediator: Okay, so "After Carol moves out of the apartment?"

Susan: Yes.

Mediator: "Susan will refund . . ." Would you like to specify what the amount would be?

Carol: My rent is $1,200 a month so half would be $600.

Mediator: Okay, so "After Carol moves out of the apartment, Susan will refund half of a month's rent ($600) to Carol." Did you want to specify dates for any of these things? When Carol leaves or when and how the refund is made? I believe you mentioned some time frames earlier when you were discussing this.

Susan: Oh, right. Carol needs to be completely out—all of her stuff and everything—by the 15th.

Mediator: Okay, so "Carol will move all of her belongings out of the apartment . . ." Is that by the end of the day of the 15th or before the 15th?

Susan: Before the 15th.

Carol: Yes, I'll have everything out of there by the end of the day on the 14th. And she needs to give me the refund as soon as I give her the key.

Susan: Yes, when you hand me the key, I'll hand you the check, assuming you're out before the 15th.

Mediator: Okay, so "Carol will move all of her belongings out of the apartment before the 15th. When she returns the key to Susan, Susan will refund a check for half of a month's rent ($600) to Carol." Does that sound right to both of you?

[Both nod.]

Mediator: Is there anything else you want in there, or does this cover it?

Carol: This is fine with me.

Susan: Yeah, this is good enough.

This example illustrates how complicated drafting decisions can be even for something very simple. The mediator was attempting to draft only what the parties were saying but realized that there was ambiguity and so asked questions for clarification. The mediator also went a bit further by asking whether the agreement should include dates, referencing an earlier point in the conversation when the parties had discussed a timeline.

There was no discussion of an inspection of the apartment for damages and no provision for what would happen if Carol did not move out before the 15th. Should the mediator have asked these questions? Or should it be left to the parties to raise such issues? Did the mediator undermine the parties' autonomy by nudging the parties toward the specifics about the amount and about timing? Or did the mediator's failure to seek *more* detail mean the parties received *fewer* opportunities to make decisions?

While we prefer that the mediator do as little nudging as possible, we acknowledge that in this situation, the mediator likely did no harm and may actually have offered a valuable service to the parties. Asking additional questions about topics that had not been raised by the parties (e.g., regarding an inspection), however, would go beyond removing ambiguity and would likely serve one party more than the other.

Agreements to Mediate and Confidentiality Clauses

Confidentiality rules in mediation are intended to motivate parties to speak freely. But parties and their lawyers are too smart for that. They know that opposing parties can find a way to use new information against them if they are motivated to do so. In fact, one of lawyers' greatest fears about face-to-face mediation sessions is that their client will say something that can be used against them. If the dynamic remains adversarial and litigious, there are many ways to use information gained in mediation against the other party.

Disclosure also provides positive opportunities. Mediation can give parties the chance to transform the litigious dynamic into a non-adversarial one by making good choices about what to disclose. Shifts toward greater understanding often occur when one side reveals new information to the other. Sometimes, sharing something that could be used against one at trial increases trust in a way that makes a trial far less likely.

We saw examples of disclosure leading to trust in stories we shared earlier in the book. For example, when Ben confirmed that Lisa had been more productive than the person who received the promotion, Lisa felt better about Ben, perhaps reducing the risk that she would sue the company but also perhaps giving her greater ammunition if she did sue. When John ("No Non-Compete" in Chapter 3) disclosed that he was planning to retire, he ran the risk that it would suggest to Bruce that John wasn't likely to pursue his lawsuit to great lengths; instead, it opened up the possibility for Bruce to buy John's company—an ideal result for both of them. Parties make these choices about what, how, and when to disclose without much regard for any technical rules that purport to make the information inadmissible or confidential.

Despite the limitations, most mediators ask their clients to sign agreements to mediate, which include confidentiality provisions. When a sponsoring agency or mediation center provides these forms, the mediator may have no choice in the matter—the mediator must let the parties know that this is a requirement of the organization. The mediator can still support party choice when doing so by presenting the form as something that needs to be signed *if* the parties wish to continue without assuming that the parties will want to sign it. The mediator can say, "Are you comfortable signing this?" This reminds the parties that they still have choices to make. They can choose not to sign the form even if it means that the mediation cannot go forward.

Dan's Take on Agreements to Mediate

Unlike any other mediator I've ever heard of, I do not use an agreement to mediate unless the parties request it or lawyers are present (lawyers always expect an agreement to mediate). I prefer not to start the process with a legal document. Such a document suggests that the parties and I should start from a place of covering our asses as opposed to opening our hearts. For me, the law provides sufficient protection of the inadmissibility of mediation communication. And I say to parties at the start of mediation, "I won't share with anyone anything that happens here," setting clear expectations, without the need for it to be in writing.

Another common provision in agreements to mediate—that the mediator cannot and will not provide legal advice—seems silly to me. The important thing is that in the process I simply do not provide legal advice not that everyone signed a document that said I wouldn't. Despite all of this, when there are lawyers present, I use an agreement to mediate because it's too hard to explain all of this to them.

Tara's Take on Agreements to Mediate

Like most mediators, I use an agreement to mediate (at least when the mediation involves a potential legal matter such as divorce). One provision I like to include is a default clause about confidentiality. It states,

> The mediator agrees not to disclose any communications, documents, or work notes made in mediation. The parties agree not to call the mediator as a witness to a litigation that is in any way related to the content of this mediation. The parties also agree not to seek production of any records, documents, or notes relating to the content of this mediation either from the mediator or from any expert or consultant retained for this mediation. The parties also agree not to disclose any communications, documents, or work notes made in mediation to a court as part of a litigation that is in any way related to the content of this mediation.

I include this provision in my agreement to mediate because I believe it is likely that the parties will enter mediation with certain assumptions about confidentiality, which may or may not be accurate. Many people have heard that mediation is confidential but are not necessarily clear about what that means. For instance, they may be confusing the word "confidential" with "inadmissible" (i.e., not admissible in court).

Rather than offering legal information, which would undoubtedly be incomplete given all of the exceptions to rules about admissibility, I limit the clause to what we are all promising each other. I am promising the parties that I will not disclose their communications to anyone. I am asking the parties to promise me that they will not try to drag me or my materials into court. And I am asking them to promise each other that they will not use mediation-related communications in court.

Given my commitment to supporting party self-determination, I would normally not ask parties to promise *anything* to each other. However, I look at their promise not to disclose information to a court as a default provision that the parties are welcome to modify. I believe having a few things in writing the parties can read before the mediation (I email it before we meet) and refer to later increases the chance that everyone is on the same page. It also may give the parties a sense of security (perhaps misplaced, as Dan mentioned) regarding whether or not the other party will attempt to use mediation-related documents or communications in court. Because mediation-related communications are inadmissible as a general rule (with some exceptions), suggesting that the parties agree to follow that rule, in my view, is not actually interfering with their self-determination. While there is no guarantee that people will not violate these agreements, I believe that starting with this provision and including it in writing has enough advantages to win the day.

I also include a clause that clarifies that decisions parties make in mediation may have legal consequences and that I am not able to offer legal guidance or protection. This is another area where I believe people may carry assumptions into the process. So including a statement about this in the agreement to mediate not only protects me (if they later accuse me of failing to provide information they wished they'd had) but also gives the parties a heads-up about my role in a way that they may be more likely to absorb and take seriously simply because it is in writing.

So even though I use a form that I drafted (okay, largely borrowed from forms I've seen others use), I do my best to support party choice even when using that form. I do this by sending it to the parties ahead of time so that they can think about it, suggest changes if they wish, and make an informed decision about working with me.

Requests We Cannot Honor

Parties sometimes ask, or expect, us to do things that we believe would be unhelpful and potentially harmful. These requests often are for us to take over in some way. As discussed in Chapter 2, when parties are caught in the vicious circle of conflict, they often feel out of control. In that state, they may imagine that the only solution is for the mediator to take control. One way parties try to relinquish control is to request that the mediator pass messages between the parties. They either do not trust themselves or the other party to behave constructively.

Sometimes parties who are meeting face to face imagine that the mediator can, and should, keep them in line. As we see it, attempting to shape, guide, or otherwise control the parties' behavior conflicts with our ability to support each party's choices in each moment.

Dan recently had this conversation with a party when preparing for a mediation with her teenage daughter.

Client: The reason I want you to be there when we have this conversation is that I want you to make sure I don't lose my temper.

Dan: I see, you're hoping I can help you not lose it.

Client: Yes, please just tell me to shut up if I'm out of line.

Dan: Well, so here are my ideas for how to help with that. First of all, you'll get to take a break at any moment if you want to, or talk privately to me. Also, if it helps to look at me, instead of the other party, you can always do that. Beyond that, I don't have a way of preventing you from losing it or from saying anything. It doesn't work when I try to stop someone in the heat of the moment. And I want you to be free to make your own choices throughout the conversation. Right now, I gather you're clear that you basically want to stay in control of yourself.

Client: That's right. And I get it that you can't really stop me. Just having you there will help.

{It so happened that this client remained incredibly calm in the mediation with her daughter.}

Occasionally, as this client did, parties will ask the mediator in advance to keep them in line or correct them if they say something that is not fair. Sometimes their hope is that the mediator will also correct the other party as it often seems clear to one party that the other party is the one who is out of line. But when in the heat of the moment a mediator tries to keep someone in line, the party is far less open to that feedback. So when parties ask in advance for that sort of intervention, it may be helpful for the mediator to be clear that they cannot provide it but they assume the party will be able to make their own more constructive choices at those moments, which may include choosing to take a break.

Another situation in which providing some guidance in the moment may feel necessary is when working with a large group.

Mediating with Large Groups

Thirty members of the Eastern Minnesota Juggling Association gathered on Zoom to process an intense conflict that had erupted among the board of directors. Some board members were present as well as regular members who had strong feelings about the situation. Dan opened the conversation as follows.

It looks like it's time to start, folks. So I will, as informally and concisely as possible, welcome you all and share a couple thoughts about how I hope to contribute to the conversation tonight. And basically, my main hope is that I stay out of the way of it because you all are the members of the organization and the ones who are intended to benefit from this conversation.

A couple things that I want to make sure you're aware of—we have hit the Record button on this thing so a video and audio recording is being made. You will all have access to that recording—I'll send an email out to you all once it's done processing after our meeting but you should know that a recording is being made. That was one of the parameters I was given for this meeting, that it should be recorded.

{The board had asked me to record the meeting when they invited me to facilitate. While it would be ideal for all the participants to be involved in that decision, I decided that since the participants were informed before-hand, and considering the challenges around getting consent from all partic-ipants, I would simply honor the board's request.}

The other parameters that I am attached to myself are that everyone present have the maximum opportunity to say what you want to say, to ask what you want to ask, and that you feel as free as possible to do whatever helps you feel that this meeting is as meaningful, productive, constructive, whatever you want it to be. And so my job is to pay attention to you all and see what I can do to maximize that for everybody present.

And the one minor challenge that sometimes happens with a conversa-tion involving this many people is that sometimes there are more people than one who want to say something at any particular time. That's one thing that I will try and help facilitate and try to do my part to help you figure out whose turn it is. My intention is always to make sure that everybody gets the turns they want.

I suppose if it turns out that a lot of people have a lot to say, it might help at some point for me to have my little timer here and put some gentle limit on the amount of time that anybody speaks. If somebody has kind of a monologue that they want to deliver, off the top of my head I'm thinking that I would start my timer and after two minutes, whoever had that longer thing to say, I'd ask them to stop and give somebody else a turn. I'm also going to pay attention to people who indicate to me that they'd like to speak next, and I assume it's helpful for me to keep track of what order people either raised their hand or used that zoom function to raise their hand. So that's all. I'll try to direct traffic and make sure everyone gets to say what they want to say.

And beyond that, I'm not aware of a need to prescribe any particular format for this meeting. Does anybody have any thoughts or concerns or questions about what we're going to do here?. . . I'm not seeing any, so where would you all like to start?

During the meeting Dan occasionally reflected and summarized, and sev-eral times he said something like, "Okay, Chuck, and then Stacy" based on the order in which people had raised their hands. For this group, that was sufficient structure. Around half of the people present spoke at some point during the meeting. Later Dan twice asked if anyone who hadn't spoken would like to say something, which led to one more person speaking up.

Another option at the start of a larger meeting is to facilitate a conver-sation with the group about structure. Should we go around the room and give everyone a chance to say something? Or should we keep it unstructured as long as that seems to be working? The art of creating a large group con-versation that is characterized by the participants making as many choices as possible involves remaining attentive to everyone in the group, acknowledging participants when they communicate the desire to be acknowledged, and offering opportunities to speak up for those who have been reticent. As with smaller groups, it's about supporting them, not controlling them.

Electronic Communications

Mediating online, either via Zoom or through email, the telephone, or other avenues of communication, can bring with it some unique challenges and opportunities. While there is much to be said about this now prevalent way of mediating, we'll focus here on some unique challenges to supporting party self-determination.

Mediations that occur over Zoom or the phone, rather than in person, leave a lot of what is happening out of sight. Among the many challenges this can create (e.g., difficulties reading body language), it also creates more opportunities for others to listen in. Someone could be listening to the call in real time, just out of sight, unbeknownst to others on the call. Or a participant could be recording the session with their phone with the intention of sharing it with others or to simply have it in their back pocket *just in case* (this can also occur in person but is probably easier when the phone can be sitting by the computer's speakers out of sight of the mediator and other party).

Some mediators have policies about this type of thing and may confirm with everyone, at the beginning of the mediation, that no one else is in the room and that the session is not being recorded. They may also include a section about this in their agreement to mediate form. As with confidentiality, having such a commitment in writing is no guarantee that the party will abide by it. Unlike confidentiality, however, there is unlikely to be a misunderstanding about this or different good-faith assumptions coming in.

If a party has decided to record the session or invite someone else to listen in without discussing it with the other party and the mediator, there is a reason for that. It may or may not be a good reason, but the party likely believes it is necessary for their protection. It is unlikely that the mediator's policy will change that belief. Therefore, to support party choice around this issue, we leave it to the parties to raise if they would like. We then support their conversation and decisions about how to handle the issue as we would any other issue.

Whether mediating face to face or online, mediators sometimes communicate with parties by email or text between sessions. This can happen because a party has a question or concern they want to raise with the mediator before the next session or it can happen because the parties want the mediator to witness (and perhaps weigh in on) communications they are having with each other.

If we try to participate in substantive conversations with clients via email, we run the risk of doing more harm than good. When messages are not sent and received in real time, there is a lot of room for miscommunication because misunderstandings cannot be as quickly discovered and corrected as they can in a live conversation. Although we have engaged in some substantive discussions using email in the past (as you read about in some of these stories), we no longer do this. Instead, we now support the parties' choice to say whatever they want to say using email while letting them know not to expect a substantive response from us. As we see it, the mediator is not in a position to help the parties understand each other better via email or text. Nonetheless, it is still possible to support the parties' choices if they wish to email us directly or to copy us on messages to the other party.

When the situation arises, we have decided to let the parties know they are welcome to email us and to share whatever they want to share but that we believe we can only help in a real-time conversation. We will then offer them such a conversation (individually or with the other party, and over the phone, via Zoom, or in person). As we see it, we are supporting the party's choice to email us (or copy us on emails) but we are not agreeing to do anything we believe will be at best unhelpful or will at worst reduce the quality of the communication, potentially escalating the conflict.

Providing Information

The Model Standards define self-determination as "the act of coming to a voluntary, uncoerced decision in which each party makes free and *informed* [italics added] choices as to process and outcome."[2] This definition raises the question of how much and what kind of information is needed, who should provide the information, when they should provide it, and who is in the best position to make those determinations. The confidentiality of the process itself, as well as the general inadmissibility of aspects of it in future proceedings, seem like the sort of things a mediator might need to provide information about. Since questions about providing substantive information about legal rights and responsibilities, tax codes, child development, and other topics arise so often in divorce mediation, we explore this question in more detail in a separate section focused on divorce below.

Procedural Complications in Divorce and Parenting Mediation

A SIMPLE QUESTION

The email from the divorce mediation client said, "Hi Dan, Would you be able to send us a checklist of things that we can go over with each other before our next meeting?" This apparently simple question raised dilemmas for me.

Should I respond with the bare minimum of topics that I knew the legal paperwork would most likely require (legal custody, physical custody, parenting time, child support, spousal support, division of assets and debts, allocation of dependent exemptions)?

Or should I respond based on the questions I had heard them raise in our first meeting, questions such as When should the kids be allowed to meet the parents' new partners? Do they want appraisals of their real estate or are market analyses sufficient? What amounts will Dad contribute to the kids' educational fund and when? and How are they going to complete the legal paperwork?

Or in an effort to maximize their opportunities to make choices, should I say only, "It's entirely up to you"? This final possibility supports the parties in raising new topics—maybe more important ones than those raised in our first meeting, questions like Should we be getting divorced? or What's the most important thing for us to establish in order to make all of these other questions much easier? or How do we reestablish trust between us so we can be the best coparents?

In this case, here's what I said.

> It's very much your choice what you talk about. In my role, I prefer not to weigh in on which topics you should cover because I want to be totally supportive of each of your choices including if either of you prefers not to talk about something. That being said, I'm sure there are checklists online of topics that divorcing couples can address. I can help you sort this out further when we meet.

Divorce is, at one level, a legal process—it requires the involvement of a judge, who needs specific documentation to finalize the divorce. Divorce clients often seek mediation for the purpose of receiving help with that documentation. They may choose a mediator over separate lawyers to avoid the cost and unpleasantness of an adversarial approach. When mediators take on the role of helping with legal documentation, they are tasked with more than purely supporting each party's choices. They need to ensure that the documentation will be acceptable to a court, which means they need to offer some guidance or direction to the parties.

As we have explained throughout this book, we believe that supporting party self-determination means empowering the parties to make their own decisions and trusting them to raise issues they view as important. Divorce and family mediators who wish to support parties in making their own choices face complications that are unique to this area. Below we have listed some common, family-specific challenges and ways to address them while maximizing party choice. Many of these suggestions overlap with our previous explanations about why we do what we do so the following bullet points will only briefly outline the ways in which family cases may be unique and how we would address them.

- Parties often expect guidance on what issues they need to address. While we like to support whatever conversation the parties choose, including whether to get divorced and how they can improve their coparenting relationship, we understand that parties also want to make sure they are thinking of everything needed to complete a legal divorce. We can respond to this need by providing a checklist but making it clear that it's entirely their choice whether they follow it. Or we can say that it is not our role to recommend what they discuss but that there are many other resources out there for that and that we want to preserve our ability to support each of them around any differences about what they discuss (as Dan did in "A Simple Question"). We might also provide, via our website, links to resources offered by others (e.g., a local court website) or those we have created ourselves (e.g., videos or blog posts answering some frequently asked questions) and point them in that direction. All of these options allow us to provide informational support to the parties without allowing that role to interfere with the role of supporting the parties' conversation.

There are no solutions. There are only trade-offs. —Thomas Sowell

- Parties often expect help completing legal documentation. If a mediator wants to provide this service, we believe that it is important to separate it from the mediation process as much as possible (recognizing it might not be entirely possible). Helping the parties complete the documentation requires some direction. When the parties see the mediator as someone who provides direction, the mediator may become less effective at supporting party agency. Since we see supporting party agency as the mediator's most important role, we are very cautious about providing documentation service.

- The Model Standards of Practice for Family and Divorce Mediation (Family Mediation Standards) ask the mediator to "structure the mediation process so that the participants make decisions based on sufficient information and knowledge."[3] As we see it, the mediator is not in a position to decide what information is sufficient or relevant. We can contribute to the likelihood that parties are satisfied with the amount of information they have by supporting their process of contemplating what information they want, by abstaining from giving them the impression that they can rely on us for necessary information, and by abstaining from pressuring them to come to decisions.

- Parties often want input on the terms of their potential agreement, particularly when they disagree. Alternative dispute resolution in family law includes evaluative and hybrid processes. In our process, we do not assume that it is helpful to give opinions or directions regarding answers to these questions and particularly when our opinion or direction will seem to support one party's position over the other's. The heart of the service we provide is support for the idea that they are in control of these decisions. They are always welcome to seek input of any kind from elsewhere (or to bring advisors into the session with them) and to discuss in mediation the advice they have received.

We assume that the drafters of the Family Mediation Standards care about the interests of children, as do we. As we see it, if we are able to contribute to parents' agency and therefore their constructive interaction with each other, we are providing a service to their children. Information from others, such as child development specialists, about children's needs may be helpful, and we support parents' discussions about how to seek and respond to such information. However, we do not believe that mediators are in the best position to give parents information or advice concerning their children. Even for mediators who are child development specialists, attempting to do so could interfere with supporting the parents' agency surrounding these issues, inadvertently doing a disservice to their children.

The challenges described in this chapter show that even when the mediator cannot fully support the parties' decisions, parties can be given choices. If nothing else, the parties always retain the choice to leave mediation. Acknowledging the parties' right to make that choice, along with any other choices available within the unavoidable parameters, can enhance party agency. As we see it, presenting the parties with the opportunity to make decisions whenever possible about even minute aspects of the process can enhance their sense of agency and help them escape the vicious circle of conflict.

Now that we've explored ways to address some procedural complications that create real-world challenges to supporting party self-determination, we are ready to face up to the realest challenge of all: lawyers.

Notes

1. When Dan writes notes of parties' potential agreements, he explains that he cannot make any representations about whether the document creates a binding contract. In this case, he simplified that point and perhaps erred in the direction of suggesting it was not binding by saying that he did not see it as legally binding.

2. American Arbitration Association, American Bar Association, and Association for Conflict Resolution, "Model Standards of Conduct for Mediators" (2005), Standard 1.A.

3. Symposium on Standards of Practice for Family and Divorce Mediation Convened by the Association of Family and Conciliation Courts. "Model Standards of Practice for Family and Divorce Mediation," (2000), Standard VI, https://www .afccnet.org/Portals/0/PublicDocuments/CEFCP/ModelStandardsOfPracticeForFami lyAndDivorceMediation.pdf.

CHAPTER 9

Self-Determination and Lawyers

People deserve support for their agency, and so do lawyers.

—Dan Simon

While our focus so far has been on the parties and the mediator, it is time to acknowledge the lawyers (mediations sometimes include other advisors, such as union representatives, but we will use the word "lawyers" for simplicity).

Some mediators see lawyers as harmful to mediation. Lawyers can appear to interfere with resolution by making legal threats or taking extreme positions, thus escalating the conflict. Lawyers can also take charge and apparently diminish their client's self-determination. Sometimes mediators find that lawyers prevent the possibility of meaningful communication between the parties. Mediators may even suspect that lawyers' financial interests decrease the quality of the process. For example, a plaintiff's lawyer may be focused solely on a large settlement and uninterested in the apology their client is after while a defendant's attorney may prefer the litigation continues so they can bill more hours.

Other mediators appreciate lawyers' contributions to the process. These mediators find that lawyers exert client control by encouraging their client to behave reasonably. Some mediators are glad the lawyers are there to protect the parties' interests so the mediator can focus on nudging them toward settlement. Some mediators may even see the lawyers as the main participants, with the mediator's role being to assist them in persuading their clients to compromise. And mediators, being human, may even notice that providing lawyers with a process that meets their expectations leads to more referrals to the mediator.

So how *should* we view and treat lawyers in mediation? If we start with the intention to support party choice, it follows that we will support their choice to include (or not) a lawyer in the process as well as their choices about how their lawyer participates. If we took action to change a lawyer's role, we would diminish the party's self-determination on that very issue. Yes, the lawyer may proceed from there to diminish the party's self-determination—there's always that risk—but we choose not to be the ones to directly interfere with the party's self-determination. Or we may believe a party is missing out on a lawyer's good advice by choosing not to include or consult with an attorney. The choice to defer to their lawyer, just like their choice to use other resources, needs to remain the party's choice.

We find that lawyers too benefit from our mirrors and lights. Contrary to the jokes, lawyers have the same sort of capacities, limitations, needs, and desires that other human beings possess. They can also get caught up in the vicious circle of conflict with the opposing party, the opposing lawyer, and even their own client. For all the reasons we believe in supporting the parties in making choices, we also believe in supporting the lawyers.

Of course, supporting the choices of all participants is not always simple. We find it challenging when a lawyer seems to interfere with their client's choices. Similar to the dilemma we face with parties who seem to be deferring too much to each other, we feel torn. We want to protect the client from losing their agency to their lawyer; at the same time, we don't want to undermine the party's agency, or the lawyer's, by trying to control those interactions.

Lawyers Interfering

As mediators, we may find it particularly challenging when we believe that a lawyer, for their own purposes, is preventing mediation from being as productive as it could be. Of course, when our goal is to support party choice, we try not to determine whether what's happening is or is not productive. We realize that conversations may take a number of twists and turns before people work their way through the vicious circle of conflict.

In the following case, Dan noticed the lawyers behaving in ways that seemed destructive but he remained focused on supporting the decision making of all participants, including the lawyers. To make it easier to keep the characters straight, we've used alliteration in naming them. They include Sam, a lumber supplier, and his lawyer, Sarah. On the other side we have Beau, a lumber buyer, and his lawyer, Bradley.

BAD WOOD

Sam, a lumber supplier, sued Beau, who owned a chain of lumber retail stores, for an unpaid bill of $32,000. Beau counterclaimed for $450,000 in damages he said one of his stores suffered when he received bad wood from Sam. In two separate actions, Beau had also sued Sam for damages due to the bad wood that two of his other stores bought from Sam. A judge dismissed Beau's counterclaim (due to Bradley's failure to meet a filing deadline). The two other lawsuits were still pending when the mediation was scheduled.

As soon as I was hired to mediate this case, I suggested to Bradley and Sarah that I start by having separate phone conversations with each side, which would include the lawyer and their client. (When lawyers are not involved, I almost always speak with each client at least once before the joint session—first to ensure they are comfortable working with me and then to give them a chance to prepare for the joint session if they like.) Both lawyers told me that their clients were not available for these calls but they would be present at the mediation.

In a perfect world I would get to talk to the parties themselves in these preliminary phone calls and support them in gaining clarity about how they want to approach the mediation. In the real world I accept that although I always let the lawyer know that I would like to talk to their client, the initial conversations are sometimes only between me and the lawyer. I could insist that I talk to the parties first, and if I did so, the lawyers and parties would likely comply, but compliance is not what I aim for when my goal is to support the self-determination of all participants.

I met with Bradley first, and he explained that in addition to the case for the unpaid bill I had been hired to mediate, there were the two other cases pending between the same two parties described above. I asked whether it might make sense to address those as well during the mediation. He said, "Absolutely not. There are different judges hearing those cases and this is the case that has been ordered to mediation."

I didn't follow his reasoning there but I dropped the subject. I also asked Bradley whether Beau and Sam might want to do business together again in the future, and Bradley said he thought that was highly unlikely given the bad blood between them now. I told Bradley that Beau was welcome to reach out to me before the mediation if he wanted to chat at all. Bradley said he would pass that message on to Beau but I did not hear from Beau before meeting him on the day of the mediation.

My initial conversation with Sarah was brief. She told me she believed that the claim of bad wood was completely bogus and added that it had been dismissed. Her client simply wanted to be paid for the wood he had delivered, for which the price was $32,000. When I asked Sarah if these guys might want to do business with each other again, she said, "No way." We wound down the conversation, and I told Sarah that her client was welcome to give me a call and have a chat before the mediation if he wanted to, and Sarah said, "Thanks, I'll tell him."

Sam called me the next day and we talked for about an hour. He filled me in on his career as a builder, which led to him having a thorough understanding of lumber and the business of it. He had purchased the current company three years earlier, and it had been very successful. He explained that he sold lumber to most of the major retailers and directly to the largest builders. He also explained that he only dealt in high-quality wood so there was no possibility that Beau had somehow received bad wood from him.

Sam also said that until Beau stopped paying and claimed bad wood, he had been a great customer. He had always paid for his lumber immediately on delivery, unlike most customers, who waited 30 days. I told him that the mediation would provide him, Beau, and the lawyers an opportunity to have whatever conversation they wanted to have.

I am always aware that the information I receive before a mediation is likely only the tip of the iceberg so I'm not tempted to think strategically about how to use the information to structure the conversation. Yet when I hear that there are other lawsuits pending between the same parties, I know it's likely that those lawsuits will come up in the conversation. I am also aware that businesses who have worked together in the past might do so in the future regardless of what their lawyers say.

When the five of us gathered in the large conference room of my office, I asked if everyone knew each other and learned that Sam and Beau had never met. They greeted each other politely. Sarah started by briefly saying that Beau owed Sam $32,000, and that was what needed to be addressed.

Bradley responded with an opening statement similar to one he might deliver in court. He emphasized that the purpose of today's mediation was only to address one of the three pending lawsuits as all three cases were being heard by different judges, and this was the case ordered to mediation. He also said that though Beau's counterclaim of $450,000 had been dismissed, Bradley intended to appeal that decision. Sarah spoke up and said, "But it's been dismissed!"

Next came several minutes of back and forth between Bradley and Sarah, which I summarized by saying, "So you have different perspectives on that counterclaim. Sarah, you're saying it's dismissed and you doubt it can be rejuvenated; and Bradley, you're saying that, first of all, you yourself *said* it had been dismissed but you believe there's a good chance that you can appeal that decision successfully."

The bickering between Sarah and Bradley, on one level, seemed beside the point, perhaps an example of lawyers' personalities getting in the way of a negotiation. To me, though, the interaction between the lawyers is always part of the story. And just like the parties, if their agency can be supported, they often find their way to a place where they are interacting more constructively—where they are able both to advocate for their client and to deal more responsively with each other and the parties.

On the topic of whether the other pending lawsuits could be addressed as well, both lawyers agreed that we were here to discuss just one of them. Sam spoke up and said that he would like to resolve all of them if possible. Both lawyers responded that no, this mediation was just for one of them. Bradley said, "I think the mediator will agree with this. The judge ordered us to mediate this case so this is the one we need to address." I said, "Just so we're clear about where I'm coming from, it's up to you all what you talk about. I don't work for the judge. And I'm hearing, Bradley and Sarah, you're saying you need to focus on this one case, and Sam, you said you'd like to discuss all of them."

I did not know what was motivating the lawyers. Maybe they believed it was to each of their client's benefit to take the position that they were only willing to talk about one case—this way, they could make it seem like they were making a concession to the other side if they agreed to talk about the other cases. Or maybe the lawyers wanted to have more work to do if this case settled. At the moment that Sam said he wanted to address all three cases, I was conscious of wanting to support him but also support the lawyers as they said otherwise. I was aware that addressing all of the cases made a lot of sense to me, but I tried not to let that interfere with supporting the conversation the participants were having.

On the issue of whether there had been bad wood, Beau and Sam seemed to come to an understanding despite their lawyers. Sam said, "We did not sell any bad wood. We get all of our product from Johnson or Westbrook. They do not sell bad wood."

Bradley said, "You are the successor in interest to a company that *did* sell bad wood. You are responsible for their liabilities."

Sarah said, "Well, that's debatable."

Beau said, "You did sell bad wood though, Man. This was right after you bought the company! I was dealing with the Jones brothers. You know what happened with them! They were shady."

Sam said, "They're no longer with the company."

Beau said, "I know, but they were selling the good wood somewhere else and pocketing the money. They sold me shitty wood."

Sam looked as if he was realizing this might be true. His former employees may have sold Beau bad wood. "Didn't you pick up this wood at our yard?"

Beau said, "No, they delivered this shit to me."

Sam said, "Huh."

Sarah seemed not to like that her client was conceding that he may have been responsible for bad wood. She spoke up and said, "Okay, guys. Hold on a minute."

Beau went on, "Those guys were doing all kinds of fraudulent stuff. I don't know where they got the crap they sold me, but it wasn't from Johnson or Westbrook."

Sarah said, "Dan, can I meet with my client privately?"

Bradley said, "Hold on a minute, Dan."

Sarah said, "Dan, can you get us back on track?"

I, of course, did not see them as being off track. The parties had just had an exchange that may have entirely cleared up their disconnect about bad wood. But I responded to Sarah by saying, "You'd like something different to be going on here?"

Sarah said, "Yes, I'd like to meet with my client alone. Bradley and Beau need to figure out what they're going to offer us, anyway."

I said, "That's okay with me, how does everyone else feel about that?"

Bradley said, "Yes, that's fine." Beau gave me a thumbs up and Sam nodded.

I led Sarah and Sam to a room down the hall and said I would check on them in a few minutes. I asked Bradley and Beau if they preferred to be alone, or if they would like me to join them. Bradley said, "Actually, Dan, I'd like to talk privately to Beau."

I said, "No problem, I'll check back with you in a few minutes."

A few minutes later, I knocked on the office door where Sarah and Sam were meeting and Sarah said, "Come in." As I sat down with them, Sarah said to Sam, "Man I do not trust that Beau."

Sam: I actually believe him, and I'd like to do business with him again.
Sarah: He seems like a snake to me.
Sam: He was a great customer—he paid in full on every delivery.
Sarah: Not that 32 grand, he didn't.
Sam: Well, he may have had a good reason.
Sarah: Well, I'm not sure he wants to do business with you.
Sam: Maybe not.

Whenever I hear a lawyer suggest to their client they should be more dis-trustful of the opposing party, I cringe inside. Sometimes it appears to serve the lawyer's interest in perpetuating the conflict. I noticed my reaction and returned to my intention to support the conversation. I reflected and sum-marized their conversation just as I would a conversation between opposing parties. After about 10 minutes, I asked if they would be ready to meet with the full group again once the others were ready, and they said, "Sure."

I checked in with Bradley and Beau and learned that they had the fol-lowing offer in mind: Beau would pay $15,000 to settle all of the claims and counterclaims in all three lawsuits. Also, he would start buying his wood from Sam again, which Beau guessed would amount to about $150,000 per month profit for Sam. But before he did that, he wanted to have dinner with Sam. Beau said he liked to know the people he did business with—he wanted to look them in the eye and let them know who he is as a person.

When we all got back together, Bradley shared that offer with Sam and Sarah. Sam asked if Beau would continue to pay at the time of delivery. Beau said, "Yes, I don't like to owe anybody anything. Except I don't like to pay for shitty wood." Sam said, "I can understand that. Okay, that sounds like a deal. And yes, let's have dinner together—I'm buying." Sam said it was a shame that the two of them hadn't met earlier, before all the litigation got out of control.

Sam and Beau were able to overcome their lawyers' idea that they should only talk about one of the lawsuits and Sarah's efforts to prevent them from talking about the bad wood. They were also able to make plans to do business together despite the assumption of both lawyers that this would be out of the question. I believe that supporting both the parties and the lawyers allowed for the best ideas to come to the surface.

Parties Deferring to Lawyers

While Beau and Sam were able to assert themselves over their lawyers' attempts to control the conversation, at other times the representative imposes more control. In the following case, Dan believed one party's repre-sentative was interfering with his client's decision making. Nonetheless, Dan consistently supported the choices of all involved.

THE ANNOYING UNION REP

The union representative, Kevin, annoyed me from the start. I felt he was treating the mediation session like his golden opportunity to prove what a great lawyer he could have been, saying things like "A preponderance of the evidence in this case proves that Jack has been the victim of discrimination in the workplace."

Jack had received a written warning based on an incident involving an argument and physical contact between Jack and his supervisor. Having a clean record prior to this incident for his entire 25 years at the company, Jack felt the letter of warning was unfair. He requested mediation with the hope of removing the letter from his record. The supervisor had also received a written warning because of the incident but did not attend the mediation. Present at the mediation was the manager, Tom, who had issued the written warnings to both Jack and Jack's supervisor, along with Kevin and Jack.

Kevin started the mediation with an opening statement in which he accused Tom of "an intentional and systematic plot to discriminate against Jack and to favor management." Kevin told the story of the incident and of the investigation that followed. He described a series of decisions that Tom had made that suggested bias in favor of management (in this case the supervisor). Jack appeared comfortable with Kevin speaking on his behalf.

I knew that Kevin had been through many of these mediations and I thought he understood that they are not hearings, that there was no point in trying to persuade me of anything, and that the chances were slim of persuading Tom that Tom had committed improper discrimination. I suspected Kevin believed that his argument would intimidate Tom and motivate him to settle the case out of fear of what might happen if Kevin were able to make his case in front of a judge.

I saw Kevin's actions as counterproductive and unhelpful for Jack, but what was I supposed to do? It is my job to support all the decisions of the participants. So every now and then I gently held up a mirror to Jack, pointing out that he had been quiet thus far. I also shone a light on his opportunity to make choices by checking in to confirm that he was comfortable with Kevin doing all the talking. And as hard as it was for me, I reflected just about everything Kevin said: "So you're saying that, contrary to what Tom is saying, this has been an intentional scheme to discriminate against Jack from the moment of the alleged incident."

"That is correct," Kevin said. "And furthermore, the evidence proves this."

One of the areas of disagreement was what exactly happened when there was physical contact between Jack and the supervisor. The supervisor had reported that Jack puffed his chest out and intentionally bumped into him. But Jack said that he was trying to walk away from the supervisor at the time and that the supervisor was following very closely behind him. When Jack turned around, it was the supervisor who bumped into Jack.

Kevin said, "It is absolutely impossible, since Jack was walking away, and then he turned around, that he could have been the one to initiate the contact. The evidence proves this."

Tom said, "What are you talking about? It's entirely possible that Jack turned around and then intentionally chest-bumped the supervisor. And why did Jack turn around anyway if he was really trying to walk away from the supervisor?"

"Don't be ridiculous," said Kevin. "Surely you understand that when someone is following closely behind you, it's natural to turn around and try to see what's happening."

Not that it's my place to evaluate this sort of thing, but it sounded to me like Jack and the supervisor probably were describing honestly what they thought happened. Each of them thought the other one had initiated the contact—and in reality, it took both of them for the contact to happen. Tom made this same point, to which Kevin replied, "Nonsense. The evidence shows that the supervisor initiated the contact."

"What evidence?" asked the manager.

"Jack's description of what occurred," said Kevin.

"But the supervisor described it differently," said Tom.

"But what the supervisor said is not true," said Kevin.

"How do you know that?" asked Tom.

"Because the evidence shows otherwise," said Kevin.

Thank goodness for what we call in transformative mediation training *Core Activity #2: Monitor and Maintain Intention When Intervening*.[1] This reminder to remain supportive and nonjudgmental helps the mediator cope with the inevitable directive urges that arise during a mediation session. Acting on these urges tends to undermine party agency. In this case, my urges included getting Kevin to shut up, getting Jack to speak up, and getting Kevin to realize how ridiculous he was being, to name a few. Core Activity #2 allowed me to notice those urges and to return to my intention to support the possibility of shifts for all, including Kevin.

> *Mastering others is strength, mastering yourself is true power.*
> —Lao Tzu

And shifts happened. Kevin appeared to feel that he had expressed himself; Tom showed amazing capacity not to be reactive to Kevin; and Jack and Tom talked through a plan that was acceptable to both. Tom agreed to rescind the letter of warning to Jack (as well as a letter of warning that had been issued to the supervisor) given the ambiguity around what actually happened in the altercation; and Jack agreed to attend workplace sensitivity training as long as the supervisor had to attend as well. It was only at this point that Jack spoke up. He said, "As long as the supervisor has to go to that training too, that's fine." At the end of the session, the mood in the room had lightened and all of the participants appeared satisfied.

There is no way of knowing what would have happened had I acted on any of those directive urges, but my guess is that Kevin would have dug in his heels or encouraged Jack to storm out of the session. As it turned out, all seemed to feel they had a good conversation, and they made a plan. In the end, everyone's agency was supported, and the vicious circle of conflict was reversed.

We hope all parties will have the chance to speak up and make their own choices about what they say and how they say it during the mediation process. In "The Annoying Union Rep," Dan needed to let go of that ideal and support Jack in making the choice he apparently wanted to make, which was to let Kevin speak for him. Dan checked in with Jack occasionally to remind him that he could choose to speak up at any point. Dan did so without implying that Jack *should* speak up. Speaking up can be empowering but only if it is freely chosen. Dan fulfilled his role by giving Jack the opportunity to decide *whether* he would speak. Only at the very end of the session, to sort out the details of their agreement, did Jack choose to speak. Perhaps Jack's choice to have Kevin speak for him, along with Kevin's fulfillment of that role, gave Jack the courage to finally speak up.

A representative's zealous advocacy can take forms other than simply speaking for their client. For example, it is common for negotiating lawyers to take extreme positions with the belief that doing so leads to the settlement landing closer to their client's side. Ray Liotta, playing a divorce lawyer in *Marriage Story*, says to his client, "Listen! If we start from a place of reasonable . . . and they start from a place of crazy . . . when we settle . . . we'll be somewhere between reasonable . . . and crazy . . . which is still crazy. Half of crazy is crazy."

> *If you choose not to decide, you still have made a choice.* —Rush

Often that strategy appears to be part of the destructive conflict cycle, which harms the parties and might also harm the lawyers, who must notice that they are part of a destructive process. In the following divorce mediation, Dan believed the lawyers were harming not only their clients but their clients' child.

BACKING INTO A CUSTODY EVALUATION

Eloise and Brandon were disagreeing about the physical custody designation for their 12-year-old child. In our mediation session, the lawyers were doing most of the talking. Not having heard from the parents, I did not know whether they had different visions about what was best for their child or if they were caught in the vicious circle of conflict and simply did not want to concede. One of the attorneys offered, "Well, we can have a custody evaluation done." The other lawyer, perhaps to communicate that she was confident a custody evaluation would be favorable to her client, said, "Yes, that would be fine."

I believe that custody evaluations are generally harmful to children, who often feel they need to take one parent's side against the other. And the evaluation almost always worsens the conflict between the parents. I thought Brandon and Eloise should try to have a conversation about parenting before resorting to such a measure. I believed the lawyers, through their gamesmanship, were causing harm to the entire family, and I wanted the parents to stop deferring to their lawyers.

At this point, I summarized the conversation as accurately as I could, trying to shine as much light as possible on the situation. I secretly hoped that when I did this, someone (a lawyer or a party) would see that they were being hasty in assuming the evaluation was necessary, but that did not happen. When I checked in with the parents, each one responded by gesturing to their lawyer, indicating the lawyer would speak for them. The one-hour session ended with the lawyers planning to exchange names of potential custody evaluators.

Another mediator in this situation might speak up and say, "Hold on, everyone. How about letting me facilitate a conversation between the parents? Maybe we can figure out a plan that works for everyone." And Dan was tempted to do just that. But doing so would have undermined the lawyers' choices as well as each parent's choice to rely on their lawyer. The mediator would be just one more professional trying to control the parents by interfering with their decision making. And that might only worsen the destructive conflict cycle, perhaps by causing the lawyers to get defensive and intensify their adversarial tactics.

Dan did his best to shine a light on the conversation by summarizing it and creating space for other choices to emerge. No other choices did emerge, though, and Dan had to let go of his feeling that another choice *should* emerge. He had no way to push the conversation in any direction without taking on the role of advisor. Supporting the agency of the participants (including, especially, the lawyers in this case) was the most helpful thing he believed he could do without causing more harm.

When mediation includes parties' representatives, the dynamics become more complex as they interact with each other, the opposing party, and their own clients. Each interaction holds the potential for us to undermine or support each person's agency. Sometimes representatives play more than one role in the mediation, further complicating the dynamics between the participants. In the following case Dan mediated, a party's lawyer was also a family member whose role became even more important after one of the parties left the session.

BROTHER LAWYER

The court referred Alyssa and Gary to its mediation program for low-income parents. Gary arrived at the courthouse with his brother Christopher, who I later learned was a trusts and estates lawyer. I greeted them and ushered them to a conference room. "Welcome, you guys. Is it okay if I say a few things about how I see what you're doing here?"

Some mediators wait until all parties are present before speaking with either of them, but I generally speak with whoever appears, whenever they appear. In this case, because I had not had a chance to speak with either party alone, I especially wanted to give each party an opportunity to share any concerns they might have privately.

Both nodded, so I continued. "This is an opportunity for you to have whatever conversation you want with Alyssa. I'm not a judge in any way. I don't talk to the judge, I'm not even thinking about who's right or wrong about anything. This is a chance for you and Alyssa to talk to each other, make whatever suggestions you want, ask each other anything, and make whatever decisions you want to make. How does that sound?"

Gary said, "That's fine. By the way, she called me. She's going to be late—she went to the other courthouse."

"Got it. And how do you feel about having this conversation with her?"

"Fine, we get along fine—it's just that she wants to change things for her own reasons."

"Okay I see."

"Yeah, I don't think there's any reason to change things. Lily is 11 and she's doing really well. The real reason Alyssa wants to change things is so she can get more food stamps.

"Ah, so maybe you could agree to that, so she gets more food stamps, but otherwise keep things the same? What's wrong with more food stamps?"

For some reason, I was off my game at that moment. It was not supportive of Gary for me to quickly suggest a solution and implicitly criticize his suggestion that it was not right for Alyssa to manipulate the system. I aspire to accept where parties are and support them in deciding where to go next, if anywhere. I don't know where my impatience came from.

Gary stood up, said "Okay, whatever," and walked out of the conference room.

Christopher said, "I think you pissed him off."

I said, "Yeah, it seems like it." I had temporarily forgotten how easy it is to unintentionally offend a client or cause him to feel pressured. I had let my urge to solve their problem overtake my intention to support Gary's own process of making decisions.

Christopher then explained more about the situation. "See, child protection services took Lily away from Alyssa three years ago and gave Gary sole physical custody. Alyssa was with a violent dude, plus Alyssa was drinking heavily. I think she's better now and that dude is gone. But Gary still doesn't want to change it back."

I said, "Got it. Let me see if Gary is still around and if Alyssa got here." I checked the waiting room and found Alyssa signing in with the deputies. I introduced myself.

"Hi, nice to meet you," she said. "I saw Gary out there in the hallway walking the other way. He just waved me off and shook his head."

I had just seen Christopher heading in the same direction so I said, "Okay, it looks like Christopher is going to try to track him down. Do you want to come back to our conference room here?"

She said, "Okay, but I don't want Christopher to be involved in this conversation. He's Gary's brother and my lawyer couldn't make it today. That's a conflict of interest or something—he's on Gary's side."

Of course I've got lawyers. They are like nuclear weapons, I've got 'em 'cause everyone else has. But as soon as you use them they screw everything up.

—Danny DeVito

I said, "Okay, cool, we can do this any way you're both okay with. Of course the whole thing is voluntary so there's no obligation to do this if you can't figure out how to do it in a way you're both okay with. And as you know, this is an opportunity for you to have a conversation. I'm here to help you do that, if you want."

She said, "Okay, Gary is a good dude. He did the right thing three years ago when he called CPS. I was having some problems and he stepped up and took Lily. But now I've been sober for three years and I don't have that boyfriend anymore so I think Lily should be with me half time. Plus he should provide half of the transportation." Alyssa opened her laptop where she had a document prepared that listed her requested changes.

When Gary and Christopher returned, I stepped out into the hallway to talk to them. I apologized to Gary, "Hey, that was out of line for me to have that attitude like I knew what you should do. That was not my place. I apologize. I work for you here and my job is to support you and Alyssa in deciding what you want to do based on what you want. If you're okay with me trying to get back on track and help you have a conversation, I'd like to do that." Gary said, "Okay, thanks. Yeah, that's fine."

I opened the door to the conference room where Alyssa was sitting while Gary, Christopher, and I were standing just outside the door. I then said in a way that all three could hear, "I'm happy to have this meeting any way you all want to. Alyssa, I understand you'd like to talk only to Gary since your lawyer can't be here, Gary, I'm not sure how you feel about that."

Alyssa said, "Yeah, I love Christopher, but he hurt me by saying in an email that I let Lily stay up until 11 p.m. That's not true, I always get her to bed at a decent hour—by 9:30 at the latest."

Christopher said, "I could just sit there and not say anything."

Alyssa said, "Okay, that works. I've got nothing against Christopher, but this should be between me and Gary."

Next we all sat down in the conference room. Gary said, "Look, you know I let you see Lily whenever you want to—I'm fine with her being at your house whenever, but I don't want to change anything legally."

Alyssa responded, "Things have changed—I've been sober three years. I should have her half of the time. Plus she's 11—she's starting her period, and she's not comfortable talking to you about that. She needs me."

Gary said, "Why do you need to change it legally though? Why do we have to be here? There's not even any problem."

Alyssa said, "I don't want to be here either."

Gary stood up and said, "Okay, we're done then."

As he walked to the door, I reached out my hand and said, "Good to meet you, good luck." In order for mediation to be as empowering to parties as it can be, support for a party's choice to end their participation is essential. I communicated my support for Gary's choice by unreservedly following the ritual of shaking his hand and wishing him well. Christopher and Alyssa remained seated, and I said, "Do you guys want to talk?"

Christopher said to Alyssa, "Yeah, do you just want to tell me what you had in mind?"

Alyssa gestured to her open laptop, "Yeah, here it is," and motioned Christopher to come look over her shoulder. "I want him to provide half of the transportation too."

Christopher said, "Yeah, maybe you could have your lawyer email this to me. I'll talk to Gary. We should be able to work something out."

Alyssa said, "You know that email you sent really hurt me. You used to be totally neutral." Christopher said, "I know. That wasn't meant for you. I felt bad about that. That was meant for your lawyer. You know, when you got a lawyer, I felt like I had to help Gary with his side of it."

Alyssa said, "I know. And I know you didn't mean for me to see that. I asked her to tell me what your guy's grounds were. She didn't want to show it to me, but I made her." Then Alyssa said to me, "Christopher is a great uncle." She then said to Christopher, "Shit, Bro, you were really there for us when Gary was out of work. I love you. But that email just wasn't true. I *do* get her to bed by 9:30 every night. I don't know where you got that—that I'm not paying attention to what she's doing and letting her stay up late. She's in bed on time."

Christopher said, "I don't know. We don't have to go into it. We can probably work something out." Christopher and Alyssa agreed that with Alyssa's lawyer in the loop, they would exchange some emails and try to come to an agreement.

Christopher provides an example of a person who is not, in a strict sense, a party to the dispute but who nonetheless plays an important role and therefore should be considered a full-fledged participant in the mediation. Technically the parties were Alyssa and Gary, the two parents of Lily. Christopher's role included his function as Gary's lawyer as well as his brother but also as Lily's uncle and even as a brother figure to Alyssa. While lawyers are often significant participants in the conversation, Christopher's relationship to the parties made him especially important. Alyssa and Christopher getting to a better place with each other likely benefited both Gary and Lily as well.

While it is rare that a lawyer is an actual family member of both parties, it is common that lawyers are entangled in the dispute beyond their simple representation of a party. Often conflict between opposing lawyers is part of the story. Sometimes one party has developed significant resentment of an opposing lawyer. Often the relationship between a party and their own lawyer is complicated as they may both wish that the other were behaving differently. We try to support participants in increasing their agency in their interactions with any of the other participants.

The Mediator's Relationship with the Lawyers

In many cases, the mediator's relationship with the parties' lawyers is a significant factor. In mediations that arise as part of litigation, the lawyers often choose the mediator without involving the parties in the selection process. That was the situation in "Bad Wood" above as well as "Wage War" below. In these cases, there is a risk the mediator will spend more time interacting with the lawyers and ensuring their needs are met but at the expense of the parties. Dispute resolution scholar John Lande has expressed similar concerns about lawyers and mediators becoming too cozy.

> As a result of the prominent role of lawyers in mediation, mediators may feel especially obliged to cater to the lawyers' interests, which often entails pressing the principals into settlement. The participation of lawyers may increase time pressure in mediation, putting additional pressure on principals. Moreover, extending lawyers' norms of adversarial bargaining and "client control" further adds to the pressure, all of which may undermine the quality of principals' consent.[2]

One aspect of our approach that is likely to decrease the risk of "client control" by the lawyers and enhance "the quality of principals' consent" is our refusal to carry messages from room to room. In Chapter 8 we discussed our policy of not carrying messages between sides if they choose to be in separate rooms since that would require us to make choices about content, tone, and responses to follow-up questions. It would also increase the chance that the parties would remain in separate rooms throughout the day and never have an opportunity to interact with each other or the opposing lawyer. When we let everyone know that we are not willing to carry messages, the parties and their lawyers usually end up meeting in the same room eventually (if not at first) and there are more opportunities for the parties to be directly involved in the communication.

As important as this principle is to Dan, he found it challenging to stick to this commitment in the following case. A combination of the lawyers' expectations, the dynamics between the lawyers, and one party's preference not to see the other party pulled Dan into a situation where he found himself carrying messages between the parties.

WAGE WAR

Johnny had a wage-and-hour claim against Marty. In my initial phone call with Johnny, his lawyer, Francisco, did most of the talking. Francisco told me the story of Johnny's employment with Marty and made the argument that Johnny had been an employee as opposed to an independent contractor; therefore, Johnny was entitled to overtime pay that he did not receive.

I checked in with Johnny throughout the call to see if he wanted to add or clarify anything. Francisco had assured me that Johnny's English was good although Spanish was his first language. At one point, I reflected back to Francisco and Johnny the entire story that Francisco had told me. I then asked Johnny what he wanted to add. Johnny started speaking to Francisco in Spanish and I heard the word "humano." It sounded like Johnny was crying, and Francisco told me that Johnny said he wanted to be treated like a human being. I reflected, "Johnny, you want to be treated like a human being." Johnny said, "Yes."

I acknowledged that I could hear that this was painful for Johnny and asked what else, if anything, he wanted to say. When it was clear that Johnny and Francisco had said everything they wanted to say, I asked them whether they wanted to talk about how they wanted to approach the upcoming group meeting, and Francisco said that the two of them would talk that over and let me know if they had any more questions or concerns. I reminded them that I see the group meeting as an opportunity to have whatever conversation they want, and I looked forward to seeing them then.

Leigh, the attorney for Marty, made it clear by email that only she, and not her client, would participate in our initial call. I was concerned that Marty would not have a chance to ask me questions and express any of his own concerns about the process but I wanted to support Leigh's and Marty's choices about the process. I scheduled the phone call with Leigh.

During my call with Leigh, she invited her senior partner, Earl, to participate. I explained that my hope was to help the parties and the lawyers have whatever conversation they wanted to have. I gathered that Leigh and Earl were accustomed to mediations in which the parties were kept separate from each other.

I said that one possible benefit of a face-to-face conversation was that the parties could address whatever was really bothering them about the situation and the conversation would not be limited to legal justifications. Leigh thought that might be helpful as she believed that Johnny had started this lawsuit because of hurt feelings. Leigh also said Marty had a strong claim that Johnny had been an independent contractor so was not entitled to overtime pay, and further, there was no evidence that Johnny had worked more than 40 hours per week. She believed that Johnny was suing Marty simply because he was hurt that Marty had stopped hiring him and insulted by the way Marty told him that he was no longer needed.

Earl explained that Marty was in a very tough financial situation and might not even be able to pay his legal bills. Earl also told me that Marty thought this lawsuit was "complete bullshit." I reflected what I heard and added that the mediation would create an opportunity to talk about the situation in whatever way the parties wanted.

Earl expressed concern that meeting together might raise the hostility between Marty and Johnny. I said that it's everyone's choice how we do it but since they were already embroiled in a lawsuit, there was not much risk of making things worse. Instead the chance to meet together might improve their relationship. This response, in which I directively suggested that a face-to-face meeting was worth considering, deviated from my general rule of being purely supportive. As mentioned earlier, I sometimes feel the need to educate lawyers about mediation's potential.

I also told Earl that as a general rule I don't pass messages between sides. I explained that I don't believe my doing so is helpful because I would not be able to convey the message as well as the party or their lawyer could. Earl said, "Okay, well I think Marty will be fine talking to Johnny directly."

Francisco called the day before the mediation to tell me that he was pretty sure Johnny would not want to talk directly to Marty because he had felt so dehumanized by Marty. I said, "That's his choice. This might be a chance for Johnny to stand up for himself and confront Marty, but absolutely, it's his call." I explained my policy of not passing messages between sides, and Francisco said, "Uh huh." I then said, "I'll show you to separate conference rooms when you get here, and you guys can decide as you go."

On the day of the mediation, the first to arrive were Earl and Marty. I introduced myself and showed them to the conference room. As I sat down with the two of them, Earl took a phone call and I chatted with Marty, who told me that he had recently had a kidney transplant. In addition, about six months earlier, the IRS had presented him with an enormous tax bill and had arranged for installments on his large debt to be withdrawn from his bank account. So he essentially had no money, and this lawsuit, annoying though it was, did not seem very important in the grand scheme of things.

At this moment, I saw through the glass windows of the conference room that someone else was arriving at the reception desk. I stepped out of the conference room and introduced myself, and it turned out to be Johnny. Johnny hung his head a bit, in a gesture I read as exuding humility. I showed him to the other conference room. Francisco arrived shortly after and I brought him to the room where Johnny was waiting. I told them I would give them a chance to talk with each other while I finished checking in with the others.

Back in Marty and Earl's room, Leigh had now arrived as well. I introduced myself to her, and Marty continued telling me his take on the situation. He told me that on Johnny's last day at work, Marty had called a meeting of all of his subcontractors to tell them he now needed documentation of their hours so he could give them accurate 1099 forms. Marty had realized he needed to do this when the IRS presented him with the large tax bill he'd mentioned earlier—part of his problem with the IRS was that he had not been documenting his payments to subcontractors. Johnny told Marty he would not document his hours, and Marty replied, "Then you can go pound sand" (which I gathered meant "Hit the road").

Having spent around 20 minutes with this group, I asked them to consider how they would like to have the conversation. "I could invite Francisco and Johnny into this room, or any or all of you three could go see them in their room . . . It's up to you." They all looked at each other, suggesting they were open to the possibilities. I said, "I'll let you ponder that, and I'll go check in with the others and ask them the same question."

In Johnny and Francisco's room, Francisco did all of the talking, mostly about how egregious Marty's behavior had been. After a few minutes, I turned to Johnny and said, "Hey Johnny—I notice you've been quiet, and that's totally fine with me, but you're also very welcome to speak up any time you want." Johnny nodded at me and then looked to Francisco, who said, "Uh huh, yeah" before continuing his story. This happened each time I checked in with Johnny.

Throughout the conversation, Francisco made the same case he had made on the phone to me: Johnny had been an employee. He was treated very poorly, had not been paid overtime, and had not been able to take restroom or meal breaks. Francisco argued that treating a vulnerable employee like Johnny this way was unacceptable and a jury would likely agree and award punitive damages. I wasn't sure in what sense Francisco was saying that Johnny was vulnerable—his immigration status, his limited English, or simply that he was the employee and Marty was the boss? But I chose not to ask.

I asked how they would like to conduct the conversation, and Francisco said Johnny did not want to see Marty. I said to Johnny, "That's totally your choice, Johnny, I just want to make sure that you know that I'd be happy to facilitate that conversation and it might give you the chance to tell him exactly what you think of how he treated you." Johnny nodded, and Francisco repeated that they would prefer Johnny not have to see Marty. I was aware that Francisco might have been the one making this decision for Johnny, but I felt I had to honor Johnny's choice to defer to Francisco. Francisco said he would be willing to join me in going to the other room to talk to Marty, Leigh, and Earl, so he walked with me to their room.

I opened the door to Marty's conference room and said that Francisco would like to talk to them, if they're okay with it. All three indicated that would be fine. After they all shook hands, I said, "So, as you know, I see this as an opportunity to have whatever conversation you want to have. Where would you like to start?"

Francisco said to the others, "I would like to know what your offer is. As you know our last request was for $45,000. You responded with an offer of $1,500, which was actually quite insulting to Johnny. You are acting as if this is not a legitimate claim, and in fact it is very legitimate and our demand of $45,000 was extremely reasonable and was a genuine effort at compromise to try to settle the case. If this case went to trial, we would ask for attorney fees as well as punitive damages which would add a minimum of another $25,000 to our claim. As you know, your client was violating the Minnesota Labor Code in a variety of ways, including failure to pay overtime, failure to provide meal breaks, and failure to provide rest breaks, and especially upsetting to my client was the disrespectful way that Marty spoke to him on the last day of his employment. This behavior is unacceptable and we feel very confident that a jury will agree with us."

I caught Marty's eye while Francisco was talking and noticed that he rolled his eyes especially demonstratively when Francisco used the word "disrespectful." I nodded in his direction to acknowledge his reaction.

Earl said, "Well, as you know, Francisco, we see a number of those things very differently. I do want to acknowledge that the demand letter you sent a couple months ago included payment plans, and we appreciate that. You may not know that Marty is in a very difficult position financially at the moment. Some of these challenges arose when the IRS came after him and he had to start reporting the payments he was making to subcontractors, like your client."

Francisco said, "Your client's ability to pay should not be a consideration here. We refuse to take that into account. He would also have to pay quite a bit to continue to defend this lawsuit."

Earl said to me, "So Dan, what's the next step here? Whose turn is it to make a counteroffer?"

I said, "You're wondering if the ball's in your court or Francisco's."

Francisco said, "We have already made an offer at compromise, and you have not made a meaningful counteroffer."

I said to Francisco, "So you're saying your demand was already a compromise, and they're the next ones who should make an offer."

Francisco said, "Yes."

I looked at all of them and said, "Well, as far as I'm concerned, this is up to all of you. Francisco, I hear you saying, you'd like to hear an offer from them."

Earl interrupted, "Okay, well I'll be happy to talk with Marty and Leigh about that possibility. Could you give us a chance to talk that over?"

Francisco stood up and said, "Absolutely." I stood up as well and said, "I'll walk back with Francisco and check in with him and Johnny, and then I'll come back and check with you guys?" Earl, Leigh, and Marty all indicated that would be fine.

As I walked down the hall with Francisco, he said, "They need to understand that we have very strong claims and that this sort of behavior by people like their client is unacceptable."

And I said, "You want them to understand that your claims are strong and that people like Marty behaving that way is unacceptable." "Exactly," Francisco said. When a mediation participant says something about the kind of person another participant is, I'm especially careful to reflect that statement. It's a sign that people are in the vicious circle of conflict and that they are viewing the other person as an obstacle or enemy rather than a fellow human. Reflecting these statements, perhaps paradoxically, can help parties shift toward more understanding and *recognition*[3] of the other's humanity.

When we arrived at the room where Johnny was waiting, Francisco said, "Could I have a few minutes privately with my client?"

I said, "Of course. I'll check on you in a little while."

When I returned to the other room, Earl said to me, "So Dan, what was his demand exactly? Did he add another $25,000 to it?"

I said, "I guess that wasn't clear. He mentioned that at trial, he'd ask for punitive damages and attorney fees of another $25,000, but I don't know whether that was a demand. I guess I'd assume that he'd let go of those claims as part of a settlement." Here I was already deviating from my policy of not speaking on behalf of anyone. I intended merely to repeat the gist of what Francisco had said in their presence but I drifted a bit toward interpretation.

Earl said, "We really can't offer much, but we don't want to torpedo the negotiations. I mean Marty has no money at the moment."

Marty said, "Yeah, the IRS will take anything that shows up in my bank account right now."

Earl continued, "So it will definitely have to be on a payment plan. But Marty, you were saying you could come up with $5,000 right now? I mean we really don't want to go up to five figures if we can help it."

Marty said, "And by the way, the thing about rest and meal breaks is completely ridiculous. He could do those things whenever he wanted. He was totally unsupervised. He was at a different site."

I nodded.

Leigh added, "I think Francisco is completely full of it. And by the way, the idea that what Marty can pay is not something they'll take into consideration is crazy. Of course it's a consideration. Marty seriously might go bankrupt and they'll get nothing."

Earl said to Marty, "So do you want to offer him $5,000?" And then to me, "What do you think, Dan?"

I said, "It's entirely up to you guys. I understand you don't feel like you owe him anything, Marty. And Earl, you're saying you'd like to try to settle it, and you don't want to torpedo the negotiations. I guess it's possible Francisco won't feel like that's enough of an offer. But it's your call."

Earl said, "Okay, well why don't you tell him $5,000 and see what happens." I paused for a few seconds to think. My normal practice was to decline to pass messages such as this. But in this case, despite having explained to both sides that I wouldn't carry messages, their expectation that I would do so persisted. And I had now seen that when Francisco talked directly with Marty and his lawyers, their differences seemed to harden. Normally I would assume there was still potential for things to shift in a constructive direction with more direct conversation, but this time, I essentially submitted to the lawyers' expectations.

I told myself that little would be lost and there was some efficiency to gain by carrying the message. It appeared to me that the important information that needed to be conveyed was just how much Marty would be willing to pay and how little Johnny and Francisco would accept. I did not know of any other way that information could be shared other than through this game of offers and counteroffers, and I even told myself that in this context, my duty to honor party self-determination meant going with the lawyers' expectations that I carry messages (contrary to everything we've said on this topic in the book and what we truly believe).

So I went to the other conference room and shared with Johnny and Francisco that Marty was now willing to pay $5,000, which he would promise to deliver within 30 days. I told them that my sense was that Marty genuinely believed he did not owe Johnny anything, that Marty said that $5,000 was certainly the maximum amount he could pay in the short term, and that even though Francisco had said it was not relevant, bankruptcy was a real possibility for Marty.

Francisco responded that he did not consider this a meaningful offer, that Marty needed to acknowledge that Johnny had legitimate claims, and that the cost of defending this lawsuit would far exceed $5,000. Francisco asked me to convey to Marty and his lawyers that if Marty made a responsible offer, Francisco would be willing to lower his demand of $45,000. But as of now, his demand remained $45,000. He also asked me to remind Marty that his violations of the law were serious. He went on to encourage me to tell them that they had an opportunity today to settle this case and that it would be a shame if they missed that opportunity.

I confirmed that I had Francisco and Johnny's permission to share with the others whatever I thought would be helpful. And I checked in with Johnny, "How are you doing? Any thoughts about anything else you'd like to do here? You're okay with everything Francisco has said?" Johnny nodded and showed no sign of wanting to do anything other than allow Francisco to handle the situation.

Returning to the room with Marty, Leigh, and Earl, I told them what had happened in the other room. Marty rolled his eyes; Leigh shook her head and rolled her eyes; and Earl said, "Yeah, I thought that might happen. So they're at 45 still?"

I said, "Yes, Francisco said that if you made what he called a 'responsible' offer, he would respond by lowering his demand. He also gave me a list of things that he thought you should consider such as the cost of fighting this and that sort of thing." Earl said, "Yeah, I mean, it's possible that if we don't settle this, Marty won't be able to keep paying us, but Marty says he'll cross that bridge when he comes to it."

Marty said, "Yeah, what can I tell you? I don't have any money."

Earl continued, "I've been trying to encourage Marty to offer somewhere in the teens, and I don't want to say it because I know Marty doesn't want to hear it, but I don't think we'll be able to settle this unless our offer has a 2 at the start of it. Marty, how about offering $5,000 within 30 days and then more over the course of time, maybe 15 more payments of $1,000 each so we can tell him $20,000?"

Marty said, "I don't want to do that, but that would be the absolute maximum. Absolutely no more."

Earl said, "I mean, I understand—you hate to pay a guy just because he wants money, but man, even if we have to do those depositions, that'll cost you like ten grand right there."

Marty said, "That's fine, but let's get a yes or a no and then we're outta here."

I said, "So you'd like to offer $5,000 within 30 days followed by $1,000 per month for 15 months for a total of $20,000, but that is absolutely your final offer."

Marty and Earl both nodded and Leigh shrugged her shoulders as if to say, "I guess so."

I stood up to walk over to the other room. And I said, "So I'll communicate that this is your final offer. And if they don't accept it and want to communicate a counteroffer to you at that point, are you going to want to hear that, or should I tell them you're only interested in a yes or no?"

Earl said, "I guess we'll hear what they have to say, but that is our final offer."

I said, "And would you like me to say anything about whether you'll keep this offer open for a while? Or is this just for today?"

Earl said, "You can tell them we'll keep that open until Monday when we're scheduled to take Johnny's deposition. They can accept it until then."

I looked at Marty and Leigh to confirm, and they both shrugged and nodded.

I said, "Okay, got it" and went to the other room. When I got there, I asked, "How are you guys doing?"

Johnny smiled and shrugged. Francisco said, "Did they make another offer?"

I said, "They did, and they asked me to let you know it's their final offer. They said they would offer $5,000 within 30 days followed by 15 monthly payments of $1,000 each for a total of $20,000. They also said that they'd keep this offer open until Monday when they said there's a deposition scheduled."

Francisco said, "Well, we very much appreciate that that is a responsible step forward toward settlement. And in response, we are willing to lower our demand from $45,540 to $41,540."

I said, "Okay, sure I'll let them know. They did say that that was their final offer so I'm guessing they'll pack up and leave when I give them this response."

Francisco said, "You should remind them that this is a golden opportunity for them to settle the case at a reasonable price."

I said, "Okay, also, I want to collect the rest of your share of my fee. Johnny, you were going to write a check?"

I believed the mediation was about to end so I genuinely wanted to deal with receiving my payment. I also felt that my asking for it at this moment was a good way to confirm for Francisco that as far as I knew, Marty's last offer really was his final offer.

Johnny said, "No problem," and opened his checkbook.

I returned to the other room and said, "Francisco asked that I let you know that they appreciate that responsible step forward to settlement and that they will now lower their demand to $41,540."

Earl said, "Did you tell them it was our final offer?"

I said, "I did."

Marty said, "Okay, that's it, how much do I owe you?" and he pulled out a credit card.

I handled the payment from Marty, helped get everyone's parking validated, shook their hands, and told them I'd be available if I could help with any further conversations or if anyone wanted to call me to debrief about today's session.

Next I went to Johnny's and Francisco's room, told them that the others were packing up and leaving, and gave Johnny instructions for filling out my check.

Francisco said, "They're really leaving?"

I said, "It seemed like it. They might still be by the elevators."

Francisco said, "Okay, tell them we'll take $30,000 plus the cost of filing the lawsuit, and our share of the rest of your fee."

I looked at Johnny and he nodded.

I stood up and said, "Okay, I'll try to catch them," and ran down the hall to find Marty and Leigh waiting for Earl to get out of the restroom. I said, "They wanted me to convey one last offer to you."

Marty said, "Okay, should we step back into the conference room?"

I said "Sure," and we waved Earl in as he passed the conference room. I shared Francisco's last offer. The body language of all three of them confirmed my guess that they would not find that offer interesting. They quickly filed back out of the conference room and headed toward the elevators. I wished them well and reminded them they could keep me in the loop if they wished.

I returned to Johnny and Francisco and told them that the others had left. Francisco asked, "How did they respond?" and I said, "They heard the offer and then went straight to the elevators." Francisco seemed genuinely surprised. Johnny remained unexpressive other than the sad smile that he had been wearing throughout.

I accepted Johnny's check, walked them out, and helped them get their parking validation from the receptionist. I guessed Francisco felt a bit insulted that they had not seemed to take his claims more seriously, and I wondered if he felt some guilt that he had not managed to obtain any compensation for his client as of yet and that the path toward obtaining any compensation wasn't clear. I also wondered whether he later called and accepted the $20,000, but I never heard.

The big question in my mind about this mediation is whether I made a mistake by switching to shuttle diplomacy. That choice likely prevented meaningful communication from occurring. To the extent Francisco was posturing in a way that was counterproductive, perhaps more direct interaction with the other side would have helped him understand more fully the limitations of what could be recovered. Maybe if Johnny had somehow agreed to be in the same room with Marty, he would have let go of some demonizing of him. It's possible Marty may have felt some compassion for Johnny and found a way to offer him more. It's actually entirely unpredictable what would have happened. If my job was to find the most the defense was willing to pay and the least the plaintiff was willing to accept, as far as I know, I achieved that, but there's no way even to know that for sure.

We have no way of knowing whether a different approach would have been more helpful to the parties in "Wage War" so we are left with our principles. Our principles include the assumption that we can enhance the agency of all of the participants. Mediations that involve lawyers create opportunities to support their agency as well as that of the parties. Parties' choices are constrained by countless factors, including sometimes their deference to their lawyers. It seems our job is to acknowledge the choices they make and their opportunities to continue making them. At the same time, we can support the lawyers in rising to the occasion and making their best choices as they manage the inevitable uncertainty of their situation.

Regardless of how involved, or even central, the lawyers are to any mediation, it is still possible to honor party self-determination. A mediator can involve the parties by suggesting a pre-mediation conversation that includes the parties and then can continue to check in with them throughout the process, reminding them that they have choices to make about how to proceed. To the extent a party wants to delegate some of the communication to their lawyer, that is their choice.

We treat the lawyers as parties in the sense that we also support their choices. As participants in the conversation, their sense of agency matters and can be enhanced as can their understanding (or *recognition*) of the opposing side and of their own client. As we see it, everyone involved can benefit from a conversation in which every participant has the opportunity to make their own choices whenever possible.

Mediations such as "Wage War" can make us feel powerless as mediators. Sometimes we cannot tell whether we helped the parties at all. Given all the uncertainty, ambiguity, and complexity of conflict situations, our choices often come down to making our best guess about what will be most supportive of the participants' agency at the time. We can feel constrained by the expectations of lawyers and others. As we will discuss in the final chapter, though, our own self-determination matters too.

Notes

1. Institute for the Study of Conflict Transformation, "Mediation: Principles and Practice, the Transformative Approach" (Training Manual 2010), 42.

2. John Lande, "How Will Lawyering and Mediation Practices Transform Each Other?" *Florida State University Law Review* 24 (1997): 844.

3. Robert A. Baruch Bush and Joseph P. Folger, *The Promise of Mediation: The Transformative Approach to Conflict* (San Francisco: Jossey-Bass, 2005), ch. 1.

CHAPTER 10

The Choice Is Yours

The highest manifestation of life consists in this: that a being governs its own actions.

—St. Thomas Aquinas

To make a long story short (we know, too late), people value their autonomy, and for good reason. They are at their best when they're able to make their own clear, conscious decisions based on their own rationales. What's more, when people are aware of their opportunities and their capacity to make choices, they do so with the greatest consideration for both themselves and others. And that feels good.

Put another way, people don't like to be told what to do. They resist efforts at coercion and even persuasion (putting us in a bit of an awkward position as we try to persuade you that this is true).

> *The only thing to do with good advice is to pass it on. It is never of any use to oneself.* —Oscar Wilde

We mediators also don't like to be told what to do. When the U.S. Postal Service started requiring its mediators to practice transformative mediation, many of them resented it. We all want to practice in a way that makes sense to us. We want to give our clients what we think they most need and want, and we have our own needs to consider as well. Just as our clients are in the best position to make choices about their conflict, we are in the best position to make choices about how we practice our craft. And the quality of our decisions is enhanced when we take full responsibility for them.

As you know by now, we (Tara and Dan) choose to practice mediation the way we believe increases parties' sense of agency. We abstain from trying to control, guide, lead, or nudge the parties. Instead, we highlight their opportunities to make choices and reflect choices they have already made. We believe this support puts them in the best position to make clear choices about how they relate to each other. We have suggested that this approach most honors what is considered to be the defining feature of mediation—party self-determination.

We have discussed the choices mediators can make when seeking to give life to the concept of self-determination, and the likely consequences of these choices. We have shared research suggesting that overall, actively supporting parties as they make their own decisions about every aspect of the process leads to the best results. This type of process allows mediators to support party self-determination while also increasing the likelihood of other desirable outcomes such as harm reduction, efficiency, and fairness—outcomes that are often, mistakenly, pitted against self-determination.[1]

We, like all mediators, operate under a set of assumptions. Those assumptions guide how we behave. Other mediators have suggested that the approach should vary depending on the case.[2] When they say that they adjust their approach to fit the case, we say, "We do, too!" In fact, that is the *essence* of our approach for *all* of our cases. We pay very specific attention to and honor each situation, each party, and each moment as a unique phenomenon. Our approach may be one size fits all, but it is *very stretchy* fabric.

Convinced though we are of the benefits of this approach, we must admit that current research does not include controlled studies of mediator interventions. There are still missing pieces in what we know about the consequences of different choices mediators make. And even if there are general trends when it comes to causes and consequences, each case is unique, and in any particular situation we have no way of knowing what would have happened had we made a different choice.

So our clarity on how to proceed when working with parties must be, to a certain extent, a matter of faith and principle. All mediators need to decide which values to prioritize and how to give life to those values. We have decided to prioritize each party's right to their autonomy with respect to us, the mediators. This means that we provide a process in which their choices govern. We do this even when a choice seems unwise and even when one party chooses to defer to another participant. And by "participant" we mean anyone other than us (e.g., the party's attorney, another advisor or consultant, another party, or a friend that the party has brought along for support).

As we discussed in Chapter 8, there are times when supporting every choice of every party might not be possible such as when the parties disagree about who should be in the room or when they want *us* to do something that we believe would harm them (including continuing with a mediation when we've realized we cannot fully support all parties). Even in those cases, we do our best to support the parties as much as possible and to help them see that there are still choices available to them.

We have chosen to view party self-determination as much more than the ability to say "yes" or "no" and instead see it as akin to agency—a psychological state that can be supported and enhanced and where parties are able to make their own choices with clarity, awareness, and intentionality. We see mediation as a process that can offer parties the opportunity to experience this agency enhancement as they have their choices supported and reflected by the mediator.

In mediation, as in the areas of social work, special education, and political science, the definition of self-determination is a source of confusion and disagreement. The ambiguity inherent in the term has provided ample opportunity for us mediators to interpret the guidelines and standards in a way that justifies how we choose to practice. And how we choose to practice arises from, among other things, our professional background, our assumptions about human nature, the first mediation training we happened to stumble upon, and our experiences of trial and error over time. All of these influences will be different for different individuals.

The tendency to adjust our definition of self-determination to our practices, rather than the other way around, may be exacerbated by another human tendency, which is to infer our attitudes from our behaviors.[3] We tend to assume that if we did something, there must have been a good reason for it. Although there may have been any number of reasons for our doing something (e.g., we were acting out of habit; we wanted the parties to see us as adding value; or we wanted to impress or please the lawyers), we are adept as are all humans at finding ways to justify and explain our behavior after the fact. And justifying our choices as upholding the value of party self-determination may be enough to end the conversation. Who can argue against that? Therefore, we think it is important for each of us to figure out how we would like to practice and why rather than try to define self-determination once and for all.

Relatedly, another bias we have (as humans and as mediators) is the tendency to infer causation from correlation.[4] For example, we might notice that our clients are in a better place at the end of a session than they were when the session began and conclude that our specific interventions were the reason. In fact, time and the opportunity to talk may have been the only causal factors. And if the parties are *not* in a better place at the end of the session, we may attribute that to specific characteristics of the parties rather than anything we did. And we may be right in both of those cases or not.

We may be motivated not to look closely at our own behavior, question ourselves, or confer with colleagues if it might mean acknowledging we are, or were, mistaken. Given how isolated from each other mediators can be, we have been free to develop our own unique ways of practicing or to exist in self-reinforcing silos with minimal cross-pollination.

All of these biases and cognitive limitations add up. One likely path toward improved practice is self-reflection. As mediator Michael Lang discusses in *Reflective Practice in Conflict Resolution*,[5] engaging in thoughtful reflection after each mediation session is an invaluable practice. Taking the time to reflect and confer with colleagues, including those who may have a very different perspective on the role of the mediator, can help us see patterns we otherwise might have missed. When writing this book together, we (Tara and Dan) experienced the benefits of frequent post-mediation debriefs.

Why Are We Such Purists?

Most if not all mediators see at least some value in the practices that transformative mediators use such as *reflecting* the parties and offering empathic support, viewing these as tools that can be used among others as needed. We are closer to purists in that regard. Although we make exceptions, we do our best to keep those exceptions to a bare minimum. Our approach to self-determination is more of a philosophy than a collection of practices—a philosophy that values the right of each person to make their own choices in each moment. We remain unattached to any goal other than supporting each party to the best of our ability as they make these choices. Remaining true to this philosophy means consistently putting all decisions in the parties' hands rather than putting only certain choices in their hands (and only if they happen to be making good choices).

> We hold that each man is the best judge of his own interest. —John Adams

Part of the reason for our refusal to take on any sort of decision making for the parties is the concern that doing so can change the entire process. If we make one decision for the parties, such as telling them who should speak first, they will start to experience the process as something requiring only their passive engagement.[6] We may then continue to make choices for them as they look to us for guidance. We would be setting a tone that we are in charge and we know what's best. They may then sit back and assume that the process will take them to a better place when, in fact, a better place consists of them proactively making their own choices.

As we see it, the way for parties to get to a better place in conflict entails making a number of decisions—decisions about how to respond to the other person, what to demand, what to request, how to manage differences, how to accept hard realities, and how to take advantage of opportunities. In our view, the last message people in conflict need from a mediator is "You sit back—I know what needs

> Make people dependent on you and you can rob them of their freedom, their dignity, their very soul. —Marty Rubin

to happen." As we see it, people in conflict need to confront the uncertainty, unpredictability, and apparent unfairness of their situation. They need to figure out what they can control and what they cannot. They may decide that they want to put some control in their lawyer's hands. We will support them in making that choice but we will not be the ones to take control from them or to accept control they try to hand us.

Our refusal to take a certain kind of control is intended to facilitate party *empowerment*. We cannot *make* parties achieve greater clarity, awareness of what matters most to them, or a sense of agency, but we can allow for it, and we can create conditions that make it more likely. We also cannot make the parties understand each other's perspective or see each other more as humans than as obstacles or enemies (also known as *recognition*), but we can stay out of the way and let their natural inclination to do so take effect. We have decided that this approach is the only way we can truly support party self-determination as we conceive of it. We also believe it is the most likely path toward other desirable outcomes such as agreements that work for the parties in the short and long term.

And it feels good to us!

The first divorce mediation training Tara took was led by an avuncular man whose mantra was "It's not your problem." To Tara, these were very welcome words and she took an instant liking to this trainer. Yet the training largely consisted of lessons on the definition of marital property, tax implications of selling the marital home, and child-support calculations, all of which suggested that the parties' decisions actually were, in many ways, the mediator's problem. Tara later attended other trainings and workshops that put less of an emphasis on content expertise and instead emphasized process expertise. These trainings suggested it was the mediator's role to move the parties through problem-solving steps and to ensure that the parties were communicating with each other respectfully. In this case, the parties' final decisions were not the mediator's problem, but the parties' behaviors within the process *were* the mediator's problem.

Dan noticed in his first mediation trainings that party self-determination was touted as a selling point for mediation. But it became clear to Dan that his trainers meant it mostly in contrast to adjudication. When he had an internship with those trainers, he noticed that his teachers had very clear ideas about what the parties should do, and the trick, as they saw it, was to get them to do it.

Now we both enter a mediation session believing that the best thing we can do for the parties is to support them where they are. And this attitude is freeing. Having mediated other ways, we know that we feel especially good when we are able to listen to people in a way that makes them feel valued and allows them to regain some of the agency the conflict may have sapped from them. Not only can we tell that people appreciate it (and it always feels good to be appreciated), but it is also a weight off of our shoulders to know that we do not have to solve their problem (as if we could).

You're giving the other person space—space to be. It is the most precious gift you can give. —Eckhart Tolle

Interacting this way works well in other relationships too. It is gratifying to empathically and nonjudgmentally support our friends as they make their own decisions. Research has shown that while both giving and receiving autonomy support among friends seems to increase well-being, *giving* this support is especially satisfying.[7] It feels good to accept people as they are and to demonstrate faith in their capacities. In contrast, it can feel like a struggle to try to change someone and to resist whatever they're doing. Although it can be tempting to try to solve someone else's problem, it also sends the message "I am more capable than you are." And when the friend doesn't take your advice, it can be alienating in addition to frustrating ("What's wrong with them? Why don't they just take my great advice?"). Deciding that it is not our place to give advice frees us from that struggle and allows us to simply connect with our friend.

Of course the role of the mediator is different from the role of the friend, and we mediators purport to have specialized skills when it comes to helping with conflict. For us that means knowing how to support party agency under all kinds of circumstances. It means supporting their choices and avoiding the temptation to pretend we know more than we do even when the parties are hoping for answers from us. Even with such clear principles, it's not so simple. Although we have decided to prioritize supporting the parties' decisions, we make exceptions. Many factors still lead to mediators making different choices. For example, Dan has a different physical presence in the room than does Tara, potentially giving us different options and our clients different expectations. Here Dan discusses a choice that he makes based on his specific options and assumptions about his clients' expectations.

Preventing Two Hugs

Often when I explain to mediation trainees that I don't try to prevent harsh conflict talk, they ask whether violence has ever broken out. They assume that my permissive attitude, in which I support whatever parties choose to say even if it includes name-calling, blaming, or other inflammatory words, will lead to escalation. I explain that in fact, my supportive attitude tends to de-escalate the conflict. When a party hears reflected back to them "You're saying that this other party is a horrible person who ought to be ashamed of themselves" (assuming that's what they said), it happens to be the response most likely to calm them down. I'm not *trying* to calm them down. I'm trying to support the choice they've made and give both parties another chance to hear it. But it tends to feel empowering to the speaker, decreasing their need to lash out.

In direct answer to the question of whether physical violence has ever broken out, I can honestly say that in my over 23 years of mediating, physical violence has never occurred. And there have been only two times when I decided to intervene directly in cases of unwanted physical contact. Both were one-sided hugs.

In one case an adult daughter attempted to hug her elderly mother and the mother crossed her arms in front of her, indicating that she did not want to be hugged. I stood up, stepped between the two, and said, "I'm sorry, I'm not comfortable with an unwanted hug happening." The same thing happened when an ex-husband wanted to hug his ex-wife.

I made an exception to my policy of supporting parties' choices in those moments. I don't know whether what I did was best for the parties. Perhaps the reluctant recipients would have warmed up to the hug. Maybe the experience would have been a meaningful, connecting moment for all. Or perhaps the hugger would have stopped on their own before the actual hug occurred, demonstrating respect for the other person's choice.

It felt like an instinctive decision in both instances. There are many post hoc rationales that come to mind to support my choice. The potential victim (or recipient of the hug) may have expected that I would protect them from unwanted contact. The unwanted hug may have been extremely offensive to the victim, more offensive than my intervention was to the perpetrator, so maybe I was decreasing the harm by stopping the hug. Maybe my reputation would suffer if it became known that I oversaw and seemed to condone acts of battery in my mediations.

Arguably I was supporting party choice even at these moments: the victim's expressed choice not to be hugged. But that argument really doesn't work because I support every other choice in mediation that parties make regardless of how the non-acting party feels about it. So the bottom line is that my hug-stopping cannot really be justified by my commitment to supporting all parties' choices. It is simply an exception I choose to make.

The Contradictions!

While we hope to have added some clarity to what self-determination in mediation can mean, semantic challenges remain. We are claiming that we mediators can provide a process where agency and understanding tend to increase and yet we cannot *try* to increase agency or understanding. We can provide opportunities for empowerment and recognition but we cannot guide people there. That's confusing. It is also confusing that we suggest abstaining from controlling or leading the process, or educating or advising the parties, and yet we claim we are doing something very powerful. We are also saying that the parties' most likely path to a satisfying settlement, a sense of increased agency, and improved mutual understanding involves us abstaining from trying to get them to those places. All of this is contradictory but true.

It is also contradictory that we refuse to act on a variety of things the parties might request of us. Shouldn't party self-determination mean we honor their requests? How can a mediator's *refusal to do something a party asks* increase party self-determination? When we refuse to comply with requests that parties make, we often justify that refusal in terms of party self-determination: "The reason I cannot do what you ask (e.g., pass messages between parties in different rooms, give advice) is because I believe, above all else, that you get to make all of the decisions throughout this process." Contradictory though it is, this makes sense to us. This book has been our attempt to explain, among other things, these apparent contradictions.

One way to describe this take on self-determination is to say that as mediators we like to keep the ball in the parties' court. We engage with the parties, pay attention to them, and reflect them, and when they ask us to take responsibility for a decision, we shift the responsibility back to them: "Oh you want me to tell you what to do? I see. You're not sure what to do so you'd like it if I could tell you what the best thing to do would be. I understand and accept that desire though I can't act on it. What would you like to do now?" (Of course we wouldn't use those exact words!). And then we step back and let them decide what to do next. As mediators, we simply believe that the best thing for the parties to do would be anything other than have us tell them what to do. So in that sense we are indeed making one decision for them, and we are, in a way, violating our principle at that moment. We would support their decision to seek advice, for instance, but we would not, ourselves, act on their choice by becoming their advisor.

We support their choices but we do not take action on their choices. We support the parties in the moment they make the choice but we also allow the space for them to change their mind in the next moment. If we took action on their choice, we would be interfering with their choice to go a different direction in the next moment. Dan sometimes says that being a mediator is like playing volleyball: When the ball comes to us, we do our best to keep the ball in the air and set it up as gently as possible for the other players so they can decide what to do next with it. Being a mediator is not like playing American football—we do not pick up the ball and run.

We support parties by using mirrors and lights to help them see the choices they are making and the opportunities they have to make new choices. We also support them by doing our best to stay out of their way. When complications arise, we respond in the way that we believe is most supportive of their opportunity to continue making choices.

Writing this book has increased our faith in the human capacity to make strong and responsive decisions. It has also strengthened our commitment to party self-determination as the primary value guiding our work. We hope this book has given you opportunities to see your path more clearly.

In the long run, we shape our lives, and we shape ourselves. The process never ends until we die. And the choices we make are ultimately our own responsibility.

—Eleanor Roosevelt

Notes

1. See Robert A. Baruch Bush and Joseph P. Folger, "Mediation and Social Justice: Risks and Opportunities," *Ohio State Journal on Dispute Resolution* 27 (2012): 1; Tara West, "Self-Determination Versus Protection: A False Choice," Institute for the Study of Conflict Transformation, https://www.transformativemediation.org/self -determination-versus-protection-a-false-choice/.

2. Jon Linden, "Mediation Styles: The Purists vs. the 'Toolkit,'" Mediate.com, https://www.mediate.com/articles/linden4.cfm.

3. Daryl Bem, "An Experimental Analysis of Self-Persuasion," *Journal of Experimental Social Psychology* 1, no. 3 (1965).

4. April Breske-Rechek, Katelyn M. Morrison, and Luke D. Heidtke, "Causal Inferences From Descriptions of Experimental and Non-Experimental Research: Public Understanding of Correlation-Versus-Causation," *Journal of General Psychology* 142, no. 1 (2015).

5. Michael D. Lang, *The Guide to Reflective Practice in Conflict Resolution* (Lanham, MD: Rowman & Littlefield, 2019).

6. See Robert A. Baruch Bush, "A Pluralistic Approach to Mediation Ethics: Delivering on Mediation's Different Promises," *Ohio State Journal on Dispute Resolution* 34, no. 3 (2019).

7. Edward L. Deci, Jennifer G. La Guardia, Arlen C. Moller, Marc J. Scheiner, and Richard M. Ryan, "On the Benefits of Giving as Well as Receiving Autonomy Support: Mutuality in Close Friendships," *Personality and Social Psychology Bulletin* 32 (2006).

References

Aknin, Lara B., Christopher P. Barrington-Leigh, Elizabeth W. Dunn, John F. Helliwell, Justine Burns, Robert Biswas-Diener, Imelda Kimeza, Paul Nyende, Claire E. Ashton-James, and Michael I. Norton. "Prosocial Spending and Well-Being: Cross-Cultural Evidence for a Psychological Universal." *Journal of Personality and Social Psychology* 104, no. 4 (February 2013): 635–652.

Aknin, Lara B., J. Kiley Hamlin, and Elizabeth W. Dunn. "Giving Leads to Happiness in Young Children." *PLoS One* 7, no. 6 (June 2012): 1–4.

American Arbitration Association, American Bar Association, and Association for Conflict Resolution. "Model Standards of Conduct for Mediators." https://www.adr.org/sites/default/files/document_repository/AAA%20Mediators%20Model%20Standards%20of%20Conduct%2010.14.2010.pdf.

Association of Family and Conciliation Courts. "Model Standards of Practice for Family and Divorce Mediation." https://www.mediate.com/articles/afccstds.cfm.

Bem, Daryl. "An Experimental Analysis of Self-Persuasion." *Journal of Experimental Social Psychology* 1, no. 3 (1965): 199–218.

Ben-Ami Bartal, Inbal, Jean Decety, and Peggy Mason. "Empathy and Pro-Social Behavior in Rats." *Science* 334 (December 2011): 1427–1430.

Bernier, Annie, Celia Matte-Gagne, Marie-Eve Belanger, Natasha Whipple. "Taking Stock of Two Decades of Attachment Transmission Gap: Broadening the Assessment of Maternal Behavior." *Child Development* 85, no. 5 (September–October, 2014): 1852–1865.

Bingham, Lisa B. "Mediation at Work: Transforming Workplace Conflict at the United States Postal Service." IBM Center for the Business of Government: Human Capital Management Series, October 2003. https://www.maxwell.syr.edu/uploadedFiles/parcc/cmc/Mediation%20at%20Work-%20Bingham%20IBM.pdf.

Breske-Rechek, April, Katelyn M. Morrison, and Luke D. Heidtke. "Causal Inferences From Descriptions of Experimental and Non-Experimental Research: Public Understanding of Correlation-Versus-Causation." *Journal of General Psychology* 142, no. 1 (2015): 48–70.

Bush, Robert A. Baruch. "A Pluralistic Approach to Mediation Ethics: Delivering on Mediation's Different Promises." *Ohio State Journal on Dispute Resolution* 34, no. 3 (2019): 459–535.

Bush, Robert A. Baruch. "Taking Self-Determination Seriously: The Centrality of Empowerment in Transformative Mediation." In *Transformative Mediation: A Sourcebook*, edited by Joseph P. Folger, Robert A. Baruch Bush, and Dorothy J. Della Noce, 51–72. Association for Conflict Resolution and Institute for the Study of Conflict Transformation, 2010.

Bush, Robert A. Baruch, and Joseph P. Folger. *The Promise of Mediation: Responding to Conflict Through Empowerment and Recognition.* San Francisco: Jossey-Bass, 1994.

Bush, Robert A. Baruch, and Joseph P. Folger. "Mediation and Social Justice: Risks and Opportunities." *Ohio State Journal on Dispute Resolution* 27, no. 1 (2012): 1–52.

Bush, Robert A. Baruch, and Joseph P. Folger. *The Promise of Mediation: The Transformative Approach to Conflict*. San Francisco, CA: Jossey-Bass, 2005.

Bush, Robert A. Baruch, and Peter F. Miller. "Hiding in Plain Sight: Mediation, Client-Centered Practice, and the Value of Human Agency." *Ohio State Journal on Dispute Resolution* 35 (2020): 591–644.

Crush, Elizabeth A., Emily Frith, and Paul D. Loprinzi. "Experimental Effects of Acute Exercise Duration and Exercise Recovery on Mood State." *Journal of Affective Disorders* 229 (2018): 282–287.

Dan Simon Mediation. "Transformative Mediation in Action: Workplace Discrimination Case Example." https://www.youtube.com/watch?v=Cq0upTnMbVc.

Dawkins, Richard. *The Selfish Gene: Fortieth Anniversary Edition*. Oxford University Press, 2014.

Deci, Edward L., Jennifer G. La Guardia, Arlen C. Moller, Marc J. Scheiner, and Richard M. Ryan. "On the Benefits of Giving as Well as Receiving Autonomy Support: Mutuality in Close Friendships." *Personality and Social Psychology Bulletin* 32 (2016): 313–327.

Dimock, Michael, and Richard Wike. "America Is Exceptional in the Nature of Its Political Divide." Pew Research Center, 2020. https://www.pewresearch.org/fact-tank/2020/11/13/america-is-exceptional-in-the-nature-of-its-political-divide/.

Donovan, Kirsten, and Cheryl Regehr. "Elder Abuse: Clinical, Ethical, and Legal Considerations in Social Work Practice." *Clinical Social Work Journal* 38, no. 2 (2010): 174–182.

Dossey, Larry. *One Mind: How Our Individual Mind Is Part of a Greater Consciousness and Why It Matters*. Carlsbad, CA: Hay House, 2013.

Eisenstein, Charles. *Sacred Economics: Money, Gift, and Society in the Age of Transition*. Berkeley, CA: North Atlantic Books, 2011.

Fisher, William, Roger Ury, and Bruce Patton. *Getting to Yes: Negotiating Agreement Without Giving In*. New York: Penguin Books, 1991.

Folger, Joseph P., Robert A. Baruch Bush, and Dorothy J. Della Noce, eds. *Transformative Mediation: A Sourcebook*. Association for Conflict Resolution / Institute for the Study of Conflict Transformation, 2010.

Friedman, Gary, and Jack Himmelstein. *Challenging Conflict: Mediation Through Understanding*. Chicago: American Bar Association, 2008.

Gately, M. J. "Manipulation Drive In Experimentally Naive Rhesus Monkeys." Unpublished manuscript, University of Wisconsin, 1950.

Gintis, Herbert. "Strong Reciprocity and Human Sociality." *Journal of Theoretical Biology* 206, no. 2 (2000): 169–179.

Haidt, Jonathan. "The Positive Emotion of Elevation." *Prevention and Treatment* 3, no. 1 (March, 2000).

History.com. "Christmas Truce of 1914." https://www.history.com/topics/world-war-i/christmas-truce-of-1914.

Institute for the Study of Conflict Transformation. "Mediation: Principles and Practice, the Transformative Approach," 2010.

Institute for the Study of Conflict Transformation. "What the Parents Know: A Transformative Mediation MP4," 2011.

Jorgensen, Erling O., Janet K. Moen, James R. Antes, Donna Turner Hudson, and Linda H. Hendrikson. "Microfocus in Mediation: The What and How of Transformative Opportunities." In *Designing Mediation: Approaches to Training and Practice Within a Transformative Framework*, edited by Joseph P. Folger and

Robert A. Baruch Bush, 133–149. Institute for the Study of Conflict Transformation, 2001.

Lande, John. "How Will Lawyering and Mediation Practices Transform Each Other?" *Florida State University Law Review* 24 (1997): 839–901.

Lang, Michael D. (2019). *The Guide to Reflective Practice in Conflict Resolution.* Lanham, MD: Rowman & Littlefield, 2019.

Linden, Jon. "Mediation Styles: The Purists vs. the 'Toolkit.'" mediate.com. https://www.mediate.com/articles/linden4.cfm.

Mdcourts.gov. "What Works in Child Access Mediation: Effectiveness of Various Mediation Strategies on Short- and Long-Term Outcomes." https://mdcourts.gov/sites/default/files/import/courtoperations/pdfs/familyfullreport.pdf.

Mdcourts.gov. "What Works in District Court Day of Trial Mediation: Effectiveness of Various Mediation Strategies on Short- and Long-Term Outcomes." https://mdcourts.gov/sites/default/files/import/courtoperations/pdfs/districtcourtstrategiesfullreport.pdf.

Montgomery, K. C., "The Relation Between Fear Induced by Novel Stimulation and Exploratory Drive," *Journal of Comparative and Physiological Psychology* 48, no. 4 (August 1955): 254–260.

National Association of Social Workers. "NASW Standards for Social Work Practice with Family Caregivers of Older Adults." https://www.socialworkers.org/LinkClick.aspx?fileticket=aUwQL98exRM%3d&portalid=0.

Nissen, Henry W. "A Study of Exploratory Behavior in the White Rat by Means of the Obstruction Method," *Pedagogical Seminary and Journal of Genetic Psychology* 37, no. 3 (1930): 361–376.

Ostrom, Elinor, James Walker, and Roy Gardner. "With and Without a Sword: Self-Governance Is Possible." *The American Political Science Review* 86, no. 2 (1992): 404–417.

Peterson, Bruce. "Time, Perhaps, to Get Courts Out of Divorce," *Minneapolis Star Tribune*, July 12, 2012.

Pinker, Steven. *The Better Angels of Our Nature.* New York: Penguin, 2012.

Qin, Hua, Pei-Luen Patrick Rau, and Gavriel Salvendy. "Effects of Different Scenarios of Game Difficulty on Player Immersion." *Interacting with Computers* 22 (2009): 230–239.

Raines, Stephen A. "The Nature of Psychological Reactance Revisited: A Meta-Analytic Review." *Human Communication Research* 39, no. 1 (January 2013): 47–73.

Relis, Tamara. "Consequences of Power." *Harvard Negotiation Law Review* 12 (2007): 445–501.

Relis, Tamara. "'It's Not About the Money'": A Theory on Misconceptions of Plaintiffs' Litigation Aims, *University of Pittsburgh Law Review* 68 (2007): 1–48.

Ryan, Richard. M., and Edward L. Deci. *Self-Determination Theory: Basic Psychological Needs in Motivation, Development, and Wellness.* New York: Guilford Press, 2017.

Schnall, S., J. Roper, and D. M. T. Fessler. "Elevation Leads to Altruistic Behavior." *Psychological Science* 21, no. 3 (2010): 315–320.

Schopenhauer, Arthur. *The World as Will and Representation.* Cambridge University Press, 1818.

Sheldrake, Rupert. "Part I: Mind, Memory and Archetype: Morphic Resonance and the Collective Unconscious." *Psychological Perspectives* 18, no. 1 (1987): 9–25.

Simon, Dan. "Transformative Mediation for Divorce: Rising Above the Law and the Settlement." In *Transformative Mediation: A Sourcebook*, edited by Joseph P. Folger, Robert A. Baruch Bush, and Dorothy J. Della Noce, 249–270. Association for Conflict Resolution, Institute for the Study of Conflict Transformation, 2010.

Spicker, Paul. "Social Work and Self-Determination." *British Journal of Social Work* 20, no. 3 (June 1990): 221–236.

Timulak, Ladislav. "Witnessing Clients' Emotional Transformation: An Emotion-Focused Therapist's Experience of Providing Therapy." *Journal of Clinical Psychology* 70, no. 8 (2014): 741–752.

Tryphonopoulos, Panagiota D., Nicole Letourneau, and Enrico Ditomasson. "Attachment and Caregiver-Infant Interaction: A Review of Observational-Assessment Tools." *Infant Mental Health Journal* 35, no. 6 (2014): 642–656.

United Nations General Assembly. Resolution 1514. 1960.

Waldman, Ellen. *Mediation Ethics: Cases and Commentaries*. San Francisco: Jossey-Bass, 2011.

Wall, James Allen, Timothy C. Dunne, Suzanne Chan-Serafin. "The Effects of Neutral, Evaluative, and Pressing Mediator Strategies." *Conflict Resolution Quarterly* 29, no. 2 (2011): 127–150.

Warneken, Felix, and Michael Tomasello. "Altruistic Helping in Human Infants and Chimpanzees." *Science* 311 (March 2006): 1301–1303.

Wehmeyer, Michael. "Beyond Self-Determination: Causal Agency Theory." *Journal of Developmental and Physical Disabilities* 16 (December 2004): 337–359.

Weinstein, Netta, and Richard M. Ryan. "When Helping Helps: Autonomous Motivation for Prosocial Behavior and Its Influence on Well-Being for the Helper and Recipient." *Journal of Personality and Social Psychology* 98, no. 2 (February 2010): 222–244.

West, Tara. "Self-Determination vs. Protection: A False Choice?" https://www.transformativemediation.org/self-determination-versus-protection-a-false-choice/.

West, Tara. "Settlements Are Like Sex." http://www.transformativemediation.org/settlements-are-like-sex/.

White, Robert W. "Motivation Reconsidered: The Concept of Competence." *Psychological Review* 66, no. 5 (1959): 297–333.

Wissler, Roselle L. "The Effectiveness of Court-Connected Dispute Resolution in Civil Cases." *Conflict Resolution Quarterly* 22, nos. 1–2 (December 2004): 55–88.

List of Quotations

Unless otherwise noted here, quotations that appear in the text are famous sayings. They are listed here in order of appearance.

Williams, R. R. "Creating a New World of Opportunity: Expanding Choice and Self-Determination in Lives of Americans with Severe Disability by 1992 and Beyond." In R. Perske, ed., *Proceedings from the National Conference on Self-Determination*, Institute on Community Integration, Minneapolis, Minnesota, 1989, 16–17.

Hamilton, A. *The Farmer Refuted*, 1775.

Wolfensberger, W. *Normalization: The Principle of Normalization in Human Services* (Toronto: National Institute on Mental Retardation, 1972).

Gandhi, M. *Young India* (March 1931), 31.

Wilson, W. "President Wilson's Address to Congress, Analyzing German and Austrian Peace Utterances," February 11, 1918.

Lord Acton, in a letter to Bishop Mandell Creighton, April 5, 1887.

Bush, Robert A. Baruch, and Joseph P. Folger. *The Promise of Mediation: Responding to Conflict through Empowerment and Recognition* (San Francisco: Jossey-Bass, 1994), 46.

Carter, J. *A Government as Good as Its People* (Fayetteville: University of Arkansas Press, 1996), 185.

Krueger, J. "We Just Disagree," *Let It Go, Let It Flow* [Album], 1977.

Dalai Lama. *The Art of Happiness* (New York: Riverhead Books, 2009).

Roy, A. "Edward Snowden Meets Arundhati Roy and John Cusack: 'He Was Small and Lithe, Like a House Cat,'" *Guardian*, November 28, 2015, https://www.theguardian.com/lifeandstyle/2015/nov/28/conversation-edward-snowden-arundhati-roy-john-cusack-interview.

Cliff, J. "We All Are One," *The Power and the Glory* [Album], 1983.

Forbes, M. S. *The Sayings of Chairman Malcolm: The Capitalist's Handbook* (New York: Harper & Row, 1978).

Buckley, C. *Losing Mum and Pup: A Memoir* (Toronto: Emblem Editions, 2010).

Seligman, M. E. P. *Flourish: A Visionary New Understanding of Happiness and Well-Being* (New York: Simon & Schuster, 2012).

Wharton, E. "Vesalius in Zante (1564)," *North American Review* 175, no. 552 (1902): 625–631.

Gawande, A. *Being Mortal: Medicine and What Matters in the End* (New York: Metropolitan Books, 2014).

Dickinson, E. "Forever—Is Composed of Nows," in *The Complete Poems of Emily Dickinson* (Boston: Little, Brown & Company, 1960).

Rogers, C. *A Way of Being* (New York: Houghton Mifflin, 1980).

Malcolm X. "Prospects for Freedom in 1965," in *Malcolm X Speaks* (New York: Pathfinder Press, 1965), ch. 12.

Chekhov, A. P. *Motley Tales and a Play*, trans. Constance Black Garnett and Vlada Chernomordik (New York: Doubleday, 1998).

Dostoevsky, F. *Crime and Punishment*, trans. Constance Garnett (New York: Bantam, 1963).

Lao Tzu. *Tao Te Ching*.

Boyle, G. "Great Read: After 30 Years of Helping Gang Members, Father Greg Boyle Is Slowing a Bit But Still Determined," *Los Angeles Times*, https://www.latimes.com/local/great-reads/la-me-c1-father-boyle-20151104-story.html.

Galsworthy, J. *Strife* (London: A & C Black, 2014).

Gawande, A. *Complications: A Surgeon's Notes on an Imperfect Science* (London: Picador, 2003).

Sowell, T. *A Conflict of Visions: Ideological Origins of Political Struggles* (New York: Basic Books, 2007).

Lao Tzu, *Tao Te Ching*.

Gawande, A. *Complications: A Surgeon's Notes on an Imperfect Science* (London: Picador, 2003).

Fromm, E. *Man for Himself: An Inquiry into the Psychology of Ethics* (New York: Henry Holt & Company, 1990).

Tolle, E. *The Power of Now: A Guide to Spiritual Enlightenment* (New York: New World Library, 1999).

Lao Tzu, *Tao Te Ching*.

Roosevelt, E. *You Learn by Living: Eleven Keys for a More Fulfilling Life* (New York: Harper Perennial, 1960).

Index

About the Authors

Dan Simon, Fellow and Board Member of the Institute for the Study of Conflict Transformation (ISCT), practices and teaches transformative mediation in Minnesota and Southern California. Dan authored "Transformative Mediation for Divorce: Rising Above the Law and the Settlement," a chapter in *Transformative Mediation: A Sourcebook* (2010), and co-authored "Transformative Mediation: Illustrating a Relational View of Conflict Intervention," a chapter in *The Mediation Handbook* (2017). Dan earned both his MA in Counseling Psychology and his JD from the University of Minnesota.

Tara West, author of *The Mediator's Approach: Five (and a Half) Paths Through Conflict* (2021), is a certified transformative mediator and conflict coach. She has been trained in facilitative, evaluative, understanding-based, and transformative approaches to mediation and has mediated in public and private settings. Tara has taught and developed undergraduate and graduate psychology courses covering topics such as socio-cultural approaches to psychology, developmental psychology, personality psychology, group processes, and the psychology of conflict resolution. Tara earned her PhD in Social and Health Psychology from Stony Brook University and her JD from the New York University School of Law.

**Association for
Conflict Resolution®**

VOICES, CHOICES, SOLUTIONS

About the ACR

The Association for Conflict Resolution (ACR) is a professional organization enhancing the practice and public understanding of conflict resolution. An international professional association for mediators, arbitrators, educators, and other conflict resolution practitioners, ACR works in a wide range of settings throughout the United States and around the world. Our multicultural and multidisciplinary organization offers a broad umbrella under which all forms of dispute resolution practice find a home. Website: www.acrnet.org; Twitter: @ACRgroup.

Editorial Board Members

.

87446549R00115